Mindworks

Becoming More Conscious in an Unconscious World

Mindworks

Becoming More Conscious in an Unconscious World

by

Alexander W. Astin
University of California

INFORMATION AGE
PUBLISHING

Charlotte, North Carolina • www.infoagepub.com

Library of Congress Cataloging-in-Publication Data

Astin, Alexander W.
  Mindworks : becoming more conscious in an unconscious world / by Alexander W. Astin.
    p. cm.
  Includes bibliographical references.
  ISBN-13: 978-1-59311-738-2 (pbk.)
  ISBN-13: 978-1-59311-739-9 (hardcover)
  1. Consciousness. 2. Self. I. Title.
  BF311.A743 2007
  158.1--dc22

                                                              2007014322

ISBN 13: 978-1-59311-738-2 (pbk.)
            978-1-59311-739-9 (hardcover)
ISBN 10: 1-59311-738-8 (pbk.)
            1-59311-739-6 (hardcover)

Printed in the United States of America

CONTENTS

PREFACE

Your conscious mind is remarkable not just because it allows you to think and feel, but also because it allows you to *observe* your thoughts and feelings as they arise in your awareness. Cultivating this ability to observe your own mind in action—becoming more self-aware or simply more "conscious"—is basically what this book is all about.

The subtitle of the book—*Becoming More Conscious in an Unconscious World*—reflects my personal belief that many of our contemporary domestic and world problems will be difficult to resolve without a substantial increase in our individual and collective self-awareness. If I live my life without much awareness of how my mind works and with little understanding of how my feelings and actions are continually being shaped by my beliefs, I am living in an "unconscious" way. Self-awareness and self-understanding, of course, are necessary prerequisites to our ability to understand others and to resolve conflicts. This basic truth—which lies at the heart of our difficulty in dealing effectively with problems of violence, poverty, crime, divorce, substance abuse, and religious and racial conflict that continue to plague our country—was also dramatically and tragically illustrated in the September 11, 2001 attacks on the World Trade Center and the Pentagon building.

Concepts like "mind" and "consciousness" refer to what I like to call our "inner" life, as contrasted with our "outer" life of behavior and action. In our modern technological society the relative amount of attention we devote to our exterior and interior lives has gotten way out of balance. Thus, while we are justifiably proud of our "outer" development in fields such as science, medicine, technology, and commerce, we have increasingly come to neglect our "inner" development—the sphere of values and beliefs, emotional maturity, spirituality, and self-understanding.

Even though most of our great religious and philosophical traditions are grounded in the maxim, "know thyself," the development of self-awareness receives very little attention in our schools and colleges, and almost no attention in public discourse in general or in the media in particular. This imbalance between our inner and outer development has enormous implications for the future not only of our society, but also of our world. Self-understanding, of course, is fundamental to our capacity to understand others: spouses, partners, parents, children, friends, coworkers, and neighbors, not to mention people of different races, religions, cultures, and nationalities. If we lack self-understanding—the capacity to see ourselves clearly and honestly and to understand why we feel and act as we do—then how can we ever expect to understand others?

The book is intended for anyone who believes that life—what you experience in your awareness from moment to moment, day after day—could stand some improvement. It is for people who feel that they worry too much, or are dissatisfied with their jobs or their relationships with others, or always feel rushed because there are too many things that they have to do. It is for people who want less frustration, guilt, irritability, boredom, or unhappiness and more love, joy, adventure, and sense of control over their lives.

The fact is that you have the ability—right now in this conscious moment—to begin reshaping your life's experience through a better understanding of how your mind works. The book is aims to provide you with some practical tools for applying this simple truth in your own life. These tools are designed not just to help you observe what is happening in your mind, but also to help you understand *why* you think and feel the way you do. This is not, however, a book that asks you to take anything on faith, or to believe what is being said simply because it comes from some kind of authority or sage. On the contrary, this book is *experiential*, in the sense that it encourages you to test out each idea that is presented on *yourself*: Does this knowledge work for me? Is this the way my mind works? Am I learning more about myself?

To facilitate this process of checking things out in your own conscious experience, most chapters include a number of mini-experiments and short exercises. I would *strongly* urge you to try out each of these experiments and exercises as you read through the book. See for yourself: Is this the way *my* mind works? Am I getting some new perspectives and insights about myself? **To make this "self-testing" easier I would suggest that you keep a small notebook and writing instrument handy whenever you take time to do some reading.**

There are few people alive today who could not benefit from a better understanding of this wonderful and awesomely complicated phenomenon we call "consciousness." Many of us would like to *change* certain things in our daily experience: certain negative feelings, thoughts, habits, or relationships. A major obstacle in our efforts to do this is that most of us really have little understanding of how the *un*conscious part of the mind works or of how the unconscious and conscious parts engage in their continuous by-play. Some people see the "unconscious" either as an unfathomable "black box" or as a sinister, dark part of themselves that is to be feared. But in truth the unconscious is neither threatening nor beyond any understanding. Many of its marvelous ways of working *can* be understood and it is in most respects your greatest friend and protector. And while your conscious mind may seem puny by comparison because it can deal with only a few thoughts and feelings at a time, it has enormous power to influence what the unconscious does. By better understanding how this influence occurs, you can put yourself in a position to create a much more interesting and satisfying life for yourself.

Like any other book, this is a collection of words, and words will never be able to capture fully or describe completely those wonderful and mysterious realities that you and I call "consciousness," "soul," "reality," "spirit," "imagination," "thinking," "feeling," or simply "being aware" or "being alive." The main point of the book is to encourage you to look at your own conscious experience in more depth and hopefully in some new ways. Maybe to *stretch* the way you see yourself and the world a bit. Some of you may even begin to make major changes in your daily experience. Others will read portions of the book and be able to say, "yes, that's how it seems or feels to me," or "wow, I never looked at it that way," or "I've got to think about that for a minute."

The bulk of the book—consisting of the first 10 chapters and portions of chapter 11—has to do with aspects of your normal waking consciousness that are directly accessible to practically all of us: thoughts, emotions, sensations, feelings, memories, fantasies, beliefs, and intentions. The rest of the book—parts of chapter 11 and the postscript—covers issues that we may think, wonder, or worry about, but that are much harder to discuss or pin down because of limitations in our language and because there is less agreement as what they mean or even as to whether some of them are "real." I speak here of such concepts as intuition, creativity, the nature of "time," "shared" consciousness, "psychic" phenomena, "out-of-body" or "near death" experiences, "transpersonal" levels of consciousness, and what are generally called "nonordinary" states of consciousness.

The title, *Mindworks*, is a play on words. There are at least three ways to take the phrase "mind works," and each of them says something about this book:

- Mind Works—The "workings of the mind," the main subject of the book;
- Mind Works—The mind "works" very hard, all the time;
- Mind Works—The mind "works" exceedingly well.

I have written this book in nontechnical language, but some of the ideas are fairly complicated. If you are now wondering whether you want to invest the time and effort required to learn about these ideas and to do the exercises, ask yourself the following questions: Is my mind simple and easy to describe in a few words? Are the things that really *matter* in my life simple and uncomplicated? How simple is it to choose the right career for myself and to make my life's work personally fulfilling? How simple is it to lead a life with meaning and purpose, find and sustain a love relationship, have a good sex life, be a good parent, or cultivate close and satisfying relationships with friends? How easy is it to find the right balance between work, family, and play? How easy is it to change the things in my life that are not satisfying and fulfilling?

Just as there are no easy answers to such personal questions, so there are no simple solutions to questions like "What is consciousness?" "How does consciousness work?" "Why do I feel and think the way I do?" and "Why do I respond to people and events the way I do?" These are some of the more complicated questions addressed in this book.

While it is probably best to read the chapters in their current order, **the book is designed so that you can skip around some and still be able to do the exercises and understand most of what is being said**. It is partially for this reason that you will frequently find references ("see chapter ...") to other chapters that provide more detail about something that is being discussed. So if you are particularly intrigued by the title of a later chapter, go to it right away and start reading.

The book has benefited tremendously from critical readings by four dear and generous friends: Dave Drew, Bob Holmstrom, Phil Oderberg, and Bob Osnos. I would also like to express my appreciation to Jennifer Yee for many hours of stimulating conversation about the draft chapters, to Mary Rabb for her help in preparing the manuscript, and to the Fetzer Institute for their generous grant, which helped to free me up from some of my professorial duties. I also owe a debt of gratitude to the late poet/author/mystic Jane Roberts, whose writings helped to convince me of the critical role that beliefs play in shaping our daily lives.

CHAPTER 1

THE CONSCIOUS AND NONCONSCIOUS MINDS

"...when you do meet yourself, you come into a permanent endowment and bequest of knowledge that is like no other experience on earth."

—Tariqavi (1970)[1]

Right now your conscious mind is occupied with reading this sentence. There may be other things about which you are also vaguely aware—the way the whole book looks, the position and feel of your body, the sounds and sights of your immediate surroundings—but your consciousness is mainly focused on these words and what they mean.

In a few seconds I will ask you to stop reading and do something else, and then to return to the reading. When you put this book down, **close your eyes and listen carefully to all the sounds around** you for 30 seconds or so. Take your time and see how many different sounds you can identify. OK, now **stop reading, close your eyes, and listen**.

If you are inside a house or apartment, you may have heard the sound of machines—the refrigerator motor, the furnace fan, or a clock ticking. If you are outside, you may have heard the sound of the wind, birds singing, people talking, or traffic in the streets. If you are riding in a plane, you no doubt heard the roar of the engines, and possibly the sound of cabin attendants or other passengers talking. If you are in a very quiet place,

Mindworks: Becoming More Conscious in an Unconscious World, pp. 1–32

you may even have noticed a "ringing" in your ears. When you were reading, you were not consciously aware of these sounds, even though the same sound waves were entering your ears, stimulating your auditory nerves, and being transmitted to your brain. Why did you not "hear" all these sounds until I asked you to stop reading and listen for them? Obviously some part of you was "blocking" these potential sounds from your awareness.

Let us try another little experiment. This time when I ask you to stop reading, **close your eyes and focus your attention instead on how your body feels**. Mentally scan your body. What sensations do you feel in your extremities, in your chest, and in your gut? What do you feel in those places where your body is touching the chair, where your feet touch the floor, and where your hands hold this book? How do your clothes feel on your body? Take your time and experience all of those bodily sensations. OK, now **stop reading, close your eyes and focus on how your body feels**.

If you are sitting down, you no doubt felt the places where your rear end or your back or arms touched the chair. If you focused on your chest, you most likely became aware of your breathing, of your chest moving up and down, of the air passing in and out of your lungs. If you focused on how your clothes feel, you may have become aware of places where they felt a bit tight. Again, we need to acknowledge that you were not consciously aware of most of these bodily sensations when you were reading, even though the nerve endings and brain centers that make it possible for you to experience these sensations were being stimulated in the same way all along.

I have one last little experiment for you to try. Get as comfortable as you can and hold this book with both hands in a comfortable reading position. Now look at the whole book. How wide are the margins at the sides of the pages? Does the cover extend beyond the edges of the two pages? Can you see anything printed on the cover or dust jacket? Now look at the top margin. How wide is it? Notice that the book title appears in the upper right margin and the author's name in the upper left margin. Did you notice these when you turned to this page? Did you notice the page numbers? Now look at your hands. Can you see your thumbs? Are the nails clean? Do they need cutting or polishing? Now I am going to ask you to focus your eyes on a single letter "A" so you can check what is in your peripheral vision. Without taking your focus off the letter, see how many different things you can identify in your visual field beyond the book. Now **focus your eyes on the letter below:**

A

How many different things in your peripheral vision did you become aware of while you were focused on the letter? The point, once again, is that while you read this book the images of <u>all</u> of these other things are impinging on your retina and being transmitted by your optic nerve to your brain. Yet while you are concentrating on your reading your conscious mind fails to "see" most of them.

Let us try to diagram this process. While you are reading, the image of the words from this page and their meaning is projected into your consciousness: you see the words and are consciously aware of what they mean. The stimulation from the other sights, sounds, and bodily sensations also gets to your brain, but not to your conscious awareness! (See Figure 1.1.) In other words, these extraneous or "peripheral" stimuli get to the brain, but they are somehow blocked by the nonconscious mind from entering your waking consciousness.

What is really happening here is that the nonconscious part of your mind is <u>examining</u> all of these other incoming stimuli and <u>deciding</u> not to bring them to your conscious attention. If you have any doubts about this, consider what would happen if you were to turn the page and find some-

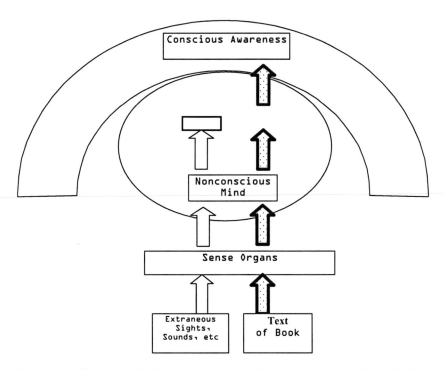

Figure 1.1. "Screening " of incoming sensory data by the nonconscious mind.

body's bold handwriting all over the margins? You would almost certainly become consciously aware of the writing, even though you had not "noticed" the plain page margins up until that point. And what if you were to suddenly get a sharp pain in your chest? You would surely notice this, even though you had not been "conscious" of your breathing or other sensations in your chest while you were reading. Finally, what if someone nearby were to speak your name loudly? In all likelihood you would consciously "hear" your name and look up to see who spoke it, even though you had not previously been aware of the other sounds that were there in your immediate environment.

It is also important to realize that your nonconscious mind is not just "funneling" the raw data—the images of the words printed on this page—into your conscious mind which then has to figure out what they mean. On the contrary, with the exception of an occasional unfamiliar word that you might have to look up in a dictionary, your nonconscious mind is <u>interpreting</u> most of these images and projecting their <u>meaning</u> into your waking unconsciousness. Your conscious mind is thus able to focus on the meaning of the words rather than on their shapes or other visual qualities. In fact, when you are reading you are probably devoting much more of your conscious attention to these meanings than to the mere visual image of the printed words.

If you have ever tried to learn to speak a foreign language, you went through a period when you did not immediately understand what a printed or spoken phrase meant; instead, you had to consciously "figure it out" before you could comprehend what the writer or speaker was trying to say (I am <u>still</u> at that stage with French!). If you say you are "fluent" in a language, what you really mean is that your unconscious mind <u>knows</u> the language so well that you can read a book or carry on a conversation in that language without having to "think" consciously about what the different printed symbols or spoken sounds mean. The "translation" work—making meaning out of the symbols and sounds—is being carried out largely by your nonconscious mind so that your conscious mind is freed up to focus on their meaning. The same thing happens in reverse when you speak: the meaning you want to convey is "automatically" translated into spoken words by your nonconscious mind.

GETTING STARTED

Perhaps the most straightforward way to start examining your consciousness is to ask, "What's there?" That is, when you look at your conscious experience, what do you find? If your were to make a list of all these different "things" that you experience during an average day, most of them would fall under one of the following three categories:

- Thoughts
- Feelings
- Sense Impressions

In other words, thoughts, feelings, and sense impressions are the "raw materials" of your conscious experience, and they can be closely connected. You can, for example, put on a CD and hear the music (sense impression), think about what you are hearing ("I wonder who the singer is?"), and also experience feelings in relation to what you are hearing (joy, sadness, etc.), all at the same time.

A very important feature of thoughts, feelings, and sense impressions is that *they are always changing.* Since the world around you is in a constant state of change, the sights, sounds, and smells that it creates for you are also constantly changing. Similarly, it is very hard to "hold" a thought in your conscious awareness for very long; instead, one thought seems to follow another in rapid succession. And while feelings or emotional states can sometimes stay in your conscious awareness a bit longer, they too tend to have a relatively short life.

Throughout the rest of this book we will be exploring how the mind works: why you experience the thoughts, feelings, and sensations that you do, and how you might go about modifying those aspects of your conscious experience that you would like to change. In pursuing these goals it will be necessary to understand how your conscious and nonconscious minds work together, and to pay special attention to the role of your beliefs, feelings, and intents. We will also consider in some depth (1) which particular thoughts, sensations, and feelings you pay attention to and why; and (2) your degree of "self-awareness," which has to do with how you focus your attention from moment to moment. In fact:

- **The first step in getting a better understanding of how your mind works is simply to become more <u>aware</u> of what is already there in your consciousness!**

If you could make a videotape of all the different thoughts, sensations, and feelings that arise in your waking consciousness during a typical day, it would be a pretty long tape and would contain a lot of different things. But if you were to play back the tape and "freeze frame" it at any given time during the day, you would find only a limited amount of material. In other words, you think a lot of thoughts over a day's time, but you can focus your conscious awareness on only one or two thoughts at a time.

The same goes for feelings: you may experience many different feelings throughout the course of a day, but you can be consciously "aware" of only one or two at a time. And despite the steady stream of sounds, sights, smells, and tactile impressions that impinges on your senses during the day, you can consciously attend to only a few at a time. Since there is relatively little "room" in your waking consciousness for all these mental events at any given time, there must be some other "place"—the nonconscious mind—where these experiences can be "stored." Otherwise, how would you be able to sit down at the end of a day and remember so many of the events of the day? To understand how all of this happens, we will seek answers in this book to questions such as the following:

- How does your nonconscious mind "decide" what the content of your conscious mind will be at any given time? What "rules" does it follow in making these decisions?
- Can you <u>change</u> these rules?
- Of the millions of different sensory impressions that you receive each day, which ones "get your attention," and why?
- Why do you experience negative emotions? How can you gain more control over your emotional life?
- What is the connection between thought and feeling?
- Why do you react to the people and events of your daily life the way you do? If some of your habitual reactions cause you difficulty, how can you change them?
- How is it that you are able to "observe" your mind at work? Who or what is doing the observing?

Let us return now to complete our discussion of the three mini-experiments. If you had encountered handwriting in the book margin, the sound of your name being spoken, or the chest pain, you would almost certainly have stopped reading in order to refocus your conscious attention on the new sight, sound, or bodily sensation. But <u>how</u> were you able to do this? And <u>why</u> did you do it? Why would you not just "ignore" these stimuli as you had been doing with all of the earlier sights, sounds, and bodily sensations that were impinging on you while you were reading? To answer such questions, we must first acknowledge some realities about the way the mind works:

- **While you are focusing your conscious attention on a task like reading a book, you are generally not consciously aware of all of the other sensory information that impinges on you.**

- **Some other (nonconscious) part of your mind is receiving and evaluating this "extraneous" sensory information.**
- **This nonconscious part of your mind has the capacity to "decide" at any time that the competing information is sufficiently important for you to redirect your conscious attention away from the reading.**

Most people probably think that such "monitoring" is being done consciously, since your response to, say, the sound of someone saying your name <u>seems</u> virtually instantaneous. But this obviously cannot be the case, since you were not "consciously aware" of all the other sounds that were coming in prior to the mention of your name. The nonconscious part of your mind, in other words, is reviewing and evaluating this incoming information, trying to decide whether it is "important" enough to interrupt your reading. During the preceding three exercises, I was asking your <u>conscious</u> mind to do the monitoring, but the only way you could really do this was to stop reading and refocus your conscious attention directly on the sights, sounds, and bodily sensations that your nonconscious mind had been "screening out" of your conscious awareness up until that point. In short, what you did was to <u>refocus</u> your attention away from the book so that you could become consciously aware of all of the other sensations that your nonconscious mind had been screening out. In other words,

These little experiments have been designed in part to illustrate a very important fact about the way your mind works:

- **The nonconscious part of your mind does much of the "deciding" about what incoming sensory information "means" and which information you will consciously pay attention to.**

Your nonconscious mind does all this "screening" and "interpretation" of incoming sensory data every waking second of every day. However, our little experiments also demonstrate a second important point about the way your mind works:

- **You can at any moment "direct" your nonconscious mind to "let through" sensory information that it had previously been screening out, so you can consciously "pay attention" to sensations that you had previously been ignoring.**

So far we have been talking only about information that comes in through your senses. But sensory stimulation is not the only thing that can interrupt your reading. Your consciousness could also be diverted by thoughts or feelings that come from "inside." These thoughts or feelings could be touched off by something you are reading, but they could also intrude on your consciousness spontaneously without any obvious association to the reading material. For example, you might find yourself distracted from the reading by the memory of some personal encounter you had earlier in the day that made you angry or frustrated. Or, you might start worrying about the fact that you soon need to start to work on some task that you have been putting off. Such spontaneous thoughts or feelings might be intense enough to make you decide to stop reading altogether.

The question is: Why would these "distracting" thoughts and feelings emerge at a particular time when you are trying to read? And why <u>these</u> particular thoughts and feelings rather than others? Clearly, the nonconscious part of your mind has "decided" that these internal thoughts and feelings are "important" enough for you to stop reading and pay attention.

If you stop to think about it, you will realize that this nonconscious part of your mind must be capable of doing a lot of other work besides storing memories: it also plays a major part in <u>producing</u> the thoughts and feelings that continuously flow into your conscious mind. In this book we will take a close look at these two parts of your mind. We shall try to understand how they communicate and work together, and how they deal with the events of your daily life to create what you call your "conscious experience."

WHAT DO WE MEAN BY "CONSCIOUS" AND "UNCONSCIOUS?"

Let us first clarify some basic terminology. When I speak of your "consciousness" or your "normal waking consciousness" I am referring to that stream of purely subjective and ultimately private experiences of which you are aware at any moment. That stream is happening right now in your consciousness. You can label these experiences with terms like thought, idea, feeling, sensation, or state of mind. Being conscious and being human and alive is the sum total of these thoughts, feelings, and sensations. That "other part" of the mind—the nonconscious part—cannot be directly experienced or observed but is rather something you can <u>infer</u> from what happens in your conscious experience. The unconscious, in other words, comprises <u>all those mental events of which you are not directly aware.</u> I realize that "unconscious" may have a more specialized meaning to students of psychoanalysis, but I will be using it in a much more generic sense to encompass all mental activity that is not directly experienced in your normal waking consciousness. I will also use "unconscious" interchangeably with "nonconscious."

In the final analysis, your "normal waking consciousness" is all you <u>ever</u> have to go on. However, by looking carefully at what goes on in your waking consciousness, you can make certain inferences about what is going on in the nonconscious part of your mind. This careful looking—what Husserl refers to as "seeing"—can also tell you something about how the two parts of your mind work together, and about how the whole mind relates to events in the external physical world. You can also figure out many of the "rules" that your nonconscious mind follows in deciding what to bring to your conscious attention, and even <u>change</u> some of these rules if you choose. This "careful looking" and what you can learn from it is basically what this book is all about.

We can draw a crude analogy here with a personal computer. The conscious part of your mind is like the computer screen: something you can directly experience and observe. The "hidden" work of the computer, which takes place inside the computer according to the "rules" set down by the operating system and other software, is like the nonconscious part of the mind: you cannot directly experience or observe what it is doing, but you know that it has a lot to do with what happens on the screen. Moreover, you can make certain <u>inferences</u> about how the software works by observing carefully what happens on the screen. Finally, if you want to <u>change</u> what you typically get on the screen, there are at least two things you can do: (1) learn more about how the software works so you can exert more control over it, and (2) change the software. In short,

- **A substantial part of this book is designed to better acquaint you with the "software" of your own mind: to understand how that software affects your day-to-day experience, and to provide you with some tools for "installing" new software if you choose to do so.**

THE "CONTENTS" OF THE MIND

So far I have been talking mainly about the <u>structure</u> of the mind—the conscious and nonconscious portions—but what does the mind <u>contain</u>? What is there in the conscious and unconscious parts? Most of these contents fall under one of the following five categories:

- **Sensations** (right now I see a computer screen and hear birds chirping outside)
- **Thoughts** (just now I am thinking about what to type inside this parenthesis)
- **Feelings** (this morning I felt sad when I read that more soldiers had been killed in Iraq)

- **Intents** (I plan to finish this book before the end of the year)
- **Beliefs** (This book is worth all the effort I have been putting in on it)

The first three—sensations, thoughts, and feelings—make up most of the content of your normal waking consciousness, while your intents and beliefs (together with many thoughts and their associated feelings) are usually "stored" in the nonconscious mind. Most of these intents and beliefs, of course, are accessible to the conscious mind, where they appear as thoughts or ideas. In other words, you can, if you wish, become consciously aware of particular intents or beliefs that you hold. While we could also add memories to the above list, memories are really <u>current thoughts</u> about something we call the "past," and most of the time they remain in the nonconscious part of the mind (see chapter 11, "The Sense of Time"). Finally, while we could also add <u>values</u> to the list, values are really beliefs about "what's right" or "what's good" (see chapter 2).

To invoke our computer analogy once again: (1) the conscious and unconscious parts of the mind are like computer hardware—the screen, the processor, and the memory; (2) your feelings, sensations, and memories and other thoughts are like the "data" that are either displayed on the screen or stored in the computer's memory;[2] and (3) your beliefs and intents are like the computer's software (more about this in a moment). Note that since the conscious mind, like the computer screen, can contain only a limited amount of information at any given moment, most of the "information" in your mind (intents, beliefs, memories, etc.) is "stored" in the nonconscious part (i.e., computer memory). There is, however, an important difference: whereas the contents of the computer screen can remain unchanged until you enter a new command into the keyboard, your conscious mind is ordinarily in a constant state of flux. Thoughts come and go. Sensory impressions—sights, sounds, smells, tastes, tactile sensations, and the physical sensations that originate from inside your body—are in a constant state of flux. Feelings like excitement, anger, happiness, worry, anxiety, and frustration arise and then dissipate. Everything that goes to make up what you call your "conscious experience" is like a steadily changing stream that seems never to stand still (in this sense, your conscious mind acts more like a computer "screen saver" that never repeats itself). And even when you are able to concentrate your attention on a particular thing or otherwise "shut out" from your consciousness most of the other incoming sensory stimulation, the contents of your consciousness do not completely "stand still."

What causes your conscious mind to be in such a state of continuous change? There are two primary sources for this stream of material that makes up your conscious experience: the "external" stimulation that comes in through your sense organs (sight, sound, smell, taste, and touch) and the "internal" thoughts and feelings that seem to arise spontaneously in your conscious mind. (There are also the physical sensations that come from inside your body, which are usually included with sensory impressions.) There is a constant by-play between the external and the internal. Sometimes your conscious awareness can be totally absorbed in something external like a good book or film or beautiful scenery. At other times you can be completely preoccupied with your internal thoughts and feelings, as when you daydream. You can even entertain both the internal and the external at the same time, as when you think about what happened yesterday while driving your car to work.

To return once again to our computer analogy: your eyes, ears, and other sensory organs are like "input devices" on a computer—the keyboard and the disc drives—by means of which "raw data" are entered into the mind. And just as the computer uses its software to "interpret" and "analyze" these data before displaying results on the screen, so does your nonconscious mind use your beliefs and intents to interpret and analyze the raw sensory data that comes in through your sense organs.

One of the problems in talking about the "contents" of the conscious mind is that being conscious is a "holistic" experience, by which I mean that everything comes in an experiential package called "consciousness" that cannot really be broken down into its parts without losing much of its essence and meaning. Therefore, in considering any thought, feeling, or other "item" that makes up the contents of your consciousness, keep in mind that how it affects your actual experience at any moment depends on the condition of all the other "parts" at that same moment. To take a simple example: you can watch a drama or sporting event on television, but your emotional reaction to that sensory experience will depend heavily on your beliefs and intents as they relate to the characters and the events being portrayed. Similarly, you can have an idea or a thought, but its *meaning* and *significance* to you depends on your beliefs and values and especially on your emotional or *feeling* state at the time. In fact, I will argue that, <u>in the absence of feelings, ideas or thoughts are basically meaningless</u> (see chapter 8, "Thinking and Feeling").

ATTENTION

One of the most important features of your normal waking consciousness is what we shall call focus or <u>attention</u>. The little experiments that opened this chapter were designed to <u>refocus</u> your attention away from the reading. You can either willfully <u>direct</u> your attention to focus on something— as I suggested you do in the experiments—or you can passively "let" it be focused—as you do when you daydream. Although the content of your waking consciousness when you are in such a passive state may sometimes <u>seem</u> like a random process, it is <u>not</u>. "If it is not random," you may ask, "then who or what is deciding what to put in my conscious mind when I am not deliberately (consciously) trying to focus my attention on something?" The answer, of course, is that your unconscious mind is doing the deciding. Keep in mind (no pun intended) my earlier definition of the unconscious as that part of your mind that does most of the very complex work of deciding what thoughts and emotions you will experience consciously and which of the many sights and sounds that are continually impinging on your eyes and ears you will <u>pay attention</u> to. In this book we will explore some of the "rules" that the unconscious follows in making all these decisions.

While it is true that you can consciously "direct" your attention to focus on certain sensory stimuli (choosing to watch a particular TV program or to read a certain book), once you have decided the general question of what you are going to "do" (e.g., watch a movie), your conscious mind passively "allows" much of your attention to particular aspects of the outside stimuli to be "directed" by your unconscious. Thus, while you can consciously choose your own books and TV programs, your unconscious does much of the work of deciding <u>which</u> of the specific characters or events being portrayed you will focus your attention on and how you will react to them and to the events being portrayed. Thus, when you discuss a TV show or a motion picture with a friend, you usually discover that the two of you had somewhat different impressions and memories of what you saw or read. And, as illustrated with our opening experiments, your unconscious also does most of the deciding about <u>distractions</u> from the film or TV show, that is, deciding when a competing stimulus is "important" enough to refocus your conscious attention away from the film or TV. These competing stimuli can be real events in your immediate environment (such as a phone ringing or a child or partner who wants your attention), but they can also be internal thoughts or feelings that come to you while reading or watching. For example, students who are "cramming" for an exam sometimes find it difficult to concentrate on their course notes because they are distracted by worries about issues such as finances, personal relationships, or how they will do on the exam! Thus, during those times when you "can't concentrate" on what you are reading or watching, your unconscious is trying to get your conscious mind to focus either on some outside distraction or on certain internal thoughts or feelings.

In fact, **when it comes to which particular thoughts and feelings you will experience and which particular sensations you will pay attention to, your unconscious does <u>most</u> of the work of deciding.** It is for this reason that people can sometimes feel that their conscious mind is "out of control," since they are unaware of all these decisions that are being made, including the "rules" that the unconscious is applying in making its choices. There are two very different ways to look at this process. If you find yourself being fascinated by or even enjoying the ideas and feelings that seem to pop spontaneously into your mind, you can look at this continuous flow as a kind of creative adventure: "Gee, that was interesting! I wonder what is coming next?" However, if you find the material that flows in spontaneously to be upsetting or disturbing, you might be motivated either (a) to try to <u>control</u> your thoughts or feelings (through meditation, drugs, psychotherapy, etc.) or (b) to <u>distract</u> yourself from your inner thoughts and feelings so that your conscious attention is focused instead on competing thoughts or on outside sensory stimuli (music, work, socializing, television, etc.). The strategy of "counting sheep" to fall asleep at night is really an attempt to distract your conscious mind from the thoughts or feelings that are keeping you awake, which sometimes include worrying about not being able to fall asleep!

As we shall see later on (see chapters 2 and 10), **any "distracting" thoughts, sensations, or feelings usually represent a <u>message</u> from your unconscious: "perhaps you could pay attention to this, rather than just being annoyed or frustrated by it."**

Regardless of whether you find your spontaneous flow of thoughts and feelings to be pleasing or displeasing, it is useful to <u>understand</u> something about this interplay between your conscious and unconscious minds. How does the unconscious do its work? Is the unconscious something to be feared or dreaded, as certain schools of psychology would have us believe? Is there an ongoing "battle" between these two parts of the mind, or are they working together cooperatively for your benefit? How does the "content" of your unconscious get there in the first place? How can you get access to that content? Is the unconscious some independent part of you that "does its own thing," or does your conscious mind ultimately determine what your unconscious mind thinks and does? How do you go about changing which particular thoughts and feelings are brought into your conscious mind by your unconscious? These are just some of the many questions about the mind that we will try to answer in this book.

First let us look in a little more depth at the conscious mind. In this way we can begin to see more clearly how the two minds work together.

THE MIRACLE OF WAKING CONSCIOUSNESS

All of this discussion about the vastness of the unconscious and the relatively small amount of information that you can contain at any time in your normal waking consciousness should not be interpreted as a put-down on waking consciousness. Indeed, the nonconscious part of the mind and all of the work that it does is only something we infer from observing what goes on in our normal waking consciousness. In short, your waking consciousness is really at the center of everything: thoughts, feelings, and sensory information all converge to help form what you call your conscious experience or, indeed, to form your life. In this sense, consciousness *is* everything. It contains everything that goes to make up "the human experience."

But the whole of consciousness is not simply a matter of the mind's contents—thoughts, sensations, and feelings. On the contrary, consciousness has to capacity to *do* things. Indeed, the power and creativity of the human being's normal waking consciousness is a remarkable thing to contemplate. When you think of monumental creations like the Egyptian pyramids, Beethoven's piano concertos, the New York skyline, or the treasures hanging in the Louvre, remember that human consciousness first imagined these things before they ever took form. In fact, the real miracle of your normal waking consciousness is that you can think anything you want. You can imagine or even visualize any event or possibility, any idea or concept, or any past, present, or future, no matter how crazy or unrealistic or trivial or grandiose it might seem. And you can do this with relative impunity. I qualify this last statement with the adjective "relative," because regularly thinking certain negative thoughts can eventually lead you to behave in ways that can have negative consequences in your life. The main point, however, is that you are free to think just about anything you want—no matter how wonderful or grandiose or fantastic and no matter how irrational or awful or despicable—because the thought by itself does not necessarily cause you or others any harm.

The human imagination is thus not constrained by anything in the physical world. You can imagine events or occurrences that might be practically or physically impossible—even events that violate physical "laws." You can imagine possible futures for yourself that satisfy your highest hopes, ambitions, or ideals, and you can "reinterpret" your past or even imagine all kinds of past events about which you have no "objective knowledge." You can look at any current problem in your life and imagine as many "possible" solutions as you want, before deciding what to "do" about the problem. Or, conversely, you can interpret that problem in the most negative and pessimistic terms, seeing no way out. It is all up to you.

Waking consciousness also steers the creative process. Your unconscious supplies the energy and the raw materials, while your conscious mind evaluates, sorts, selects, organizes, and eventually converts these raw materials into creative events and products. The very essence of creativity resides in the freedom of the conscious and unconscious parts of the mind to conceive, think, visualize, and imagine almost anything. A key element in the creative process thus involves <u>trusting</u> the unconscious so that there is the freest possible flow of insights, ideas, and "inspiration" between the two parts of the mind. In fact, sometimes the best thing your conscious mind can do to free up your creativity is simply not to <u>do</u> (i.e., think) anything, but simply to lay back and let the unconscious "do its thing" (see postscript).

Your conscious mind also possesses the capacity to <u>observe</u>, to <u>judge</u> and to <u>evaluate</u>. (Chapter 3 discusses this observing and judging capacity of the conscious mind in detail.) The "judging" feature of your personality is in certain ways similar to what Freud called the "superego." Popular conceptions of the superego speak of it like a "conscience," constantly judging our thoughts and actions as good or bad or right or wrong. But the judging/evaluating capacity of waking consciousness is far more than that. It can imaginatively "test out" alternative solutions to problems, simulating the likely consequences of each one in order to select the "best." It can estimate the likely consequences of various courses of action for you and for others. It helps you to develop your notions of right and wrong and to formulate a personal code of ethics. It can examine your life critically and help you to decide not only when change is needed, but also what kind of change is most likely to be of benefit. Our language is replete with words and phrases that describe the many functions of this evaluative/judging capacity: self-assessment, valuing, critical thinking, moral judgment, taste, discernment, and esthetic sensitivity.

Given that the content of the conscious mind at any point in time usually consists of some mixture of thoughts, feelings, and sensory impressions (sights, sounds, etc.), how would you describe your "conscious content" right now? This is a tough question because nobody's mind ever really "stands still;" rather, it is in a continuous state of change! Even so, if I pressed you on the matter, you could probably share with me some of your most immediate thoughts and impressions. For example, on the "impression" side you might tell me that you were seeing this book and this page and the words you were reading. You might also say that you were sitting in an uncomfortable position, that you had an itch, or that you also heard a dog barking, a refrigerator running, or the roar of a jet engine. Your state of mind, in other words, usually includes <u>sense impressions</u> of one sort or another, although as I tried to show in the opening experiments, when you are reading or otherwise concentrating on an intellectual task, you are not likely to "notice" (focus your conscious attention on) most of these impressions unless your unconscious judges them to be especially unusual or important.

Regardless of whether you would be able to share any sense impressions with me, you could almost certainly tell me something about what you were <u>thinking</u>. You might simply report back an idea that was being expressed in the book. Or, you might have an opinion about what you were just reading: "That's an interesting idea," "I'm not sure I understand what he just said," "That doesn't make sense," "That seems self-evident," and so on. Or, you might have an <u>associated</u> memory: "That passage reminds me of a conversation I had with a friend last week."

Finally, we come to your <u>feelings</u>. Often this is the most difficult part of your state of mind to describe, because feelings can be very subtle, especially when you are doing something "unemotional" like reading this book. You might well tell me that you are not feeling anything in particular right now, but if you stop for a moment to reflect carefully on your current feeling state, there will be very few times when you cannot discern at least *some* kind of feeling or feeling "tone." For example, upon reflection you might realize that you feel "relaxed," or "bored," or "laid back," or "content," even though the feeling did not exactly "register" until I asked you to focus your attention on it. In a way, your more subtle feelings provide a kind of background or context in which your thoughts and sense impressions arise. For this reason, among others, the meaning or significance of any conscious thought or sense impression can vary according to the feeling context in which it arises.

THE CENTRALITY OF FEELINGS

While we humans can be justifiably proud of our ability to think and reason logically, the essence of being alive and conscious is our capacity to <u>feel</u>.[3] Our capacity to feel is what makes it possible to love, to care, to be joyful, and to experience the beauty in art and music. Our more subtle feeling states, such as wonder and curiosity, provide the impetus for us to learn, discover, and create. Other powerful feelings—like fear, jealously, anger, envy, guilt and depression—are at the root of our most serious personal and social problems. Finally, many feelings are intimately connected to our <u>beliefs</u>, which, as we shall shortly see, help to shape much of our conscious experience (see chapter 2).

For all of these reasons, in this book we shall place a major emphasis on identifying and understanding your feelings, their incredible variety, and how and why they emerge into your consciousness. Chapter 5 will thus be devoted exclusively to feelings and emotions and what they mean. And given the central importance of feelings to almost all aspects of our conscious experience, we will devote major parts of four other chapters to an analysis of specific types of feelings: Chapter 6 ("Motivation and Intent"), chapter 7 ("Body and Mind"), chapter 8 ("Thinking and Feeling"), and chapter 9 ("Consciousness and Community").

"TIME"

Another important issue that we shall examine is the role of *time* in your conscious experience. Where in time do you focus most of your conscious thought? How much of your waking consciousness do you devote to thinking about things that are happening <u>now</u>, as opposed to things that happened in the past or that might happen in the future? Note that the time focus of your thoughts is intimately connected to your beliefs and especially to your emotional life. Negative emotions, in particular, are typically connected either to thoughts about <u>past</u> events—as in the case of hatred or guilt—or to thoughts about future events—as in the case of anxiety or fear. Positive emotions like love and joy, on the other hand, are more often connected to your present situation.

Your time sense is also closely connected to the activities of your everyday life and to the emotional states that accompany these activities. You are likely to feel hurried, anxious, or frustrated when you think you lack the time to do the things you believe you should do. And when you believe you have plenty of time, you are more able to feel relaxed, content, or serene. Finally, when you believe you are spending <u>too much</u> time doing something, you are likely to feel bored or impatient.

The role of your time focus will be discussed in much more detail in chapter 11, as well as in the various chapters that deal with feelings and emotions: chapters 5, 6, 7, 8, and 9.

INTENTIONALITY AND SPONTANEITY

The ordinary content of your waking consciousness can be looked at in two ways: with and without the operation of conscious "intent." When conscious intent is present, you have the sense of <u>deliberately</u> thinking about certain things, making your body do certain things, or affecting external events in certain ways. "I'm trying to remember that man's name" is an act of conscious intent, as is "that house plant is beginning to wilt, so I'm going to water it," or "It's getting stuffy in here, so I'm going to open a window." Conscious intent, in other words, is an active, goal-oriented process that appears when you deliberately try to affect either the content of your consciousness or the events or circumstances of your daily life. Since your intentions, desires, and motives play such a key role in shaping your conscious experience, we shall explore them in detail in chapter 6 ("Motivation and Intent").

Conscious content that arises in the absence of conscious intent can be termed "spontaneous." These are the thoughts, images, and feelings that arise when you daydream or meditate or that occur without any apparent motive, will or intent. With certain spontaneous material, of course, it is possible to <u>deduce</u> a purpose or intent. Thus, if you begin to think about tomorrow, you might say to yourself: "I must be anxious about all the things I have to do tomorrow." But such material nevertheless <u>occurs</u> spontaneously, no matter how much you choose to "analyze" it after the fact. While the material appears spontaneously (without conscious intent), your decision to analyze it is an intentional choice.

Although most of the content of your ordinary waking consciousness is spontaneous, it is possible to control your conscious content intentionally for sustained periods of time. You ordinarily call this "concentration." Concentration refers to those times when you are trying to memorize something, learn a new skill, solve a problem, or otherwise focus your complete attention on a particular task or event like reading a book, listening to music, learning a new language, solving a puzzle, or watching a movie or play. Concentration usually shuts off spontaneous material. Indeed, when you say you are "having difficulty concentrating," you usually mean that spontaneous material is arising when you "don't want it to." These spontaneous thoughts or feelings are thus seen as competing with your conscious desire to focus your attention on something else. When the same spontaneous conscious material reaches a point where it literally overwhelms most of a person's efforts at will-oriented consciousness, we usually call it "obsessive" thinking. When such out-of-control spontaneous content is heavily emotional, it can take many different forms: anxiety, depression, desire, excitement, and so forth.

Even though spontaneous thoughts, feelings, and actions occur without any apparent intent, these "unintentional" events can tell us a good deal about the nonconscious mind. Let us look first at actions. What can you learn about yourself by looking at actions that you take more or less spontaneously, without consciously intending or willing them?

Spontaneous Action: A Window to the "Unconscious"

If you feel something that itches you, you scratch it. If you touch something that is very hot, you withdraw. If you feel too cold, you snuggle to get warm. We call these actions "spontaneous" because you can do them without first thinking about them. Ah, but these are mere instinctive reactions, you say; they do not tell me much about my unconscious because they are wired in by my genetics. But wait a minute. What happens when you are driving on a freeway and the guy ahead of you jams on his brakes? Do you first think "there's danger ahead, I'd better put on the brakes," before you actually apply the brakes? No. There is no time for that. You hit the brakes spontaneously just like you withdraw from the hot object, without even thinking about it. There is no way that this can be an instinctive response, since your genes do not know anything about cars, freeways, or speed. What really happens when you respond in this manner on a freeway is that the <u>nonconscious</u> part of your mind has processed an enormous amount of complex information and directed your foot to apply pressure to the brake. The information that gets processed includes the relative speeds of the two vehicles, the distance between them, the condition of the shoulder or possible passing lanes, the condition of your brakes, and so on. And all of this analyzing and directing of action is happening in a fraction of a second! The same goes for many other spontaneous actions, especially those that involve possible physical danger.

The basic lesson to be learned from such examples is this: there can be an <u>intelligence</u> and a <u>wisdom</u> behind your spontaneous actions. Spontaneous actions, in other words, are not necessarily crazy, random, or irrational. This discussion, in short, highlights another fundamental principle:

- **The <u>source</u> of your spontaneity—your nonconscious mind—can be both highly intelligent and wise.**

Think about all of the complicated physical activities that you can carry out in a wise and intelligent fashion with little if any involvement of the conscious mind: Riding a bicycle, eating, singing in the shower, brushing your teeth, getting dressed, playing the piano, taking a walk, driving a car. Make your own list. Each of these activities involves highly complex perceptual, analytical, and motor skills. Judgments are being rendered. Decisions are being made. Parts of your body are being directed to carry out highly sophisticated activities. And all the while your conscious mind can be preoccupied with other things.[4] That larger, mostly unconscious part of the self that directs spontaneous activities can indeed act in an intelligent and wise fashion.

But what about those times when your "spontaneous" actions cause you pain or difficulty, those occasions when you say or do things that you later regret? In most such instances your actions can be traced to negative or otherwise dysfunctional <u>beliefs</u> (see chapter 2 through 9). In such cases what your nonconscious mind is doing is simply <u>acting</u> on these beliefs. Clearly, the key to avoiding such counterproductive "spontaneity" in the future is to identify and, where necessary, to change those beliefs that underlie your actions (see chapter 10).

So far we have been talking about spontaneous <u>actions</u>. What about thoughts and feelings? What can you learn about your unconscious from the countless "uninvited" feelings[5] and thoughts that emerge spontaneously into your normal waking consciousness? This will be a little harder to answer, since the <u>intention</u> underlying spontaneous feelings and thoughts is usually not as easy to discern as is the intention underlying many spontaneous physical actions. Sometimes, however, you can find useful clues as to the meaning or intent behind certain feelings or emotions if you look at the <u>actions</u> that they initiate. Take one very powerful emotion, fear. Fear can lead you to run away from or otherwise avoid those situations that provoked the fear in the first place ("flight"). Fear can also cause you to attempt to destroy or disable whatever precipitated the fear ("fight"). In both instances you might conclude that the purpose of the fear is to protect you from danger. Similarly, sexual feelings or feelings of love, affection, or gratitude might prompt you to touch or embrace the person to whom the feeling is directed, suggesting that the function of such positive feelings has something to do with your need to have physical contact with, affiliate with, or nurture another person.

But what about those many spontaneous feelings and thoughts that do not consistently lead to particular actions? In order to address this very large question, we first need to consider the relationship between thought and feeling. Do thoughts cause feelings? Do feelings cause thoughts? Can it work both ways? Many people seem to believe that since feelings like fear and anger are very "primitive," they are "inferior" to thoughts, which are at a "higher level." In this view, feelings might lead to or cause thoughts, but not the other way around. Upon closer examination, however, there is good reason to believe that <u>emotions arise from thoughts</u>; that thinking, in other words, is often more "basic" than emotion. Let us consider a few examples.

Suppose you are flying on a commercial jetliner that suddenly encounters moderate air turbulence which causes the plane to shake. An experienced flyer probably would not pay much attention to the shaking. But if you are a first-time flyer, you might well feel fearful. Now what has taken place within you that generates this emotion? Clearly, the shaking of the airplane has somehow been <u>interpreted</u> as a possible threat. In all likelihood, some part of your psyche has gone through a <u>reasoning</u> process something like this: "The plane is no longer flying smoothly. Is something wrong with the aircraft? Could we crash?" If the shaking is especially violent or atypical, even the more experienced passenger might apply the same reasoning process and end up feeling anxious or fearful.

What, then, can we say about the mental processes involved in this example? Basically, some part of your mind has analyzed ("thought about") certain sensory information (shaking of the plane) and concluded that the information may signify a physical threat to you personally. The particular logical or thinking process that you have applied to the information has thus <u>caused</u> you to feel fearful. The more experienced traveler may not experience fear because she analyzes the same sensory information differently.

One of the most important points to keep in mind here is that the "thinking" that gives rise to the emotional state is largely "unconscious." Like the "unconscious thinking" that helps you drive your car effectively while you carry on a conversation with someone in the front passenger seat, the thinking that gives rise to your fear response happens <u>very</u> <u>fast</u>. So fast, in fact, that you are left with the impression that the emotional response is instantaneous! In other words, it <u>seems</u> to you like the sequence of events is simply

shaking → *fear*, rather than
shaking → *analysis* → *fear*.

Yet the only way to explain why you felt fearful and the more experienced traveler did not (*shaking* → <u>*not fear*</u>) is that the two of you <u>analyzed</u> or <u>interpreted</u> the shaking differently.

Let us examine a more subtle and complex emotion: jealousy. Suppose you are newly married and that you and your spouse are attending a party. After a while you notice that your spouse is engaged in an animated conversation with an attractive person of your gender and suddenly you experience a feeling of intense jealousy. That feeling may in turn prompt any one of a number of different actions on your part, but let us first analyze the feeling of jealousy that you are experiencing.

While the feeling seemed to emerge into your consciousness almost instantaneously (*event* → *feeling*), the only way to explain it is in terms of how you <u>analyzed</u> or <u>interpreted</u> the basic sensory information (seeing your spouse or partner having an animated conversation with an attractive person of your gender): *event* → *analysis* → *feeling*. Once again, your "analysis" was done very rapidly and largely unconsciously.

There are many possible ways in which your analysis might cause you to feel jealous. Perhaps you interpreted their conversation as flirtatious, assuming that your partner was sexually or romantically interested in the other person. Perhaps you have doubts about your partner's affection for or loyalty to you. Perhaps you have doubts about your own attractiveness or sex appeal, and saw the other person as more attractive or appealing. Perhaps all of these unconscious thoughts occurred in response to your witnessing their conversation.

Jealousy, like fear, is an intense emotion that often leads to action and to other emotional states. In the instance of the party, many actions and new emotions are possible. You might walk away, pretending you did not notice them. You might interrupt them, telling your partner it is time to go home. You might even join the conversation, competing with the other person for your partner's attention (*event → analysis → emotion → action*). At the same time, any one of an array of secondary emotions may arise in your conscious mind: fear, anger, sadness, anxiety, self-doubt, self-pity (*event → analysis → emotion → emotion*). The fact that other people confronted with the same situation might react with emotions that are different from yours once again underscores the fact that the same event is being <u>interpreted</u> (analyzed) differently.

In short, this discussion underscores another fundamental principle about the workings of the conscious and nonconscious parts of the mind:

> **Most of your conscious emotional reactions to life events are based on unconscious thought and analysis.**

BELIEFS

So far our analysis has barely touched on the most important part of the relationship between thought and emotion: the central role of <u>beliefs</u>. In both of the examples given—and indeed in almost any other example you can think of—<u>your emotional reactions to events are conditioned by your beliefs</u>. In other words, any time you react emotionally to an event, it is because the event is being <u>interpreted</u> or <u>analyzed</u> in terms of your particular beliefs. In the case of the air turbulence "causing" you to feel fearful, perhaps you believe that air travel is very dangerous. The more experienced traveler, on the other hand, may believe that it is very safe, or that a certain amount of air turbulence is "normal." In the case of your feeling jealous of your partner, we have already suggested a number of beliefs that could trigger your emotional reaction: beliefs about yourself, beliefs about your partner, or beliefs about your relationship. In fact, there are many other beliefs that could also trigger an emotional reaction in response to your partner's party conversation: beliefs about what is "proper" public conduct for strangers or partners at a party, beliefs about the "intentions" of strangers who flirt at parties, beliefs about how others at the party are perceiving what your partner is doing, and so on.

We have now reached a point when we can outline, as least superficially, the circumstances that give rise to conscious experience of various emotions:

$$belief(s) \ \rightarrow \ event \ \rightarrow \ analysis \ (\text{via beliefs}) \ \rightarrow emotion$$

I have put beliefs first in the chain of events because the event is analyzed within a belief framework that has been formed prior to the occurrence of the event. In other words:

Your beliefs provide a framework for your nonconscious mind to interpret the events of your life.

Note that, <u>in most cases where you consciously experience an intense emotional response to an event, you may not be conscious of the beliefs that shaped your analysis</u>. All you perceive is the event and the emotion. But "where" is the belief? Clearly, it resides somewhere in your unconscious.

It is hard to appreciate how rapidly the nonconscious part of the mind is able to bring emotional responses into consciousness by processing your experiences through your belief system. In fact, this "analysis" of incoming information that takes place in your nonconscious mind occurs so fast that you usually assume that no analysis has taken place at all; rather, you believe that the incoming information is the direct <u>cause</u> of the emotional state: "He 'made' me jealous." "She 'made' me feel guilty." It <u>seems</u> so automatic that you seldom stop to reflect on the complex unconscious processing that just took place. Thus, when you regularly experience negative emotions in response to a particular person, you might say, "he sure knows how to press my buttons." The information—the person's words or actions or just his mere physical presence—seems to "trigger" the emotional response. Pushing buttons and pulling triggers are mechanical acts that have instantaneous consequences. We use such metaphors because they express our sense that the emotional response is (a) automatic and thus beyond our control, and (b) instantaneous, that is, that no "analysis" or "processing" of the other person's words or actions has occurred. In other words:

Since the unconscious analysis of life events through our belief system is so rapid, most of us believe that our emotions are "caused" by life events.

Under these conditions, it is no wonder that we often blame other people for our negative emotional states, since it <u>seems</u> like we were helpless to react in any other way. Psychotherapists sometimes refer to this problem as "not owning" our emotions or "not taking responsibility" for the emotional states that we experience in response to others. However, it is difficult for the client to "own" emotional reactions to others as long as there is no understanding of the unconscious processing that is going on. Rather, the speed and predictability of the emotional response leads the client to assume that there <u>is</u> no processing:

other person → emotion

Reaching a state where you have achieved some understanding of the unconscious processing mechanism is sometimes called achieving "insight." However, there are very different <u>levels</u> of insight that are possible. Sometimes you may act without even recognizing or acknowledging the emotion that gave rise to the action (e.g., reacting angrily toward your partner at the party without realizing that you are also feeling jealous). And even if you have achieved that limited level of insight ("I left the party early because I was jealous and angry"), you may not be aware of the particular action or event (e.g., the attractiveness of the other person, your partner's apparent interest) that "triggered" the negative emotion. Being able to associate the feeling with the external precipitating event thus provides a bit more insight: "I got mad because she was flirting with someone else who is very attractive." However, you may regularly feel anxious or depressed or angry or fearful and yet not be able to associate the repeated occurrence of such feelings with any particular type of "cause." Still another level of insight is thus to recognize <u>patterns</u> in your emotional responses: "she always manages to do something that angers me." In fact, the phrase "she pushes my buttons" reflects a significant level of insight, not only because it acknowledges the emotion and recognizes the habitual pattern (*she → emotion*) but also because it implicitly acknowledges ownership ("<u>my</u> buttons") and the presence of <u>some</u> unconscious processing and analysis that precedes the emotion. The only problem with the "button pushing" level of insight is that this type of metaphor suggests a certain level of helplessness (the reaction seems almost "wired in") and that it does not necessarily encourage any further understanding of the belief systems ("wiring diagram?") through which the life event is being processed. If the life event is unique and something you can simply avoid in the future, then this level of insight may be enough. But if similar events cannot be avoided in the future, then it may well be worth investigating the processing mechanism, which is, of course, your <u>belief system</u>. Thus,

The key to understanding your emotional reactions to life events is to understand the relevant beliefs[6] that you employ to make meaning out of these events.

Let us see if we can illustrate these somewhat abstract ideas with an example from the mental health field. Some schools of psychotherapy are cognizant of the important role played by beliefs in the shaping of emotional states (although they may use somewhat different terms than I am using to describe the process). Let us say the client recently got very jealous and angry at his wife at a party. When a client recounts such an event, the therapist may try to help the client identify the particular beliefs which helped shape the emotional response. (Sometimes the event <u>itself</u> first has to be identified!) This therapeutic technique is sometimes referred to as a "clarification" or even an "interpretation." The basic problem with this approach—reasoning backwards from emotions to events and beliefs—is that <u>intense emotional states often interfere with the reasoning process</u>. Try being "objective" about your own sexuality or attractiveness when you are feeling intensely jealous of your spouse! Try being objective about <u>anything</u> when you are really angry! Clearly, in such cases your chances of being able to identify the relevant beliefs will be improved if your wait until some of the intense feeling has subsided.

Therapists who recognize this problem will often try to help clients first understand their beliefs without necessarily associating these beliefs with the occurrence of unpleasant emotional states. Indeed, there is some real risk in <u>assuming</u> that the client's emotional response is predicated on particular beliefs without first establishing clearly what the client's relevant beliefs really <u>are</u>. Therapists are on shaky ground when they interpret emotions without really understanding the client's relevant beliefs.

Even though we are not usually consciously aware of how our beliefs are <u>affecting</u> our conscious emotions from moment to moment, most of us, including many psychotherapists, fail to realize that:

- **Most of your beliefs are accessible to your conscious mind**!

Some views of the human psyche portray the "unconscious" as a hermetically sealed vat of impulses and memories that is largely cut off from your normal waking consciousness and which can be unsealed and explored, if at all, only through many years of intensive psychoanalysis or psychotherapy. The fact is that much of this "unconscious" material is <u>potentially</u> available to normal waking consciousness, even without a therapist's help, providing, of course, that you are willing and determined to make such an effort at self-exploration. Some specific <u>memories</u>, of course, might be extremely difficult to bring into waking consciousness, especially memories of events that happened a long time ago. Your current <u>beliefs</u> about yourself, others, and the world, however, <u>are</u> largely accessible to your normal waking consciousness, although it might well require a bit of planning and effort to identify these beliefs. However, given the critical role that beliefs play in regulating your feelings and behavior, such an investment of time and energy would seem to be well worth the effort.

Later on we will discuss some techniques for accessing your beliefs (see chapters 2 and 10). But perhaps the most important point to be learned from this initial discussion so far concerns the problem of powerful emotional states like anger, fear, jealousy, depression, and anxiety: <u>the key to</u>

changing your negative emotional responses to events is to change your beliefs. (Specific techniques for changing beliefs will be discussed in detail in chapter 10.)

As we shall see in the next chapter, beliefs are usually about "concepts" like yourself, others, good, evil, truth, and so on. For example, if you encounter a panhandler while walking down a busy city street, you may automatically (unconsciously) attribute certain meaning to that encounter by identifying the person with a concept such as a "homeless person," a "dangerous person," a "bum," a "beggar," an "alcoholic," a "mental case," a "dirty person," a "sad person," a "suspicious character," or whatever. And, depending on your beliefs about such concepts, you will simultaneously experience certain feelings—apprehension, discomfort, fear, disgust, anger, defensiveness, guilt, compassion, humor, etc. (See especially, in chapter 9, the section on "Getting to Know You.") These cognitive interpretations of and affective reactions toward the other person are, once again, attributable to the (largely unconscious) processing of the incoming sensory data (the person's presence and appearance) through your concepts and beliefs. For this reason, your particular conscious experience of such an encounter might be very different from the experience of someone who holds different beliefs about concepts such as wealth and poverty, mental illness, the "work ethic," cleanliness, race, crime, welfare, or politics. These differences in conscious experience might also lead to different behaviors: ignoring the panhandler, stopping to converse, giving money, lecturing the person about the value of hard work, and so on. Indeed, since a person from another culture who has never experienced panhandling or homeless people would almost certainly process that same encounter through a different set of beliefs, that person would probably have an entirely different conscious experience of the same encounter, and thereby react in a very different manner. In short:

- **Your beliefs influence not only your emotional reaction to a particular event, but also the meaning you make of that event and how you act in response to it.**

A BRIEF SUMMARY: "MIND AS COMPUTER"

One way to try to summarize the major ideas about the conscious and unconscious parts of the mind that have been presented so far is to resort once again to our personal computer analogy. While I remain skeptical about efforts to use computers to "model" thinking and feeling (i.e., the experience of being conscious), I believe that there are many parallels between computers and the human mind in their basic operations. This should probably come as no real surprise, since the computer is, after all, a creative product of the human mind, which is basically designed, like the mind, to do certain "mental" work. Indeed, the computer (or perhaps its ancestor, the abacus) may be the first human invention that has been deliberately designed to carry out mental work. However, as we shall see shortly, I still find it necessary to include a human being—the computer operator—as one of the basic "parts" of the computer, simply because a computer cannot really do anything without a conscious, intentional operator to tell it what to do. In the same way, a brain and a body and an unconscious mind are not of much use without waking, intentional consciousness.

Any functioning computer requires at least the following four basic structures: hardware, software, data, and a human operator. Hardware is the physical machine itself, which must include a memory, the ability to make computations, and the capacity to both receive and display data (i.e., "input-output" devices like a keyboard and a screen). Software comprises a set of rules for processing data ("computing") that are coded in the form of computational instructions to be carried out by the hardware. The operator is the person who (a) decides what input data are to be given to the computer and which parts of the software are to be activated and (b) views and interprets the "output" data that are printed out or displayed on a screen.

There are direct parallels between each of these four computer structures and your mind. Let us start with hardware and software. "Computer hardware" is very much like your brain and body, which regularly receive "input" data through your senses, processes those data in the central nervous system and produce "outputs" in the form of conscious thoughts, feelings, sense impressions, and bodily actions. These outputs, of course, constitute your conscious experience and your behavior. "Computer software" is very much like the beliefs, intents, and concepts that reside in your nonconscious mind, since these provide the framework for screening the incoming sensory data and giving it meaning, for shaping your conscious thoughts and feelings, and for directing your bodily actions. The brain, sensory organs, neuromusculature and peripheral nervous system, in other words, make it possible for you to act physically and consciously to experience sense impressions, thoughts and feelings. However, the beliefs that reside in your nonconscious mind are crucial in determining what particular meaning you will make out of your daily experience, which particular thoughts and feelings you will experience consciously, and what particular actions you will take. In the same way, the computer hardware is what makes it possible to receive input information, process it, and produce output information, but it is the software that determines how the incoming data will be processed and, ultimately, what the output will look like.

The computer operator determines what raw data ("instructions") will be given to ("input" into) the computer. These data activate the software which, in turn, instructs the hardware in what to do. The computer operator is thus very much like your conscious mind, which controls much of the raw "data" your nonconscious mind will receive. Since the daily events of your life constitute most of the "raw data" that are "input" into your nonconscious mind, your conscious mind ultimately "controls" much of your daily experience through the choices it makes. In other words, since the conscious choices that you make throughout your life—friends, lovers, enemies, education, employment, career, place of residence, and so on— will obviously have a major effect on the kinds of life events you will be exposed to, these same choices help to determine much of the "raw data" that will be input through your senses. The same is true of your conscious choices of hobbies, reading material, entertainment, travel and life-styles—each of these choices helps to shape the raw "data" that you input into your nonconscious mind. (This book is a simple case in point: your conscious decision to read it has not only caused you to be exposed to particular "raw" sensory data—mostly of a visual nature—but has also caused you to ignore a lot of other sensory data, that is, recall the experiments that opened this chapter.)

In short, the parallel structures in the computer and the human mind can be summarized as follow:

Computer Analogue	Human Consciousness
computer operator.....................	normal waking consciousness
computer hardware................... (input devices)	brain/nervous (sense organs)
software....................................... (installed in hardware)	beliefs, concepts, and intents ("stored" in unconscious)
(*Input Data*)	
"raw" data..............................	sensory stimulation ("experience")
software commands.................	conscious intent
Output data..............................	change in conscious experience

Note that there are basically two types of input data that the computer operator can give the computer: (1) "raw" data, and (2) "software commands." To take a very simple example, if I had a long list of numbers that I wanted to add up on the computer, I would (1) enter or input the raw data—the numbers—into the computer, and (2) enter or input the software commands, which would in turn cause the machine to add them up. In the same fashion, my waking consciousness can either (1) expose my nonconscious mind to certain "raw" sensory data or (2) directly "command" the brain and the nonconscious mind to carry out certain tasks. In the first instance, I can choose to expose my conscious and unconscious minds to new "input data" by changing my external environment, for example, by reading a new book, listening to new music, changing my friends or habits, traveling to a new place, and so forth. In the second, I can to a certain extent directly "command" the nonconscious mind to try to recall certain events or to change its "screening" rules for sensory data. Thus, before you began this chapter's opening experiment, the initial raw data was the image of the printed words on the pages of this book. When you closed your eyes and "commanded" your nonconscious mind to stop screening out all the sounds around you, you stopped reading this book and suddenly became conscious of many sounds that you previously had not been "hearing" while you were reading. And just as you can change the "rules" by which computers analyze raw data by changing the software, so can you change the meaning that your nonconscious mind gives to the events of your life ("the raw input data") by changing your beliefs. And just as you can change a computer's output by changing the raw data that you input, so can you directly change your conscious experience by choosing different friends, jobs, place of residence, hobbies, reading material, entertainment, or other lifestyle choices that determine the much of the "raw data" that are input through your senses.

There are, of course, important differences between computers and the way your psyche operates. The most important difference is that the "software" of the nonconscious mind includes much more than beliefs, concepts, and intents. The nonconscious mind "knows" most of the things that you have learned throughout your life—from cognitive skills like reading and speaking to motor skills like walking and driving a car that you can perform with only minimal involvement of your conscious mind. The nonconscious mind is also the repository for all of your memories, not to mention the source of your intuition, inspiration, and creativity. While it is true that computers can "memorize" information and even "learn" certain kinds of "skills," there is nothing in the structure or function of computers that is analogous to human intent, desire, emotion, intuition, inspiration, or creativity.

Another major difference already noted between consciousness and personal computers is that the content of your normal waking consciousness is continually changing, even if you try to control it. In fact, your conscious experience never really "freezes" like the information that you might choose to display on the computer screen. For this reason, playing a video game is probably more like human consciousness than is analyzing data on a personal computer, since both the "inputs" (the player's manipulations of the controls) and the "outputs" (the display on the video screen) are continually changing. And just as an expert video game player must be attentive to the outputs and be knowledgeable about how the software operates—that is, how the outputs that appear on the screen will be affected by inputs that he makes through the manual controls—so is a psychologically well-functioning person both a careful observer of his or her conscious experience and knowledgeable about the system of beliefs and intents ("software") that help to shape that experience.

A FINAL QUESTION: WHO IS IN CONTROL?

With all the by-play that happens continuously between the conscious and unconscious minds, it is interesting to consider the issue of who is "calling the shots." Certainly a great deal of the material that flows into your normal waking consciousness <u>seems</u> to be sent there by your unconscious mind, regardless of whether or not your conscious mind asks for it. And yet it is also true that you can intentionally focus your conscious mind so completely on a task that very little "unasked-for" material from the unconscious can enter your consciousness. At these times it is as if you are instructing your unconscious: "Go away and don't bother me. I want to focus all of my attention on this particular thing."

Yet at other times—for example, when you daydream—you more or less "relinquish control" to your unconscious, as if to say, "OK, now you can take over and I'll just sit back and watch what happens." At still other times—for example, when you cannot stop yourself from being preoccupied with worry, guilt, fear, depression, or other intense thoughts or emotions—it seems like the unconscious has completely taken control away from your conscious will.

This discussion raises an important issue regarding the "autonomy" of the unconscious: Does the unconscious always take its cues or "orders" from the conscious mind, or does it have "a mind of its own?" Some psychological theories, for example, portray the mind as a kind of battleground between its conscious and unconscious portions, with the socialized, rational, conscious mind struggling to control the primitive, irrational urges of the unconscious mind. One way of looking at this issue is to realize that the beliefs and intents that govern the workings of the nonconscious mind are <u>your</u> beliefs and intents. If you were consciously to examine these beliefs and intents one at a time, you would no doubt "agree" with most, if not all, of them. Apparent "conflicts" between the "two minds" thus arise either because you (a) have embraced conflicting or inconsistent beliefs or intents or (b) are not presently aware of the connection between your "unwanted" thoughts and feelings and the particular beliefs or intents underlying them. (Techniques for identifying your most important beliefs and intents are presented in chapters 2 and 10.)

This book is thus predicated on four basic premises concerning your beliefs and the conscious and unconscious parts of your mind:

- The conscious and unconscious parts of your mind are basically engaged in a cooperative effort on behalf of your psychological well being and personal development.
- Many of the concepts, beliefs, and intents that guide the activities of the unconscious are accessible to the conscious mind.
- Healthy psychological development and creativity are hindered when the unconscious becomes host to a great many negative or conflicting beliefs.
- One of the keys to psychological health and the freeing of creative talents and energy is to recognize your negative or contradictory beliefs and, where necessary, to abandon or revise them.

OVERVIEW OF THE REST OF THE BOOK

The steady stream of thoughts, feelings, and sensations that flows through your waking consciousness has been heavily influenced by the countless concepts, intentions, and beliefs that are "stored" in your nonconscious mind. A good way to begin asserting more control over your conscious experience is to (a) start getting better acquainted with your beliefs and with how they affect your reactions to events and shape your experience (chapter 2) and (b) become a more astute observer of what goes on your consciousness from moment to moment (chapter 3). As you begin to do this it is especially important to become more aware of what you pay attention to (chapter 4) and of your different feeling states (chapter 5), especially those feelings that have to do with your intents and desires (chapter 6), your body (chapter 7), your thinking (chapter 8), and especially your relationships with other people (chapter 9). It is also important to recognize that certain powerful emotions like anger, fear, and guilt can be very dysfunctional and disempowering because they divert attention from the present moment (chapter 11).

Becoming better acquainted with your beliefs and intents and with how they condition your emotional reactions to events can be a very useful and liberating experience, but the key to making major changes in your life experience is to change or relinquish those beliefs which are not serving you well, especially certain negative or otherwise limiting beliefs about yourself and others in your life (chapter 10). Making such changes can also help to free up your creative and intuitive potential and enhance your spiritual life ("Postscript" chapter).

NOTES

1. From *Wisdom of the Idiots* by Idries Shah by permission of The March Agency Ltd on behalf of the Estate of Idries Shah.
2. Strictly speaking, since sensations and feelings can be <u>experienced</u> only in the conscious mind, it is the <u>memory</u> of them that is "stored" in the non-conscious mind. It is possible, of course, that upon recalling particular memories you might <u>re</u>-experience their associated sensations or feelings.
3. With apologies to Rene Descartes.
4. Some philosophical schools, of course, and Zen in particular, maintain that we all need to learn how to focus our consciousness <u>only</u> on the particular activity: "when I eat I eat, when I sleep I sleep." For an extended discussion of the "splintering" of consciousness between two or more activities, see chapter 4.
5. For most of this book we will use the words "feeling" and "emotion" inter-changeably.
6. Of course, in the case of certain neuroses or other severe psychological disturbances, the relevant beliefs might involve significant distortions in other people's motives or intentions or even in "historical" events.

CHAPTER 2

THE NATURE OF BELIEFS

Your beliefs form the core or your personality. They are the "lenses" through which you view the world and the "filters" that determine much of what you pay attention to in your daily life. Your beliefs also play a major role in determining your emotional reactions and in shaping the desires and intents that underlie your actions. Your beliefs, in other words, literally create much of what you call your "conscious experience."

In the preface I tried to stress the fact that you should not take anything that is said in this book on faith, and that you should instead use your own conscious experience as a laboratory for checking out the ideas being presented. To facilitate this process of "personal testing," this and subsequent chapters include a number of simple exercises that you can do to illustrate or demonstrate what is being written.

Just what are your beliefs? In a nutshell, a belief is a thought or idea which asserts one or more of the following:

- What is true.
- What is good.
- What is important.
- What is possible.

The sum total of your beliefs about what is currently true, good, important, and possible constitutes your worldview.

Mindworks: Becoming More Conscious in an Unconscious World, pp. 33–57
Copyright © 2007 by Information Age Publishing
All rights of reproduction in any form reserved.

Beliefs about <u>truth</u> have to do with "what is" or "what's real": the way things were, are, or will be. "People are basically good" is a belief about the way things are. Such beliefs are assertions not only about what is true or what is false, but also about what is real or not real. A belief about what is true or real states that a certain past, present, or future condition or event actually happened, is now happening, or will happen. Beliefs about the past or future usually have to do with events: "My parents didn't get along together" is a belief about past events, while "Next week I'll go on a diet" is a belief about future events.

Beliefs about truth and reality have enormous power in your life, not only because they are so numerous, but also because you tend to take most of them for granted. That is, they represent your version of the "real world." While you might occasionally question your beliefs about what is good, important, or possible, given that such beliefs obviously involve some degree of judgment, you are much less likely to question your beliefs about what is true or real because you think they are based on "reality" rather than perception or judgement.

Beliefs about <u>goodness</u> have to do with your morals, your sense of good and bad or right and wrong:

- "Love thy neighbor."
- "Masturbation is a sin."
- "Children should be seen and not heard."

These beliefs also carry enormous power in your daily life, in part because they often have a strong <u>emotional</u> component. In particular, such moral beliefs are often at the root of powerful emotional states like guilt and anger.

Beliefs about <u>importance</u> have to do with the value or priority that you assign to things in your life: "When it comes to choosing my career, economic security always comes first." There is obviously a connection between importance and goodness, in the sense that you generally believe it is "important" to be good and not to be bad, but these two types of values can also be in conflict. A common example in contemporary American society would involve the twin concepts of money and greed. Thus, while many people in our society apparently believe in making as much money as possible (importance), many of these same people probably also believe that "greed is wrong" (goodness). Beliefs about what is important can also have a strong emotional component, especially if they take the extreme form of "what's essential" or "what's necessary."

Beliefs about <u>possibility</u> have to do with the way things could (or could not) be: "I could never succeed in that job." While such beliefs are probably fewer in number than beliefs about what is true, good, or important, they exert tremendous influence in your life because of what they enable you to do or <u>prevent</u> you from doing. Obviously, if you believe something is highly improbable or impossible, you will not exert much effort in attempting to realize it.

Here are some simple examples of each of these four types of beliefs using the theme of "punctuality":

<u>Truth</u>: "I am (was, will be) always late for meetings."
<u>Goodness</u>: "Punctuality is a virtue."
<u>Importance</u>: "It's essential that I be on time for that meeting tomorrow."
<u>Possibility</u>: "Harry will never learn to be on time."

Another critically important role played by your beliefs is that they form the basis for your <u>desires</u>, <u>purposes</u>, and <u>intents</u> (see chapter 6). For this reason, your beliefs help to provide a basis for most of the choices you make in life and, ultimately, for your behavior and actions.

In summary, since beliefs have to do with your sense of right and wrong, of what is true, of what is important, and of what is possible in life, they play a central role in forming your intents and in shaping your decisions. In other words, you base many of your choices and actions on what you think is right, true, important, and possible.

"CORE" BELIEFS

Given the fact that each of us harbors literally thousands of beliefs about almost every topic, it is important to distinguish between "core" beliefs—the main subject of this chapter—and superficial beliefs which tend to be situationally determined and which are usually not worthy of much reflection or consideration. The latter kind of beliefs include straightforward notions about physical reality—"when I drive home after work today I will find my house in the same place where I left it this morning"—that we take for granted and that really do not merit much consideration in this book. By contrast, "core" beliefs—your notions of right and wrong, your

---

EXERCISE

(a) Pick one of the following concepts: punctuality, honesty, courage, money, success, love, and happiness; (b) write down four of your beliefs about that concept, one each for what you believe to be true (or false), right (or wrong), important, and possible.

conception of who you are, your purpose in life, and so forth,—operate over long periods of time and can potentially influence your behavior in many subtle ways. More important is the fact that many of these core beliefs, unlike most superficial beliefs, are associated with various kinds of <u>emotional</u> states (see below).

THE POWER OF BELIEFS

Note that your beliefs are, by definition, "real"—they are <u>your</u> beliefs—but they are not necessarily true or valid. You might believe, for example, that all people are basically greedy and selfish, and that there is no such thing as true generosity or altruism. Such a belief is certainly real—you embrace it in your waking consciousness—but it is not necessarily true or valid.

How, then, do you know if your beliefs are true? This question would be easy to answer if most beliefs had to do with factual circumstances that could be easily checked: "I believe that this person is over six feet tall" or "I believe that I have at least $100 in my bank account." But how do you verify the belief that all people are greedy? The fact is that most beliefs, especially those that can have profound and lasting effects on your life and behavior and thus on your conscious experience, are not easily proved or disproved. Here is just a small sample of such beliefs:

- Most people cannot be trusted.
- My spouse loves me.
- My boss does not appreciate me.
- Most teachers are lazy and incompetent.
- You cannot trust a [fill in the racial, ethnic, religious or national group].
- People of the opposite sex find me attractive.
- If I sin I will be punished.
- Sex is dirty and evil.
- I have no aptitude for math.
- I can drive just as well when I have had a few drinks.
- People do not respect me.
- I should always follow my doctor's orders.
- My family does not appreciate me.
- I am a good leader.
- God knows all my thoughts.
- School is a waste of time.

- There is no way I will ever amount to anything.

The list could go on for pages. The point to keep in mind is not just that such beliefs are difficult to disprove, but that <u>they tend to be self-validating</u>. If I believe that most people are greedy and selfish, it will certainly present no problem for me to find plenty of examples of greedy and selfish behavior. Or if I believe strongly that children need to be more firmly disciplined, it will be easy to identify plenty of "misbehaving" children who have been "spoiled." Or if I believe my spouse loves me it will be easy to find plenty of supporting "evidence" in her behavior toward me. In other words:

- **Your nonconscious mind uses your beliefs as guideposts to direct your conscious mind to pay attention to events that support these beliefs.**

For example, if your believe that most people are greedy and selfish, your nonconscious mind will direct your conscious mind to pay attention to events that confirm that belief—a small child refusing to share his ice cream cone with another child—and to ignore events that contradict that belief—one child offering another a taste of her ice cream cone.

Since most of us are inclined to take our beliefs for granted, we seldom reflect on or question them. One of the major purposes of this book is thus to encourage you to become more conscious of your beliefs and to develop the habit of examining them critically. Even on those rare occasions when we do become aware of particular beliefs, most of us are inclined to think in terms of their origins: "I believe this because such-and-such happened in my childhood." While experience no doubt plays a central role in shaping your beliefs, what many of us fail to realize is that **beliefs play a major role in shaping your experience**. Beliefs not only represent the mental filters through which you interpret the daily events of your life, but they also serve to shape these events. If I believe that my boss does not appreciate me, this belief will not only affect how I interpret his behavior toward me, but will also tend to <u>change</u> his behavior toward me because it will affect how I relate to him. In other words, my belief about my boss can set up a chain of events that will ultimately make my belief "true":

My belief about my boss → I act on my belief → My boss reacts to me → My boss's behavior confirms my belief.

Let us look at this process in a little more detail. If I feel that my boss does not appreciate me or my work, such a belief can affect what I do, and these changes in my behavior can in turn affect how he treats me. For example, in response to the belief that my boss does not appreciate me, I might come to resent my boss, feel sorry for myself, lose enthusiasm for work, complain to other employees, or take it out on fellow employees. Look at how my boss might respond:

My Reaction to my Belief that I am not appreciated	Possible Effect of my Reaction on my Boss's Beliefs
I show resentment toward my boss or toward others	"This is a disgruntled employee who puts out bad "vibes""
I feel sorry for myself	"This employee is always whining about something"
I lose enthusiasm for my work	"This employee's work is only mediocre"
I complain to others about the boss	"This employee is a troublemaker"
I take it out on subordinates or coworkers	"This employee doesn't know how to work with others"

Note that each reaction on the boss's part represents a critical response toward me, which will ultimately serve to validate my belief that "I'm not appreciated." If the boss expresses any of this criticism to me directly, I will likely respond: "See, I just knew he doesn't appreciate me." Indeed, these responses from the boss may well help to generate a whole new set of beliefs: "My boss is a mean-spirited person." "My boss is always ragging on me." Self-generated beliefs of this kind tend to be mutually reinforcing: "My boss doesn't appreciate me because he doesn't like me, and he doesn't like me because he's a mean-spirited person." "I'm in danger because I work for an evil boss." In other words, strongly held negative beliefs tend to generate an ever larger web of mutually reinforcing negative beliefs, and acting on these beliefs tends to bring events into our lives which reinforce the entire belief system: "Here is my boss criticizing me again. See? I just knew he's mean-spirited, that he doesn't like me, and that he doesn't appreciate me."

It is possible, of course, that I might react to my belief about not being appreciated in a different way. For instance, I might try to work even harder in the hope that the boss might take more notice of me and show more appreciation. Or I might make more of an effort to bring my accomplishments to the attention of the boss through memos, staff meetings, or casual conversation. I might even ask to have a special meeting with my boss to discuss my problem, or possibly even to test my belief: "How do you feel about my work?" However, in order to take any of these actions, it is first necessary either to entertain contrary beliefs (e.g., "maybe he really does appreciate my work, but I just don't realize it") or temporarily to suspend my belief ("maybe he's really capable, under the right circumstances, of coming to appreciate me and what I do"). This is much easier said than done, of course, since we all have a tendency to cling to our beliefs, especially when they are enmeshed in a larger web of mutually reinforcing beliefs and when they are seemingly "validated" by the events of our daily lives (i.e., the boss's current behavior toward me). It is especially difficult to question or relinquish a belief that we have been clinging to for a long period of time, since we have probably generated a complex web of supporting beliefs and experiences that have to do we our notions about "reality" and possibly even our sense of self.

Under the right circumstances, the greater wisdom of the unconscious mind is able recognize when particular beliefs are not serving us well. This wisdom may appear as a spontaneous idea: "Maybe my boss will appreciate me more if I just work a little harder." However, the force of our need to continually validate our beliefs is so great that we may sometimes engage in what amounts to a self-deluding "test" of these beliefs. For example, I might try to court my boss's approval by spending extra hours on the job or by undertaking special projects, but do it in such a way that I can cling to my original belief no matter what the boss does in response. If the boss fails to respond immediately because he is preoccupied with other things, I can conclude: "See, I knew all along he doesn't appreciate me." Or, if the boss takes notice and says something positive, I can tell myself: "He's only trying to pacify me; I know he doesn't really mean it." I may even guarantee no response or even a negative response in the way that I bring my "extra effort" to the boss's attention.

In the scenario just described, you might reasonably ask, what is the "truth?" Does my boss <u>really</u> "not appreciate" me? What if my boss really <u>did not</u> like me from the beginning? When it comes to most beliefs about significant others in our life, the belief is usually more important than the "truth." And even if such a negative belief about my boss <u>is</u> initially "true," there is a very good chance that my boss will come to dislike me even more, especially if I exhibit some of the defensive behavior already mentioned: feeling sorry for myself, acting sullen, unresponsive, or recalcitrant, gossiping, taking it out on fellow employees, and so forth. In other words, regardless of whether a newly formed belief is initially true, it can literally change your life experience in such a way as to become true! Thus, in much the same way that we speak of a "self-fulfilling prophesy," beliefs tend to be self-validating:

- **Your beliefs to a certain extent "create your reality."**

In summary, then, there are at least two ways in which beliefs help to shape your conscious experience:

- Selective <u>Attention</u>: **You tend to pay conscious attention to those life events that confirm or validate your beliefs and to ignore events that are inconsistent with those beliefs.**
- Selective <u>Action</u>: **By acting on your beliefs, you tend to create events in your life which will confirm those beliefs.**

Why is it so important that your beliefs be valid or correct? This question will be easier to answer once we have considered the many roles that beliefs play in your daily experience. However, for now let me offer what is perhaps the most basic answer:

- **In order to feel reasonably safe and secure and to function effectively in this continually changing world, it is necessary to <u>trust</u> your beliefs, especially your beliefs about present and future truth: <u>the way things are</u> and <u>the way things will be.</u>**

If the events of your daily life prove to be inconsistent with these beliefs, and you continually find your beliefs being contradicted by your experience, you will soon lose confidence in your ability to make decisions and to act. A person who is afraid to act—or acts inconsistently or irrationally—because his beliefs seem to be continuously at variance with his experience would be seen as "neurotic," at best, and—if the perceived belief/experience discrepancy is great enough—as insane or "psychotic." In other words:

- **Having your beliefs regularly confirmed by your experience is important to your sanity and your sense of well being.**

If you have any doubts about how important it is to your mental health to have your beliefs regularly confirmed by your experience, consider just three of the many beliefs that you must rely on simply to drive a car:

EXERCISE

(a) Write down a negative belief that you hold about someone you know; (b) Think of the last time that person did something that is consistent with your belief; (c) Now think back over all the time that you have known this person and ask yourself: "has this person ever done or said anything that contradicts, or is not consistent with, my belief?" Think hard, and try to be as honest with yourself as you can.

- "When I press my foot on the brake, the car will slow down."
- "When I turn the steering wheel to the right, the car will turn right."
- "Oncoming traffic will remain on the opposite side of the road."

While these obvious examples may seem trivial or even a bit silly, could any of us get behind the wheel of a car if we could not trust in such beliefs?

Imagine how difficult it would be for you to get through an ordinary day if you could not trust the many hundreds of similar beliefs that we all take for granted. When you climbed out of bed this morning, did you first examine the floor to make sure that it was safe to put your feet down on it? You probably did not even think about this simple physical act because you <u>believe</u> it is safe to roll out of bed without looking at the floor. (This belief proved to be a serious mistake for some residents of Los Angeles immediately following the early morning Northridge earthquake of 1992, because the bedroom floors in some households were littered with broken glass!) You brush your teeth, drink the water, and eat your breakfast without being concerned that you might poison yourself because you <u>believe</u> that the toothpaste, water, and food are safe. You ride the bus or the train or fly on an airplane because you <u>believe</u> it will go to your desired destination and get you there safely. Or, you do not take written directions with you when you drive to work because you <u>believe</u> you will remember which turns to take along the way. In short, you must rely on literally hundreds of similar beliefs simply to function.

While these may seem like trivial examples, the fact is that the only way that you can get through a normal day <u>and</u> retain your sanity is if most of your beliefs—and the expectations that are predicated on these beliefs—are confirmed. You must, in other words, be able to <u>trust</u> your beliefs and that trust must be regularly confirmed by your experience. Otherwise, an average working day would be dominated by fear and apprehension. In an extreme case, you might not even be able to leave the house because of the fear and paranoia that would result from the many uncertainties that lie ahead. In short:

- There is no way that you could make the hundreds of seemingly petty decisions that you have to make during an ordinary day unless you also have a good deal of trust in your beliefs and in the intents and expectations that derive from these beliefs.

BELIEFS TEND TO BE LIMITING

While some beliefs can be liberating, many are limiting. This is especially true of beliefs about possibility, because most such beliefs have to do with what is <u>not</u> possible. Beliefs about groups—racial, religious, national, political, ethnic—also tend to be very limiting for you personally, since they tend to <u>stereotype</u> the group in your mind and thereby condition (limit) the manner in which you can perceive and act toward members of that group (see chapter 9, under "Getting to Know You"). While most stereotypes are negative or derogatory, sometimes they are favorable or positive (we refer to these with words like "favoritism" or "bias"). Positive stereotypes also limit your ability to experience people as they really are because they tend to blind you to their limitations and shortcomings or exaggerate their virtues.

But those beliefs about persons or groups that constitute our negative stereotypes give rise to some of humankind's most dangerous and destructive behavior. Perhaps the most extreme form of such limiting stereotypes arises during times of war, when one group acquires dehumanizing beliefs about its opponents: if you believe that your opponent is subhuman (e.g., a "gook"), it becomes much easier for you to brutalize, enslave, imprison, or kill that opponent.

Negative beliefs about yourself can also be extremely limiting because in believing that you are a certain way—"I am a procrastinator"—you automatically assume that it will be difficult, if not impossible, for you to behave in some <u>other</u> way. Indeed, given the strong investment in the "rightness" of your belief systems, believing strongly in the idea that "I am a procrastinator" limits your ability <u>not</u> to procrastinate! Of course, if you qualify such a belief (for example: "I have a tendency to procrastinate"), such a belief may represent a more accurate description of some of your past behavior. But is it true of you <u>all of the time</u>? Most of the time? How much of the time? Does the "fact" that you may have procrastinated in the past mean that you must always procrastinate in the future? Perhaps you have a tendency to procrastinate only under certain circumstances. What <u>are</u> these circumstances? Do you usually have a "good" reason for procrastinating? Do you take on too much responsibility? Perhaps you sometimes put things off because you are tired, or because you have something to do that you believe is more "important." Is "procrastinate" really the right word? Are you being unfairly harsh on yourself? Have you set unrealistic and unreasonable expectations for yourself? If you want to minimize the limiting effect of such negative beliefs about yourself, it is important to begin asking yourself such questions.

NEGATIVE BELIEFS

What is a negative belief? This question should be addressed in at least two ways: (1) the content of the belief itself, and (2) the limiting <u>effect</u> of

EXERCISE

(a) Write down a negative or critical belief about yourself; then (b) write a few sentences explaining why you believe this; finally (c) can you think of anything you have done in the recent past that is inconsistent with this belief? Think hard and do your best to be honest with yourself.

that belief on your creativity and psychological well-being. Let us first look at content.

A negative belief is one that tends to belittle, diminish, criticize, or otherwise denigrate yourself, other persons, groups of people, objects, concepts, or events. Here are some typical examples of negative beliefs:

"I'm no good at math."
"I think too much about sex."
"My father didn't love me."
"Most [name the group] can't be trusted."
"Abstract art doesn't take any real talent; anyone can do it."
"School is boring."
"Most people are selfish and greedy."

Each of these beliefs is clearly negative in content, since it expresses a derogatory stereotype or limiting viewpoint about the object: me, my father, [the group named], abstract art, school, and most people. However, a more important consequence of holding such beliefs is that they limit your <u>experience</u> of that object. Believing that "I'm no good at math," for example, will probably prevent you from even <u>trying</u> to develop your math skills. Believing that "I think too much about sex" will almost certainly inhibit your sexual fantasies and limit your enjoyment of these fantasies. And when you encounter a member of the group that "can't be trusted," your lack of trust will limit your ability to experience that person as he or she <u>really</u> is. Whenever you see a work of abstract art, it will be difficult for you to enjoy it or see any artistic merit in it. Your belief that school is "boring" will not only make it difficult for you to enjoy schooling in the future, but it may also deter you from even <u>continuing</u> in school. Finally, your ability to experience the <u>real</u> motives underlying other people's behavior will be limited if you are prepared to see their behavior in negative terms such as selfishness and greed. This last type of belief is especially insidious and limiting, because it is easily reinforced through your own selective perception: since almost all of us are capable of acting in a selfish or greedy fashion at least once in a while, you will have no trouble spotting evidence of greed and selfishness in other people if you <u>look</u> for it.

These considerations underscore the following point: to minimize the limiting effect of negative beliefs on your life, it is extremely important that you take the trouble to:

- <u>identify</u> your key negative beliefs (especially beliefs about yourself).
- scrutinize, question, and analyze these beliefs <u>critically.</u>
- determine how these beliefs are affecting your <u>experience</u> and your <u>behavior.</u>
- be willing to consider <u>changing</u> those negative beliefs that are not serving you well.

Obviously, following these suggestions could involve a good deal of your time and effort. For this reason, chapter 10 will provide a lot more in the way of specifics about how to identify and change limiting or negative beliefs.

Perhaps the most important thing to realize about negative beliefs is that they usually have an emotional component, and sometimes a very powerful one. The emotionality of negative beliefs comes in part from your commitment to their "rightness," but the <u>content</u> of the belief itself very often has an even stronger emotionality associated with it. For example, the belief that "expressing emotions is a sign of weakness" may be associated with feelings of contempt or anger and, at deeper levels, with anxiety, shyness, insecurity, or fear. Negative beliefs about others are frequently associated with feelings like contempt, anger, or fear, while negative beliefs about yourself are typically associated with feelings like guilt, anxiety, and depression.

Some of our most intensely felt negative beliefs have to do with death and dying. These negative beliefs may give rise to the hope that you will "live a long time" or the wish that you could "live forever." Most of us believe that we will die someday, but the most negative beliefs usually have to do with the <u>meaning</u> of death. To many people, death means personal extinction, the end of consciousness, the end of self. This belief is especially strong among people who have been raised in the traditions of positivism or scientific materialism, which maintain that human consciousness—the central topic of this book—is nothing more than a by-product of biochemical and electrochemical processes that occur in the brain and body. They thus believe that when the brain and body die, these processes come to an end, and consciousness is thereby terminated: "Since physical death means the end of consciousness, 'I' no longer exist once my physical body dies."

People who embrace this particular set of beliefs about death may say,

I "wish" it were not so—I would like to believe that there is such a thing as God or reincarnation or an afterlife existence—but in my scientific heart I know that this is just wishful thinking, that there is really nothing beyond physical existence.

If such people hold this belief strongly enough, they will reject outright any contrary evidence—mystical or other paranormal experiences—as "sheer coincidence" or "just my imagination."

We have already mentioned that strongly held negative beliefs are usually accompanied by intense negative emotions such as fear, envy, or anger. In the case of negative beliefs about death, older people tend to envy younger people, and fear of death is an almost universal emotional response. These emotional states can sometimes motivate us to seek alternative beliefs that will relieve the negative emotional state. This seeking can take many forms. If you fear that death may be the "end" of you, or are someone who is not absolutely convinced of the scientific/materialist position (i.e., if you are an "agnostic"), you may be motivated to seek evidence that would contradict that position. For example, you may seek specific evidence that consciousness or the "self" can exist independently from (or beyond) the physical body (e.g., "out-of-body" experiences, "near death" experiences, "channeling" of deceased personalities, "séances" where one communicates with personalities who have died), or you may merely seek evidence that appears to contradict the presently known laws of science (telepathy, psychokinesis, precognition, etc.).

Most organized religions, of course, are based on a set of alternative beliefs to the "death is the end of it all" belief. It seems likely that the initial appeal of formal religion to many people is that these alternative beliefs about the meaning of death do not generate the same negative emotions (fear in particular) that the "death is the end" belief generates. Many religions, to be sure, promote beliefs that are based on fear ("God will punish you if you sin"), but they also offer the believer some sense of power and control over the outcome ("I can avoid punishment by confessing my sins, through God's forgiveness, or by not sinning").

Embracing the beliefs of certain organized religions may thus help to alleviate the fear associated with death, but these alternative beliefs can have their own emotional downside. Negative beliefs about sex, for example—that it is dirty and sinful, a kind of "necessary evil" for procreation—can generate strong feelings of guilt whenever sexual feelings arise in consciousness, especially among adolescents. Even if a believing teenager manages not to act on these sexual feelings (e.g., by not masturbating and by avoiding sexual contact with others), simply <u>having</u> sexual feelings and fantasies can produce strong guilt feelings: "God knows all my thoughts, and he will punish me for thinking or feeling this way." Thus, if the teenager believes that she should be punished for having certain sexual thoughts (or, worse, for acting on these thoughts by masturbating or having sexual contact with others), she may act so as to bring some form of "punishment" upon herself: failing in school, fighting with friends, anxiety, depression, defying parents, and so on.

Guilt is a very powerful emotion because it is closely connected with a whole array of beliefs relating to your self-concept or, to use a more contemporary popular phrase, your "self-esteem." Obviously, guilt feelings tend to be associated with poor self-esteem: "I am a bad person because I have sinned or done wrong." Guilt occurs when your behavior (including your thoughts and feelings) fails to conform to the standards that you have set for yourself. These standards, of course, are defined by your beliefs about goodness (right and wrong) and about importance, that is, what you should accomplish: "It is wrong for me to have certain sexual fantasies;" "I should get straight A's in school; "I should never tell a lie;" "I should always obey my parents." When your thoughts, feelings, or actions fail to conform to such standards (i.e., when your experience goes against your beliefs about right and wrong and about what kind of person you should be), guilt feelings are triggered. These feelings, in turn, can contribute to lowered self-esteem.

One way to look at negative feelings like anger or guilt is that they are <u>signals</u> from your unconscious mind either that (a) your beliefs about goodness or rightness have been violated, or that (b) negative beliefs about yourself have been confirmed by some thought or other event in your life. Similarly, a feeling of anxiety or fear may be a signal that one or more of your beliefs about what is true or important has been contradicted by your experience.

BELIEVING AND WISHING

Let me suggest a new way for you to look at your "wishes": A wish is a thought that emanates from a negative belief about your present circum-

---

EXERCISE

(a) Think of a recent time when you felt guilty about something. Then, (b) write down all of the relevant beliefs that you can associate with that feeling. Finally, (c) repeat the exercise using a recent time when you got very angry about something.

stances: "I believe that this [present negative situation] is true, but I would prefer that it were not true." Some typical examples:

"I wish my boss appreciated me." (Negative belief: "My boss doesn't appreciate me.")
"I wish I were more attractive." (Negative belief: "I'm not attractive enough.")
"I wish I had more money." (Negative belief: "I'm poor" or "I'll never have enough money.")

Wishing is slightly different from hoping and a lot different from wanting (see chapter 6) "I 'wish' my boss would change" is pretty much to say that "I doubt he will" or "He won't!" "I 'hope' my boss will change" is to say that he might change, but that it is pretty much out of your control. "I 'want' my boss to change" is to suggest that you personally might be able to do something about it. In short,

- **Wishing reveals some of your most deeply held negative beliefs.**

Since the beliefs that underlie your wishes are so strong, "wishing" that something were different is usually accompanied by a sense of futility: "Deep down in my heart I 'know' that it won't change." People who entertain fantasies that contradict their most deeply held beliefs are often said to be engaging in "wishful thinking." In fact, we often use clichés like "wishing won't make it so" to discourage wishful thinking. Negative beliefs that generate wishful thinking are so firmly held that we sometimes believe that things can change only through supernatural processes or magic like the "wishing well" into which we throw coins or the "birthday cake wish" we make when we try to blow out all the candles at once.

By focusing a lot of your conscious attention on wishing, you can easily be distracted from the most important issue: the negative belief that gives rise to the wish. What are some of these negative beliefs? How do you form them? How should you deal with them?

EXERCISE

(a) Jot down at least three personal wishes (they might have to do with yourself, others, the society, the world, etc.). Then, (b) next to each wish write down the negative belief(s) implied in the wish.

BELIEFS AND CONCEPTS

Like most languages, English contains a number of words that we humans have developed in order to label or describe our conscious experience. "Belief" and "concept" are words that describe two closely related conscious phenomena. A concept organizes, or groups together, things that are different but that share certain qualities in common. "Fruit" and "emotion" are both examples of concepts. "Fruit" includes diverse objects like cherries, pears, apples, and bananas. Similarly, the concept of "emotion" includes different mental states like anger, joy, depression, and fear. The purpose of concepts like fruit and emotion is to organize what otherwise would be an almost endless list of different phenomena. We organize them around their similarities (edible plant products, subjective mental states). Concepts also include very abstract phenomena such as virtue, beauty, and honesty.

Beliefs are usually <u>about</u> concepts. If I believe that "Fruit is good for you," the concept is "fruit." Similarly, if I believe that "Emotions should be kept in check," the concept is "emotions." Sometimes a belief involves several concepts, as in "Men who express their emotions don't deserve our respect," where the concepts include "men," "respect," as well as "emotions."

CONCEPTS: THE BUILDING BLOCKS OF BELIEFS

Your beliefs, as we have seen, express your personal point of view about the nature of things. You have beliefs about yourself (what kind of person you are, have been, could be, or should be), about other individuals (your parents, friends, neighbors, coworkers), about groups or classes of people (by race, gender, age, sexual orientation, religion, politics, educational level, social class, occupation, region, nationality, etc.), and about money, family, work, love, truth, success, death, illness, God, and life in general. Given that beliefs are usually about concepts, let us look at both in a little more depth by examining some simple beliefs about the concept of <u>honesty</u>. The following beliefs all use honesty to state what is <u>true</u> (the way things are, were, or will be), what is <u>possible</u> (the way things could be), and what is <u>good</u> or right (the way things ought to be).

The way things <u>are</u>:	"Most people are honest."
The way things <u>were</u>:	"Henry lied to you."
The way things <u>will be</u>:	"Next time Mary will tell you the truth."
The way things <u>could be</u>:	"He'll never tell you the truth."

The way things <u>ought to be:</u> "Parents should never lie to their children."

All of the beliefs in the above list are about the concept of "truthfulness" or "honesty," but each belief also includes one or more other concepts like "most people" and "parents." The simplest beliefs thus involve two types of concepts: the "subject" and the "assertion." Take the following belief:

"I am an honest person."

In this example, "I" is the subject and the assertion that I am making about myself is that I am "honest." In the above examples I have varied the subjects: Most people, Henry, Mary, he, and parents. The subject of a belief can thus be an individual like yourself, someone else, or a entire group like parents or Americans, but it can also be another living thing ("<u>Dogs</u> require a lot of care"), an inanimate object ("<u>Guns</u> are dangerous") or an abstract concept ("<u>Beauty</u> is in the eye of the beholder"). Sometimes the subject is merely implied, especially when it comes to your beliefs about <u>goodness</u>: "honesty is the best policy" (the implied subject here being "you," "people," or "everybody").

Another kind of concept is contained in the assertion, that is, whatever the belief claims be true about the subject. In each of the five simple beliefs shown in the above list, the assertion has something to do with the concept of honesty or truthfulness: that the subject either was, is, could be, will be, or should be either honest or dishonest. Obviously there are many thousands of other assertions or claims that you can make about any subject, simply because there are so many other concepts you can draw upon. When the subject is a person, for example, you can believe that that person is intelligent, shy, untrustworthy, pushy, lazy, generous, mean, strong, beautiful, loving, and so on. When the subject of your beliefs is a group or class of people—Baptists, New Yorkers, lawyers, teenagers, African Americans, housewives, used car salesmen, liberals, rocket scientists, homosexuals, Republicans, Texans, Italians, the elderly—you have almost as many descriptive concepts to draw upon to form your beliefs as you do in the case of beliefs about individuals. Beliefs about entire groups are sometimes called "stereotypes," and when such beliefs are negative or derogatory, we sometimes call them "prejudices." Stereotypic beliefs that are positive or complimentary can go by many names: chauvinism, bias, favoritism, partiality, and ethnocentrism.

Many individual beliefs are really part of much more complex <u>webs</u> of interrelated beliefs. Consider the following set of interrelated beliefs:

"People should always tell the truth."
"Lying is a sin."
"I shouldn't lie."
"I deserve to be punished if I lie."
"God knows everything I do."
"God will punish me if I lie."
"I am a liar."
"God is going to punish me."

THE FUNCTION OF CONCEPTS

A major purpose of beliefs and concepts is to make sense of out of your experience. The stream of sensations—visual, auditory, proprioceptive, and so forth—that continually impinges on your conscious mind would be impossible to respond to in any meaningful way if you did not have a framework of concepts and beliefs with which to organize them.

Take the concept of "tree." Since no two trees are exactly alike, every new tree that you encounter would be a completely novel sensory experience that would probably command your attention if you did not have a "tree concept" which allows you to assess and classify most trees. Imagine how it would be if you were visiting a friend's house for the first time and had no concept of "tree." Let us say the friend had a dozen or so trees of varying type and size in her front yard. Since you have never seen your neighbor's front yard before, as you attempt to walk to the front door your attention would be drawn to each tree in turn: "Wow! I've never seen anything like that before! I wonder what that is! Amazing!" It might take you a half hour just to get to the front door! And imagine how long it might take you to walk through a few acres of forest!

Most of the time when you visit someone's house for the first time you do not even "notice" the trees in her front yard. I put "notice" in quotes because, unless you have your eyes closed, the sensory images of her trees

---

EXERCISE

(a) Pick one of the following concepts: honesty, beauty, sexuality, intelligence, and virtue. Then, (b) write down a belief about yourself that uses the concept. Finally, (c) write down three similar beliefs: one each about a family member, another person you know well, and some group of people. (d) If you have the time, repeat the exercise with one or more of the other concepts.

will certainly impinge on your retina and visual cortex and thus be "seen" (even if you don not directly "look at" any one tree, the image of most of the trees will impinge on your peripheral vision). (Recall the exercise in the first chapter when I asked you to stare at the letter "A.") But why do you not "notice" the trees? That is, why do you not direct your conscious attention toward the trees?

This is a very critical question. In fact, in understanding how the conscious and unconscious minds work together to process all of the information that is continually coming in through your senses, it may be <u>the</u> most important question. It is also a critical question in understanding the roles that concepts and beliefs play in shaping your conscious experience.

Let us start with concepts. As you grow up you develop literally thousands of concepts. You, like me, have a concept that you call "tree." You and I have also seen many trees in our lives. Seeing "a tree," then, is not a novel experience for either one of us. There is thus some kind of "tree concept" that resides in your unconscious, and it is likely to be very similar—but probably not identical—to the tree concept that resides in my unconscious. When the sensory image of a tree impinges on your retina and is transmitted to your brain, your unconscious instantaneously classifies that image ("that's a tree") and evaluates it: "Is this tree something special? Is it important or interesting enough to justify my conscious attention?" If your nonconscious mind answers "no" to this question— "Ho hum, just another ordinary tree, nothing exceptional, not worth my conscious attention"—your conscious mind will not be instructed to "notice" the tree. Your nonconscious mind is, in fact, continuously classifying and evaluating all of your other sensory impressions as you walk towards your friend's front door: the lawn, the bushes, the house, the sidewalk, the doorstep, the front door, and so on. All of this sensory information is coming in, and your unconscious is busy classifying and evaluating all of it simultaneously. The concepts like "tree," "door," and "house" that reside in your unconscious thus provide a framework not only for classifying and organizing all these sensory impressions ("that's a tree," "that's grass," "that's a front door knob"), but also for evaluating or judging whether each impression is worthy of your conscious attention. Since your normal waking conscious mind can focus on only a few things at a time (see chapter 4), the unconscious—which can examine a lot of things at once—must prioritize all your sensory impressions to decide which ones are most worthy of your attention. How, then, does your unconscious judge the "importance" or "worthiness" of a sense impression?

One way it does this is to judge its <u>novelty</u>. The unconscious is on the lookout for new and unusual sense impressions. And here your concepts come into play: Not only do you have a "tree concept," but you probably have many tree concepts. Note in the preceding paragraph I used the phrase "ordinary tree." Most of us probably have such a concept, which means that we will not consciously take note of or pay attention to most trees we encounter because they fall into our "ordinary tree" concept. I remember that when I first traveled from the east coast of the United States to southern California, I "noticed" the palm trees, eucalyptus trees, and other exotic vegetation. My eastern concept of "ordinary tree" did not include such things, so my unconscious directed my conscious attention to the "novel" vegetation of southern California. You and I and most other people probably have slightly different beliefs about which kinds of trees are novel as opposed to ordinary, but in all likelihood the giant sequoias and ancient redwoods of northern and coastal California are not "ordinary" to almost anyone! If such trees come within your visual field, you are most likely going to "notice" them.

Concepts like "tree" refer to specific objects. All of us also have larger-scale concepts like "scenery" or "landscape." When people who have grown up in the desert-like climate of southern California visit the eastern United States during the summer, they often "notice" the landscape: "I had no idea how green it is." In contrast, I seldom "noticed" how green the eastern landscape is during the summer while I was growing up there because the greenness was part of my concept of "ordinary" or "average" summer landscape. My unconscious thus did not evaluate it as "novel." The visitor from southern California, however, whose "ordinary" summer landscape tends to be more barren and much less green, "notices" the greenness and lushness of the eastern summer landscape. The point to emphasize, however, is that it is the unconscious that is initially doing all of this classifying and evaluating and that it is using "degree of novelty" as one of its yardsticks to determine whether or not you should focus your conscious attention on any particular sensory impression. Novelty, of course, is determined by your particular concepts and beliefs.

Our concepts are really much more sophisticated than this discussion suggests. Let us say you have an "average" tree in your own front yard. Most of the time when you walk past this tree you may not pay conscious attention to it (your unconscious is perceiving the tree, but it is probably saying "this is the same old tree" or "just the tree in my front yard," so it has decided that there is nothing very novel to justify focusing your conscious attention on it). What is interesting about this is that the unconscious is usually able to identify it as the "same" tree, even though your sensory impression of it is never exactly the same. In other words, when you walk past the tree your sensory impression of it is never exactly the same because you are never in exactly the same spot. In fact, if you went across the street and looked at the tree, if you walked around the tree while looking at it, or even if you climbed up in it and looked very closely at it, it would still be "the same tree in my front yard," even though in each instance your actual sensory image would be very different. Psychologists call this phenomenon "perceptual constancy," which means that your perception of a particular object ("what is it?") can remain the same, even though the actual sensory information that you receive from it can vary widely from one occasion to another.

In short, a major function of concepts is to help you to organize, make sense of, or give meaning to what would otherwise be a distracting and confusing flood of sensory impressions. This is particularly true of higher-order concepts that combine many simpler concepts into a whole. Thus, instead of perceiving each of the individual trees, bushes, rocks, blades of grass, and flowers in your friend's front yard as discrete objects, you perceive "landscaping," a "front yard," or a "pleasing entryway." Instead of seeing tires, a windshield, a hood, a roof, doors, bumpers, and a trunk, you see a "car." Instead of seeing dozens of different makes, models, and colors of individual cars, trucks, and buses moving along a highway, you see "traffic." Concepts, in other words, can help you summarize or integrate a lot of complex and diverse sensory material into a meaningful whole. They can also help you to see similarities and connections between seemingly disparate sensory phenomena: an orange and a banana and a grape are thus connected in the sense that they are all "fruit," even though they look and feel and taste very different. And a dark-skinned seven-foot male basketball player and a light-skinned newborn baby girl are both "people," even though they bear little physical resemblance to each other. Concepts thus help you to make linkages among seemingly different sensory experiences.

Another thing to keep in mind is that certain concepts can carry a good deal of <u>emotional</u> content because of the beliefs that you harbor about them. Consider concepts such as the following: politicians, free enterprise, homeless people, family values, communists, the "unborn," the "super rich," terrorists, child molesters, motherhood, welfare recipients, honor, gangbangers, and patriotism. (See exercise below.)

Let us stop for a minute to review all the different functions and purposes of concepts that we have discussed so far.

EXERCISE

(a) Pick three of the above concepts and identify one or more feelings that you can associate with each one; (b) for each concept, write down the belief that gives rise to the feeling.

- Concepts provide the framework that the nonconscious part of your mind uses to sort through and classify the mass of incoming sensory stimuli. One purpose of this sorting and classification process is to help your unconscious decide where to focus your conscious attention: what is it, and how significant, novel, or important is it?
- Concepts aid this choice process by providing your unconscious with guidelines which help it determine what is most novel in your current sensory experience. Your conscious mind is thus directed to focus on the most novel information.
- Your nonconscious mind will also tend to direct your conscious attention to concepts that you associate with strong <u>emotions</u>.
- Concepts also help you to make <u>meaning</u> out of your experience by (a) organizing diverse stimuli into larger conceptual "wholes," and (b) detecting similarities (making "connections" between) seemingly different sensory experiences.
- Concepts are usually organized hierarchically, so that the more complex, higher-order concepts like "scenery" and "landscape" are composed of many simpler concepts like "tree" and "grass."
- Concepts are always personalized, so that concepts like "ordinary tree" or "emotion" seldom mean exactly the same thing to different people.

The Limitations of Concepts

While concepts provide us with a very convenient "shorthand" to facilitate communication, they also have a downside: they inevitably <u>distort</u> reality. Thus, while it is true that bananas and grapes are both "fruit," they are not "the same," or even close to it: they look, feel, smell and taste very different. Similarly, while Leonardo DiVinci's *Mona Lisa* and a preschooler's finger painting are both "paintings," they are also very different from each other and have very little in common. In other words, while concepts like <u>idea</u>, <u>tree</u>, <u>animal</u> and <u>feeling</u> are very "efficient" ways of referring to or covering a lot of different things with just a few words, in using such concepts we run the risk of ignoring the rich diversity of things that can fall <u>within</u> each concept.

In fact, the "things" that we include under most concepts are often <u>themselves</u> concepts! "Grapes," for example, is a concept, since grapes come in many different varieties, and even <u>within</u> a given variety, no two grapes are exactly alike. As a matter of fact, most nouns—excluding for the moment so-called "proper" nouns—are really concepts. Nouns refer to persons, places, or things, and unless we are referring to a <u>particular</u> person, place or thing, each noun that we use is really referring to a concept (a <u>class</u> of persons, places, or things, with no two members of the class being exactly the same).

But what about "proper" nouns? If I speak about "my son Paul," exactly who or what am I talking about? Am I referring to the person I last talked to on the telephone 3 days ago, the person I last saw 5 days ago, or the person as he is right now? And what do I mean by "right now?" The person as he was when I wrote the previous sentence, or the person as he is as you read this sentence? Or do I mean all of these "Paul's?" And just what does "all" mean? Can "Paul" be all of these "Paul's" at once, since he, like you and me, is continually changing and developing as a person? What I am really suggesting here is that all nouns are, to a certain extent, concepts, and to that extent they can be either ambiguous and/or distort reality.

This discussion suggests that one of the major limitations of concepts is that they tend to remain static with time, while the phenomena that they describe are frequently changing. The implication here would seem to be that, the older the concept, the less accurately it describes whatever it is supposed to represent.

CHANGING CONCEPTS AND BELIEFS

Because we have so many operating concepts like "tree" and "ordinary tree," we are inclined to forget that almost any concept, especially one that involves judgemental aspects like "ordinary," can be challenged or even changed. The easiest way to do this is to be <u>mindful</u> (see chapter 3). Let us take the tree in your front yard. If someone were to ask you about it, you might say it is "a tree" or "a nice tree" or "an average-sized tree." But how often do you ever <u>really</u> look at it? Have you stood near it and examined the bark up close? Have you touched it to see how it feels? Have you stood away from it and looked at it from different angles to see how its shape changes? Have you watched how it reacts to wind or observed how it looks after a rain or a snow? Have you noticed how it looks during different seasons or at different times of the day? What kinds of birds and insects inhabit it? If you were to make the effort to do some of these things—to be more "mindful" of the tree—you would almost certainly change your concept of "the ordinary tree in my front yard." You might even develop some feeling for the tree!

The purpose of this last paragraph is to underscore the following point:

- **You can change your concept of, or beliefs about, something simply by focusing your conscious attention on it.**

In fact, being mindful can change your concept of or beliefs about almost any thing, event, person, and even yourself! (We will deal with the issue of how to change your beliefs in much more detail in chapter 10.)

Why do you even need concepts and beliefs? Could not your normal waking consciousness simply "take in" raw sensory information without classifying, judging, evaluating, and prioritizing it? Certain meditative practices actually attempt to train the mind to do just this ("to be non-judgemental" or to become a "pure observer"; see chapter 3), but there is still the matter of focus: your normal waking consciousness seems to have certain limits in terms of how many things it can focus on at once (see chapter 4). And the more you focus on one thing, the less "aware" you become of everything else. While there is little doubt that you can "expand" your awareness through meditative practice, there would still seem to be certain limits in terms of how many things you can incorporate in your conscious mind at one time and how much attention each one gets. Thus, the need to "prioritize." (For further discussion of the process of "splitting" our conscious attention between two or more activities, see chapter 4.)

But why should there be any limits? Perhaps the best way to answer this question is to recognize that there is a more practical issue here: <u>you must be able function effectively and safely in the physical world of time and space in which you live</u>. Certain physical and mental tasks almost demand that you be able to focus your entire conscious attention and shut out virtually everything else from your normal awareness. This requirement for intense focus is certainly important for optimal performance of demanding intellectual tasks like reading or creative tasks like writing and performing music, but it is absolutely necessary when you are performing motor tasks that involve potential physical danger. For example, if you are driving your car on a country road and encounter another car headed directly at you just as you are rounding a sharp curve, you need to be able to focus your entire conscious attention immediately on the task of avoiding a collision. You must be able to create this focus instantaneously and maintain it until the danger is past.

BELIEFS AND THE UNCONSCIOUS

Imagine the nonconscious part of your mind as a great repository of thousands of different beliefs about yourself, others, and the world around you. Since your nonconscious has the job of processing, sorting, and analyzing your ongoing experience and deciding what to bring to the attention of your normal waking consciousness, it uses all of these beliefs in much the same way it uses concepts: to organize, "screen," and "evaluate" incoming information. This process of screening the mass of incoming sensory stimulation through your beliefs, however, is much more complex than the "screening for novelty" that your concepts help you perform, in part because your beliefs (especially your negative beliefs) often have an emotional component, and sometimes a very powerful one.

You might believe, for example, that "expressing emotions [the concept] is a sign of weakness" or that "ancient redwood trees [the concept] are magnificent." The negative belief about "expressing emotions" may be associated with feelings of contempt or anger and, at deeper levels, with fear. Similarly, if you believe that the redwoods are "magnificent," it may be that being in their presence, or even just thinking about them, might evoke feelings of wonder, awe, or spirituality. But we have already noted another feature of beliefs that makes them different from concepts: you ordinarily have a <u>stake</u> in your beliefs. That is, since your beliefs represent your personal views about reality, it is very important to you that these beliefs be "right," especially when it comes to beliefs about <u>truth</u> or "the way things are." In other words, you have an emotional investment in the "truth" of your beliefs.

SUMMARY

Your beliefs form the core of your personality. They reflect your personal notions about what is real and true, what is moral and good, what is important, and what is possible. You harbor literally thousands of different beliefs about yourself, other people, groups, and abstract concepts like honesty and beauty. While beliefs can be freeing and liberating, many beliefs tend to be limiting. Concepts, the basic building blocks of beliefs, are mental tools for organizing and classifying the masses of sensory data that impinge on each of us every second of every day.

Your nonconscious mind serves as the repository for your beliefs and concepts, where they provide the "lenses" or "filters" that you use to make meaning out of the events of your life. Your beliefs also shape your desires and intents and determine most of your emotional reactions to events. Given that you have a strong emotional investment in the "truth" and "rightness" of your beliefs, they not only help you <u>interpret</u> your experiences but also help to <u>shape</u> those experiences. In this sense, then, a good deal of your personal experience is literally "created" through your beliefs.

CHAPTER 3

MINDFULNESS AND THE "WITNESS"

"Mindfulness is the miracle by which we master and restore ourselves."
—Thich Nhat Hanh (1987)[1]

A remarkable feature of human consciousness is that it can observe itself. Thus, your conscious mind is capable not only of <u>having</u> thoughts and feelings, but also of judging, analyzing, or simply paying attention to or "noticing" these thoughts and feelings as they arise. In other words, each of us is capable of experiencing that special state of mind where there seems to be a separate "you" that is observing what you are thinking, feeling, and doing.

You can analyze or judge your thoughts and actions, but you can also just <u>observe</u> them without judging or analyzing. This process of merely observing or witnessing the events that make up your conscious experience <u>as they happen</u> is called "mindfulness." It is one thing to have a thought; it is quite another to observe the thought as it arises in your awareness. Being mindful of a thought means that you are aware of or realize your thought: "This is my thought." "I am having this thought." "Here I am thinking about..." Similarly, you can say or do things "mindlessly" without really being aware of what you are doing or saying, or you can observe yourself as you speak or act. When you are in that state of mind where you are observing what is happening right now in your mind and in your life in a conscious way, your "witness" is present in your consciousness and you are being "mindful."

Being aware of your thoughts and feelings as they emerge in your waking consciousness may sound like a pretty simple thing to do, but it can be very difficult. You can, for example, become very angry about something and not "realize" how angry you are until you <u>say</u> or <u>do</u> something that you end up regretting: "Wow, I didn't realize at the time how angry I was." We have even developed linguistic conventions for differentiating between mindful and mindless actions. For example, when you say "I caught myself doing that," you mean that you suddenly became mindful of what you were doing, whereas previously—before you "caught yourself"—you were not being mindful.

THE THREE OBSERVERS

That self-observer or "little person inside your head" can take on several different roles with respect to what it is observing. Three of the most common roles are what I like to call the Judge, the Analyst, and the Pure Observer or "Witness." Since it is difficult for more than one of these to be present in your consciousness at the same time, you sometimes find your sense of self-awareness shifting rapidly from one role to the other. Keep in mind that those different forms of self-awareness should not be seen as "separate you's," but rather simply as different "states of mind" that you can assume in observing yourself and your experiences.

The Judge

The Judge is basically concerned with formulating preferences. However, the Judge can appear in two very different forms that I like to call the "Discerning Judge" and the "Moral Judge." The Discerning Judge basically makes distinctions according to taste, excellence, or quality. When your Discerning Judge is focused on your present experience, it might make judgements such as: "This food is too salty," "This is beautiful music," "That person over there is very handsome," "I'm a good dancer," "This painting is poorly done," "He's an excellent speaker," and so on. In short, when your Discerning Judge is active, you are judging the quality or excellence of something.

The Moral Judge, on the other hand, comes very close to being what psychoanalysts would call the "superego." When your Moral Judge makes its appearance in your consciousness, it is there to tell you that what you are experiencing or what is currently happening is either good or evil, right or wrong, or positive or negative. Your Moral Judge often makes such judgments about the actions of others—"John is being extremely selfish"—or about events in which you are not directly involved (e.g., political or other "news" events), but for the present discussion we shall focus our attention on its role as a judge of your actions, thoughts, and feelings. Your Moral Judge can decide that something you are doing or thinking is positive or good (i.e., when you give yourself a "pat on the back"), but in most of us it has a strong propensity to find fault: "That was a dumb thing to do." "You think too much about..." "Boy, you really screwed that up." "There you go again, making the same mistake!"

How does your Moral Judge make all these judgments? Where do its standards of right and wrong come from? The answer, of course, is that it relies on your beliefs. More particularly, your Moral Judge relies on your personal beliefs about goodness—"right" and "wrong"—and importance—the kind of person you think you ought to be, that is, the "standards of performance" you set for yourself. When you do or think or feel something that you believe to be "wrong," or fail to reach the behavioral standards that you have set for yourself, your Moral Judge may appear to remind you of your "transgression." There are many hundreds of different beliefs that can come into play here:

"It's wrong to..."
"People should..."
"I should always..."
"I should never..."

When you think or feel or do something that results in a critical self-assessment by your Moral Judge, you can be sure that one or more of your "right and wrong" beliefs about yourself is involved. Again, this self-criticism usually occurs because you think you have either (a) failed to meet the standards you have set for yourself or (b) thought, felt, or done something "wrong" (i.e., that contradicts one or more of your beliefs about right and wrong). The most common emotion that accompanies that self-critical judgment, of course, is guilt. And the beliefs that have the capacity

EXERCISE

(a) Complete each of the four sentences above. Then, (b) think of a recent time when you said or did something that violated one of those beliefs. How did you feel?

to generate the strongest guilt feelings typically have to do with such things as honesty, trust, responsibility, loyalty, aggression, and sexuality.

Your unconscious usually does the work of comparing your thoughts, feelings, and actions with your beliefs, and "signals" your consciousness either by activating your Moral Judge or by causing a feeling of guilt or regret to enter into your awareness. As with much of its other work, the unconscious can do this processing and signaling very rapidly. Often you will not even be consciously aware of what the relevant beliefs are! However, with a little reflection, you can usually begin to get in touch with those beliefs: "Why is my Moral Judge being so hard on me? What beliefs are involved here?" Or, "Why am I feeling so guilty about this? What beliefs about right and wrong am I violating, or what expectations have I set for myself that I have failed to meet?" (See chapter 10 for more detail on examining and changing your beliefs.)

Your Moral Judge can also make an appearance when your conscious experience activates (i.e., confirms) a negative belief about yourself: "I think too much about..." "I lack the ability to..." "One of my weaknesses is..." For example, if you believe that you are neglecting or not spending "enough" time with your spouse or partner, and you have to cancel a dinner date with that person because of something else that has come up unexpectedly at work, you might feel guilty and/or be paid a visit by your Moral Judge because that negative belief about yourself has just been confirmed: "Here I am once again neglecting my partner." Note that negative beliefs about yourself are usually predicated on other beliefs about right and wrong, for example, your beliefs about how much time a "good" spouse or partner should spend with the other person, or whether you really "deserve" to spend time alone with yourself. (See chapters 2 and 10 for more discussion of negative beliefs.)

The Analyst

This second type of "observing self" is more of an investigator or scientist than a judge. It seeks to <u>understand</u> your thoughts, feelings, and actions rather than merely to judge them. Thus, the Analyst necessarily

---

EXERCISE

For each of the concepts just mentioned—honesty, trust, responsibility, loyalty, aggression, and sexuality—write down one or more of your personal beliefs about that concept.

EXERCISE

(a) Recall a recent time when you felt guilty about something you said or did. (b) Write down the relevant belief(s) about right or wrong that you thought you violated.

makes an appearance when you attempt, as discussed in the preceding paragraph, to identify the beliefs that may have caused your Moral Judge to be self-critical. There is, in fact, a lot of by-play between the Moral Judge ("You sinned!") and the Analyst ("Why do you believe you sinned?"). The Judge can thus provide an incentive for the Analyst to go to work: "Here I am criticizing myself; why am I doing this?" Obviously, the work of the Analyst can be very useful in helping you understand your beliefs and how your unconscious works with these beliefs. As a matter of fact, most of the exercises included in this book are designed in part to activate your Analyst.

The Analyst is also frequently involved when your Discerning Judge is activated. For example, if your Discerning Judge concludes that a movie you are watching is "poor," your Analyst may well come into play to explain why: poor script, poor acting, and so forth. Similarly, if you look in the mirror and your Discerning Judge says "you don't look so good today," your Analyst may well appear to try to explain why: "You need to get more sleep," "You could use a new haircut," "Maybe you should lose a few pounds."

The Pure Observer or "Witness"

This is the Observer that is essential to achieving a state of "mindfulness." Since it does not try to judge, evaluate, or explain the thoughts, feelings, sensations, or actions that it is observing, it is sometimes also referred to as the "Witness." The Witness[2] merely "realizes" what is happening in your consciousness—a thought, an image, an emotional state, a sensory impression—without judging or analyzing.

One difficulty that we encounter in trying to describe or define the Witness is that "it" does not have any characteristics or <u>do</u> anything except observe. If anything, it is simply a "state of mind" where you are fully aware of what is happening in the moment without analyzing or judging whatever you are observing. In this sense, we could also describe the Witness as <u>a state of pure awareness</u>.

To activate your Witness, teachers of meditative practice will sometimes advise you simply to "take note of" whatever "arises" in your consciousness. If you are "breath watching," chanting a mantra, or using some other meditative technique for focusing or narrowing your conscious attention (see the exercise on page 72), the advice is usually to "merely note" any thought, feeling, or sensory impression that occurs and then "return" your attention to the breath, mantra, or whatever.

Once again, it is important to realize that the Witness, the Analyst, the Discerning Judge and the Moral Judge are not really "separate you's," but rather different <u>states of mind</u> that can appear and then dissolve in rapid succession. Further, the Analyst and the Moral Judge rely heavily on your beliefs about reality and truth (the Analyst) and goodness and morality (the Moral Judge). The Witness, on the other hand, functions primarily in a belief-free framework because it is focused on what <u>is</u>, without judgement or analysis.

There is obviously a fine line between the Witness and the Analyst, since it can sometimes be difficult to know whether you are "merely" observing, as opposed to observing <u>and</u> analyzing. (One reason why "Witness" is probably the better term is that the word "Observer" may imply some form of analysis.) But the Analyst and the Judge really <u>need</u> the Witness, since it is virtually impossible to analyze or judge without first becoming aware of whatever is to be analyzed or judged. However, the more you get into analyzing or judging something that you have observed, the more difficult it becomes to continue observing, to remain mindful of what is happening now. So keep in mind: **It is very easy for your Witness state to "slip" into an analytical or judging state, especially when you are "witnessing" the behavior of others.**

For example, imagine that you are conversing with several other people, and you find yourself disagreeing strenuously with something one of the people just said, so you say to that person, "I think that's a dumb idea." Your Witness may appear briefly to "note" or "realize" your critical comment, but then quickly give way either to (a) your Analyst, who may ask, "why did I say that?" or (b) your Moral Judge, who might say, "you shouldn't have been so nasty!" The Analyst and the Moral Judge can sometimes get hooked up in a dialogue:

> Moral Judge: "There you go again, shooting your mouth off."
> Analyst: "Why did I say that? Am I carrying some kind of grudge against that person?
> Moral Judge: "You should be ashamed for saying that."
> Analyst: Why am I feeling guilty?

Sometimes such internal dialogues can be useful, but they have a potentially important downside: <u>They focus your attention away from the present moment</u>, thus causing you to become <u>un</u>mindful. Thus, while your Analyst and Moral Judge are chatting away, you may not be able to comprehend fully what the other people are saying now or to participate meaningfully in the continuing conversation because your conscious attention is focused more on your internal dialogue. In fact, in focusing too much on your internal dialogue you may find it difficult to keep track of the conversation and end up saying or doing something "foolish" or possibly even "insulting." You are much more likely to act in such a way when you lapse into a state of <u>un</u>mindfulness.

This discussion should make it clear that the Witness, when present in your waking consciousness, always keeps observing, since that is all it does. The Moral Judge and the Analyst, by contrast, seize upon a mental or physical event and then focus on that event (which is now a "past" event), thereby diverting your attention away from the "now." The Witness, of course, can appear in your consciousness to observe your Moral Judge or your Analyst in action, in which case you have returned to a state of mindfulness. When this happens—when your Witness appears to observe your Moral Judge or your Analyst at work—it becomes difficult for the Moral Judge or the Analyst to continue functioning. In other words, **you cannot continue judging or analyzing past events and remain fully mindful.** For this reason, neither the Judge nor the Analyst can "observe" the Witness. (Besides, there would be nothing to "judge" or "analyze"!)

The Witness can be of enormous value in helping you to become more aware of how your own mind works. All of us are capable of "observing" or "watching" ourselves—our behavior, our sensory impressions, and especially our thoughts and emotions. Becoming a good Witness of these internal mental processes is what many schools of meditative practice are all about. Indeed, cultivating your Witness is probably the beginning to what Buddhists call "enlightenment," to what some Hindus call "self-realization," or to what some Christians might call "the Kingdom Within." But keep in mind: While it is one thing to have or experience certain thoughts and feelings, it is quite another to be aware of the thoughts and feelings as you are having them. And it is still another thing to be a nonjudgemental observer of these internal mental states.

BEING MINDFUL OF FEELING STATES

Let us try to make all of this a little more concrete. You can be angry—experience anger—and not be consciously aware that "I am angry." It is the Witness, of course, that recognizes the feeling of anger. The Witness can also become aware of physiological reactions such as heavy breathing or muscular tension. This is "mindfulness." However, when you get angry and your Witness is not present, you will probably <u>act</u> on your anger in some way. These actions often include aggressive behavior directed at the perceived source of the anger. For example, if you feel angry in response to something someone has said, you might say something nasty to the person. Or, if you stub your toe painfully, you might curse or even throw something. If your Witness makes you at least partially aware of how you are reacting, this "mindfulness" could well trigger the appearance of your analyst: "Wow, I must be pretty angry. I didn't realize [i.e., wasn't mindful of] how angry I was." Your Analyst, in other words, rather than sensing the anger directly (as your Witness would do), <u>deduces</u> it from the "angry" behavior.

This discussion suggests that aggressive or violent responses to anger are most likely to occur when your Witness is absent. In other words, you tend to react to emotional states "automatically" when they occur in the absence of your Witness. We might also describe such reactions as "mindless."

A very different scenario emerges when your Witness is present to "watch" your emotional state. For example, if you get angry about something but remain mindful, your Witness will simply make you aware of it: "I am angry." "I am furious." "I am really pissed off." Or if you feel fearful, your Witness realizes it and simply notes it: "I'm scared!"[3] One thing that can make it hard for you to be mindful of intensely negative emotional states like anger, guilt, and fear is that you often have strong negative <u>beliefs</u> about such emotions. Consequently, when you experience one of these emotions, your Moral Judge is often tempted to make an appearance, shoving your Witness aside, and criticizing or blaming you for being in such an emotional state. Negative emotions like fear and anger are, after all, often seen by our culture as a sign of weakness, and many of us have formed strong negative beliefs about such emotions. No wonder, then, that so many of us inactivate our Witness when we experience negative emotions, because being aware of such states as they arise in consciousness can sometimes pose an irresistible temptation for your Moral Judge to make an appearance. If you are already feeling angry, jealous, or fearful, and you harbor strongly negative beliefs about such emotions,

---

EXERCISE

Take a sheet of paper and write down some of the "automatic" responses that you are likely to exhibit when you experience intense emotions like anger, guilt, jealously, frustration, sadness or sorrow, sexual excitement, and happiness or joy.

why compound the problem by also becoming mindful and then self-critical? Why add to the problem by putting yourself down for "allowing" yourself to get into such a "bad" state? The problem with such denial of feeling, of course, is that your nonconscious mind probably knows not only that the feeling is there, but also that your conscious mind is denying it! The challenge of mindfulness, of course, is to develop the capacity to be aware of intense emotional states as they arise without allowing the Moral Judge to take over.

Our resistance to acknowledging negative emotions is sometimes so strong that we will actively deny the reality of such emotions even when others point them out to us: "Whaddaya mean angry? I'm not angry!!" Or, "You're crazy. I don't feel jealous toward that person." Take these last two quotes and substitute other emotions like envy, greed, "lust," or hatred. How many times has each of us said such things to others when they have observed our emotional state?

Psychotherapists would be likely to label such statements as "defensive," but what is really being "defended" against is either (1) the external judgement of others, which can lead us to feel hurt; or (2) the negative self-judgement (i.e., guilt) that our Moral Judge would be tempted to make if our Witness were around to acknowledge the negative feeling that we are experiencing.

Indeed, sometimes you will deny the observations made by others about your negative feelings or behavior with particular vehemence because your Witness is trying to make an appearance. You vaguely sense that the "bad" emotional state may indeed be present and you are afraid of being "found out." By denying the other person's observation with sufficient intensity, you hope to convince them (and yourself) that they are in error and thereby "cover up." This is very similar to what happens during an argument when your opponent finds a significant flaw in your position, but you continue to argue that position even harder to try to convince your opponent (or yourself!) otherwise. What is really happening here is that you are able to "sense" that your opponent may have scored a significant point because your Witness is once again partially present, but your determination to "win" the argument drives you to argue even more intensely in an effort to compensate for the "vulnerability" that your opponent has detected. However, the most important point to keep in mind is that

- **Your Witness is always there, at least in the background of the unconscious, trying to help you see things as they really are.**

The real power of the Witness is that it is able to acknowledge a strong emotional state without passing judgment on it: "I am angry." "I am sad."

"I feel frustrated." "I feel guilty." "I feel jealous." "I'm afraid." One obvious advantage of being able to observe your emotions in a nonjudgemental fashion is that you are then in a better position to bypass the Judge and to invoke the Analyst to help you understand your emotional state: Then, instead of the Moral Judge saying "I shouldn't be angry," your Analyst may ask "Why am I angry?" "What happened to make me feel so sad?" "What is it that makes me feel so frustrated?" "Why should I feel so jealous of this person?" "Why am I feeling so guilty?" Keep in mind, though, that this kind of analysis, like judging, can shove your Witness aside and take you out of the moment.

Being a nonjudgemental Witness of your negative emotional states is a lot easier said than done. Powerful emotions like anger have a way of "swamping" your normal waking consciousness to the point where there is little opportunity or "room" for your Witness to make an appearance. Sometimes it is only the Analyst that comes into play, and only after you have already acted on the intense emotional state. In the long run, of course, it is more useful to cultivate the habit of having your Witness present to recognize your feelings and your behavior as they occur.

Cultivating the Witness

Cultivating the ability to activate your Witness is well worth the effort. Being in that state of mind can be of enormous value in helping you to recognize your habitual modes of responding to events in your life, especially those kinds of events that generate strong emotional states such as fear, guilt, and anger. Your Witness, with some help from your Analyst, can also be of great assistance in your efforts to change the conditions of your life.

Basically, your Witness is fully aware of what you are doing, thinking, and feeling right now. When we say that someone "wasn't aware of what he was doing," we usually mean that the person was acting on some strong emotion mindlessly, that is, without the Witness being present.

EXERCISE

Think back over the past 24 hours and recall at least one time when (a) your Discerning Judge made an appearance; (b) your Moral Judge made an appearance; and (c) your Analyst made an appearance. Can you recall at least one time when you were fully mindful of how you were feeling?

While this discussion of being mindful or having your Witness fully present in your consciousness has been limited so far to the process of witnessing your own mind and behavior, it should be stressed that **mindfulness is the state of being fully aware of <u>all</u> the events of your life as they occur.** Each of us has the ability to activate our Witness, even in highly stressful moments, but few of us have cultivated the <u>habit</u> of doing so. Of all the "good" habits that you may have learned throughout your life—from brushing your teeth to saying "thank you" when someone gives you something—few, if any, are as valuable or as useful as the habit of activating your Witness so that you can be "mindful."

When you are not being mindful and are just thinking, feeling, and acting, "you" have, in effect, <u>become</u> your thoughts, feelings, and actions. Becoming mindful under such circumstances thus requires that a portion of your consciousness "separates" from your thoughts, feelings and actions and begins to <u>observe</u> them. Such an alteration of consciousness is precisely what is meant when we speak of "activating your Witness," "becoming mindful," or simply "witnessing." It is not always easy to cultivate the habit of being mindful, in part because your thoughts, feelings, and actions can be very compelling, almost magnetic. We even have a language for this: "I got so 'caught up' in what I was doing that..." Or, "I was 'lost' in my thoughts." Or, "I didn't 'realize' what I was doing." Such phrases represent different ways of saying that the Witness has been "lost" in the moment.

At this point it is important to note that mindfulness is not necessarily an absolute state and that there can be <u>degrees</u> of mindfulness at any moment. For example, since the realities of modern life often require us to focus our attention on what is happening in the external physical world—thus making it virtually impossible to maintain awareness, say, of our breathing or of how our body feels— it is clearly impossible for most us to be fully mindful all of the time. Nevertheless, it is still useful to develop the ability to maintain a state of at least partial mindfulness whenever circumstances permit.

One reason why it is difficult to be "mindful" all the time is that the mere act of "being mindful" changes your conscious experience! Rather than simply <u>having</u> thoughts and feelings, they become objects to be observed. This is the "uncertainty principle" that plagues any attempt to observe your own conscious experience: your conscious experience changes as a result of your attempt to observe it! (Your consciousness is, of course, in a state of continual change, regardless of whether or not your Witness is present.) About the only way to get around this problem is to recruit your Analyst to examine your memory of what was happening in your consciousness when you were not being "mindful": What was I feeling and thinking about at that time? How did I react in that situation?

This is not to say that you cannot learn a lot about how your mind works by being mindful about what is happening in the moment, but rather to recognize that there is also plenty to learn about how your mind works when the Witness is not present (including the issue of <u>why</u> your Witness was not present), and about the only way to do this is to reflect on your memory of what went on in your consciousness during those times when you were not being mindful.

WHO <u>ARE</u> YOU ANYWAY?

This last discussion raises an interesting question: is it possible to maintain a strong emotional state <u>and</u> be mindful of it at the same time? When you come to think about it, being mindful almost forces a part of your consciousness to become a bit detached from the rest of your experience (i.e., from the part of your conscious experience that you are being mindful <u>of</u>). In other words, "you the Witness" seems to become something separate from "You the thinker and feeler" or "you the doer." This "separate you" becomes mindful of—witnesses—your thoughts, feelings, and actions. The question then becomes, <u>who are you</u>? The language used here is revealing: when my Witness is present, I say that I am merely observing my mind and my behavior. Clearly, since I have identified me with the Witness, to a certain extent I have detached my sense of self from the thoughts, feelings, and actions that "I" am observing. But how can "I" be just the Witness, since these are also <u>my</u> thoughts, feelings, and actions? Mystics, poets, and philosophers have wrestled with this problem for a long time, and about the best resolution I have come across can be summed up as follows: "I <u>have </u> a mind (thoughts and feelings) and a body (actions), but I <u>am not</u> my mind and body."

An interesting characteristic of this separate "I, the Witness" sense, is that it seems to have a kind of permanence about it when you consider it in the light of the rest of your conscious experience. Thus, while my thoughts, feelings, and actions are continually changing ("fleeting") and my body continues to change throughout the aging process, and while the physical world around me is also in a continuous state of change, that part of me that has been witnessing all of this is always there and remains pretty much unchanged: I—the Witness—am always "me." In other words, as you age, almost everything that your Witness can observe changes—your body, your beliefs, your memories, your behavior, your skills and accomplishments, your relationships with other people, the physical environment in which you find yourself—and yet the "you" that is that Witness is always the same, always there, waiting to witness these changes. No doubt this capacity to sense that there is a "self" that is separate from thoughts, feelings, and physical actions is why humankind has been able to conceive of something like a "transcendent self" or "soul" that exists apart from (or "beyond") the mind and body and that predates physical existence and "survives" physical death.

Cultivating Mindfulness

On the following page is a simple exercise in mindfulness meditation. For much more detailed self-instruction in this very useful and powerful set of techniques, I would recommend any of the books by Jon Kabat-Zinn (1994), Thich Nhat Hanh (1987), Lama Surya Dass (1997), Sylvia Boorstein (1995), Kathleen McDonald (1990), or Gunaratana (1992).

Since even the most experienced meditators have difficulty remaining mindful all the time, it is useless to set "goals" for yourself in terms of how long you can remain mindful. In this connection, it is useful to remember that when you are meditating there are at least two very different ways that you can get distracted by thoughts, feelings and sense impressions. Perhaps the most common experience is to be "attracted" to a "stray" thought so that you begin associating with it. For example, if you shift your attention away from your breath and start thinking about some difficult task you have to perform later in the day, you may start mentally "rehearsing" the task by thinking about how you are actually going to carry it out. When this happens, your Witness has disappeared from consciousness.

The other form of distraction occurs when your Witness is replaced either by your Judge or Analyst. For example, when the thought about the upcoming task arises, your Analyst might appear and say, "Why am I thinking about this task? Am I worried about being able to handle it well?" Or, your Moral Judge might appear to say, "There you go again forgetting about watching your breath and letting yourself get distracted by your thoughts. You need to learn more discipline in your meditating." When either thing happens during meditation, you can simply reactivate your Witness, take note of what your Judge or Analyst is doing, release it and then return your attention to the breath. One of the real benefits of meditation is that it can help you not only to develop the capacity to recognize the Judge or the Analyst whenever they appear, but also to cultivate the ability to activate your Witness whenever it can be of assistance to you in your everyday life. In fact, one of the major goals of this book is to help you become more mindful more of the time.

EXERCISE

(a) Find a quiet place where you will not be disturbed;

(b) seat yourself comfortably—a firm chair or cushion on the floor is ideal—relax, close your eyes, and focus your attention on your breathing;

(c) become fully aware of your chest rising and falling and of the way the air feels moving in and out of your lungs; try to maintain this focus of attention by following each breath in and out; stay relaxed and alert; if you like, focus your attention on a specific place in your nose where the breath passes by on each inhale and exhale;

(d) whenever you find your mind wandering away from the breathing—that is, whenever you "become mindful" that you are no longer fully focused on your breathing—simply "take note" of whatever you are feeling or thinking about and, without any judgement or analysis, return your attention to your breathing;

(e) see if you can "breath watch" in this manner for at least 5 minutes (or longer if it feels comfortable).

(f) At least once a day, try to become fully mindful of whatever is happening: what you are thinking, feeling, and doing in the moment, what others are doing, and so forth. Try not to judge or analyze; just observe.

(g) Repeat these exercises for several days; you can become much more adept at being mindful with just a few weeks' practice.

SOME FINAL THOUGHTS ON MINDFULNESS

Since mindfulness involves being fully aware of what is happening <u>in the present moment</u>, your "time sense" plays a major part in determining whether you are being mindful. That is, you cannot be in a mindful state if your conscious attention is focused either on memories of past event or on fantasies about possible future events. For this reason, chapter 11 is devoted to a detailed consideration of your "sense of time."

When you are "watching" your breathing or your thoughts as they arise in your awareness, there seem to be two different phenomena: the breathing or the thoughts, and whoever or whatever is doing the watching (i.e., the "Witness"). Contrast this with ordinary daydreaming, where you <u>have</u> thoughts but without the Witness being present (i.e., there is no conscious watching of the thoughts as they arise). Of course, if you become mindful of the fact that you are daydreaming, then in all likelihood the daydreaming will stop, at least temporarily. In other words, one critical difference between daydreaming and mindfulness meditation is that the latter process ordinarily involves a heightened <u>awareness</u> of the activities of the mind. When you are in such a state of awareness we would say that "your Witness is present."

Let us now return once again to consider the "simultaneity" question: when you are engaged in mindfulness meditation, is your Witness present <u>while</u> you are having thoughts, or does it appear immediately <u>after</u> you have those thoughts? Does thinking "drive out" the Witness? And does the Witness's presence preclude thinking? Is the Witness, in other words, able to be "aware" only of the immediate <u>memory</u> of what you were just thinking? We can pose this question in a more general way: Can you think and be mindful at the same time? Or does your conscious focus shift back and forth very rapidly between mindfulness and thinking? If you believe that you can think while <u>simultaneously</u> being mindful of those thoughts, consider the following possibility: could it be that this rapid shifting back and forth between thinking and mindfulness creates the <u>impression</u> that the thoughts and the state of mindfulness are occurring simultaneously, much like motion pictures where the rapid projection of successive still images creates the impression of continuous movement? Let us try one more exercise.

Perhaps by now you are asking "what's the point of this exercise." My main purpose is to give you some practice in distinguishing between two of the three states of mind that we have been focusing on in this chapter: the Analyst and the Witness (the third state, of course, is the Judge). The two questions that end the exercise are basically asking you to activate your Analyst. Keep in mind that it is one thing to be mindful—simply to be aware of your thoughts as they arise—but what happens when you start <u>judging</u> or <u>analyzing</u> these thoughts? In effect, you have replaced one set of thoughts—the ones that you initially "observed"—with a second set of thoughts (i.e., judgements and analyses of the first set). But in order to do

---

EXERCISE

(a) Get yourself into a comfortable meditative state where you are being as mindful of your breathing as you can; (b) wait for the first unrelated thought to arise in your consciousness. Now ask yourself:

- Did the thought arise while I was being mindful? Or did the thought replace my mindful state?
- Was I subsequently mindful of the thought while I was having it? Or did the thinking stop as soon as I became mindful of it?

this you must first be <u>aware</u> of the initial thoughts, and the only way this can happen is for your Witness to appear long enough to observe them. In other words, the Witness makes a brief appearance, but is quickly replaced by the Judge and the Analyst. We can diagram this sequence of events as follows:

> **Thought** → **Witness** (awareness of thought) → **Judge/Analyst** (more thinking)

Note that the initial thought process is replaced very briefly by the Witness, and that the Witness is, in turn, replaced by the Judge or Analyst, at which point you once again cease being mindful.

Let us conclude our discussion by briefly raising another subtle but very important issue posed by the concepts of mindfulness and the Witness: the <u>dualism</u> implied in the notion that there is a distinction between the Witness ("you") and what is being witnessed or observed (your thoughts, sensations, emotions, etc.). For example, in the two simple meditation exercises it was suggested that you "watch" (focus your attention on) your breath, which implies that there is, on the one hand, the "watcher" (the Witness, you), and, on the other, the "watched" (your breathing). But how can "you" be something separate from your breath and your thoughts? And who or what is doing the watching? Is it not all part of the same package that we call consciousness? <u>Your</u> consciousness?

CONCLUSION

Mindfulness really has to do with being able to focus your full attention on whatever is happening in the moment. You can thus be "mindful" of what other people are doing or saying, of the sounds, sights, smells, and feel of your physical surroundings, of your feelings, or of the sensations coming from within your body. Since each of us is capable of being mindful, at least for brief periods of time, the real challenges are (a) to develop the capacity to become mindful whenever it is in your interest to do so; and (b) learn how to maintain a state of mindfulness for longer periods of time.

NOTES

1. From *The Miracle of Mindfulness* by Thich Nhat Hanh, copyright (c) 1975, 1976, by Thich Nhat Hanh. Preface and English translation copyright (c) 1975, 1976, 1987 by Mobi Ho. Reprinted by permission of Beacon Press, Boston.

2. Henceforth I shall be using the terms Witness to refer to the Pure Observer.

3. Your Witness does not really speak or label what it observes; rather, it is merely aware of whatever is going on in your conscious mind.

CHAPTER 4

ATTENTION AND FOCUS

What is your consciousness "doing" right now? In all likelihood its principal activity—your "focus of attention"—has to do with reading the words on this page—comprehending, reflecting on, or thinking about what is written here. Our language includes several ways of describing how your consciousness is focused: "concentrating on...," "paying attention to...," "absorbed in...," and so forth. How we use such words is also revealing. For example, when we say that something is the "focus" of attention, we imply that there may be other things in our consciousness that are not in focus or "blurred" (meaning that they are "there" in our consciousness but that we are not "paying attention" to them) because our focus is directed elsewhere. To take another example: if you are walking behind someone on a narrow path and the person ahead encounters an obstacle, that person may call back to you, "mind your step," which is really a warning to focus your consciousness on (be *mindful of*) where you are walking ("step") so you do not stumble or fall. Similarly, teachers tell their pupils to "pay attention" when they believe that some students' consciousness may be focused on something other than what the teacher is saying or doing.

A simple but very important truth about the mind is that the **quality of your life is very much a matter of what you pay attention to**. Another important but seldom-recognized truth is that you can exert a good deal of control over what you pay attention to. And by combining these two

Mindworks: Becoming More Conscious in an Unconscious World, pp. 77–100
Copyright © 2007 by Information Age Publishing

truths we reach an even more important conclusion: **you can substantially improve the quality of your life by changing what you pay attention to.**

What, exactly, do we mean by "attention" and "focusing" your attention? Right now your focus of attention is on this book; otherwise, you could not understand what is written here. The opening exercises at the beginning of chapter 1 asked you temporarily to <u>shift</u> your attention away from the book to the sounds around you and then to how your body feels. Let us try a similar exercise with your vision (before reading any further try the exercise below).

Were you able to do it? Were you able to keep your attention focused on both <u>at the same time</u>? Or did you find it shifting rapidly back and forth between the two? If you are not sure, try it again.

Attention and focus can also be illustrated by means of an analogy. Imagine yourself on a dark night flying over the city or town where you live in a helicopter that is equipped with a powerful searchlight. The town has been blacked out by a power failure, so the only way you can see anything below is by shining the searchlight on it. The searchlight is thus like your normal waking consciousness and the darkened town below symbolizes all the various things on which you <u>might</u> focus your conscious attention: thoughts, feelings, or incoming sensory information (sights, sounds, etc.), and so on. And just like your consciousness, which can focus on only a very limited amount of material at any given moment, the searchlight can illuminate only a tiny area of the town at a time. You can, if you wish, deliberately choose to point your searchlight at certain familiar neighborhoods, streets, or buildings, but you can also use it to explore parts of the town that you do not know well. In the same way, you can, if you choose, focus your conscious attention on familiar thoughts, places, people, or activities, or you can make choices that will bring entirely new things to your attention. In other words, just as you can point your searchlight at a great many new and different things in the town below simply by flying over unfamiliar neighborhoods, **so is there an almost limitless variety of new things that you can choose to focus your attention on simply by**

EXERCISE

Look up from this book and do a quick survey of all the sights around you. (a) Find one object and focus your full attention on it for a few seconds; then (b) find a nearby object and shift your attention to that second object for a few seconds; finally, (c) try focusing your attention on both objects at once!

<u>changing your environment</u>: taking a walk or a drive, watching television, going to a movie, listening to music, reading, calling someone on the telephone, going to a bar, visiting with friends, making love, daydreaming, taking some time out for reflection or meditation, and so on. And you also have a great many options in terms of <u>where</u> you decide to walk or drive, <u>what</u> you choose to watch or read, <u>whom</u> you call or visit, <u>what</u> you decide to talk about, and <u>what</u> you daydream about or meditate upon. And even when you are doing something physical like walking or driving a car, you still have a wide range of choices as to what you will <u>think</u> about while you walk or drive. In short, **you ordinarily have a good deal of control over the things that you pay attention to.**

The miniexperiments given at the beginning of chapter 1 were designed in part to demonstrate two important principles concerning what you pay attention to:

- **At many times during a typical day you have complete freedom to shift your focus of conscious attention.**
- **In changing your focus of attention you can "order" the nonconscious mind to "let through" certain sensory information that it had been screening out of your conscious awareness.**

ATTENTION AND FEELINGS

One obvious reason why it is important to exercise your freedom to choose what to pay attention to is that there can be very different <u>feelings</u> associated with the different things that you can choose. Take television as one example. Certain kinds of programs can make you laugh and feel good, while others can excite you, depress you, intrigue you, bore you, irritate you, or even make you angry. And watching a lot of TV can sometimes make you feel sleepy, or even a bit guilty—that you are "wasting time" when you should be doing something "more constructive." Similarly, when you are daydreaming or in a reflective mood, the particular <u>subjects</u> that you choose to reflect upon can generate all kinds of different feeling states.

EXERCISE

Write down of at least five thoughts or ideas, other than this book, that you could choose to focus your attention on right now.

THE "SPLINTERING" OF CONSCIOUSNESS

One of the most remarkable and interesting qualities of human consciousness is that it can be involved in doing more than one thing at a time. I like to call this the "splintering" of your conscious attention. Under certain conditions splintering can be the opposite of mindfulness, especially when the main focus of your conscious attention is on something other than what is happening in the moment. Splintering can occur in many different ways, and under many different circumstances. Sometimes it can be useful and helpful, and at other times it can be dysfunctional. Here are just five simple examples of splintering:

- driving your car while you talk on a cell phone or converse with a companion in the passenger seat.
- jogging while you listen to the news on a walkman.
- setting the table while you worry that the guests might arrive before you are ready for them.
- getting dressed while you plan what you will be doing at work that day.
- eating dinner while you watch television.

You could no doubt add many more personal examples to the list. Note that each of these five examples combines "thinking"—talking, listening, worrying, planning—with some sort of physical activity (running, driving, dressing, eating, etc.). While you would need to devote at least some of your conscious awareness to the physical activity, the <u>focus</u> of your attention is on the thinking activity. Note that if you were to focus your attention instead on the physical activity—for example, if while jogging you were to concentrate on what specific movements your body is making, how the ground feels under your feet, how other parts of your body feel—you could not continue the "thinking" activity (i.e., listening to the news), and your consciousness would no longer be splintered. We could say, instead, that you had become "mindful" of the jogging, since you were focusing your entire attention on that physical activity while it was happening. You could, of course, shift your attention away from the running and back to the news, in which case you would cease being mindful and your consciousness would once again be splintered.

In short, you "splinter" your consciousness whenever you engage in some kind of physical activity while your focus your conscious attention on something else.

The concept of splintering can be illustrated with a photographic analogy: when your consciousness is splintered it is like a photograph of a person, where the person is in sharp focus, while the background—say, some scenery—is somewhat blurred. Considering the picture as a whole (i.e., your entire conscious awareness), the background scenery is there, to be sure, but it is not really "noticed" when you first look at the photograph because the main focus of attention is the person. Note that while each of the five physical activities in the above list requires little, if any conscious thought, they all require at least some conscious monitoring of incoming sensory information. But this sensory monitoring is only in the "background" of your awareness because your focus of attention is on your thought process. In most of the five examples this "background monitoring" involves your senses of vision and touch: When you drive your car you need to be able to <u>see</u> ahead and <u>feel</u> the steering wheel and pedals, and when you jog you need to be able to <u>see</u> ahead and <u>feel</u> your body and the ground underneath. Since you do not really need these two senses to think, you are thus able to monitor the physical activity in the background of your consciousness while you think about or concentrate on something else. And even though you can carry on several unrelated physical activities at once—driving or running while scratching your head—while you are thinking about something else, it would be very difficult to for you to be <u>mindful</u> of any of these physical activities without abandoning the thought activity. Thus, in order to "realize" that you are scratching your head while you are driving your car, you would probably have to stop thinking about whatever else you were thinking about, at least temporarily.

Since you are obviously able carry out <u>several</u> different physical activities at once—scratching your head while you jog or singing while you take a shower—, an interesting question arises: can you "think" about more than one thing at the same time? A few moments ago we tried this with objects in your visual field. Now try it with thoughts (see exercise below).

Can you manage it? Most people find this very difficult to do. Instead, they find their attention shifting back and forth very rapidly between the two. If you think you were able to do it, check it out again: were not you really just shifting your attention very rapidly between the two? As it turns out, about the only way you can do this is to conceptually "merge" the two things into a unit. But then, of course, it is no longer two things.

EXERCISE

Pick two words, two ideas, or two recent events or experiences, and try to focus your attention on both of them simultaneously.

"Self-Conscious" Splintering

A subtle but very interesting form of consciousness splitting occurs when you become aware that it is you who is thinking or feeling or involved in some kind of physical activity. Becoming self-conscious in this way may seem to be a little like mindfulness, but it is not the same thing. In the case of physical activity, this self-conscious sense of "I" can take at least two forms: the "I" who is performing the activity—"Here I am doing this—, or the "I" who experiences the activity—"This is happening to me." There is thus both an active, will-oriented "I" who makes decisions and strives to create and achieve, and a more passive "me" to whom events "happen." (Our grammar—which differentiates clearly between the subjective and objective cases and between the active and passive voices—reflects these two senses in which the self-conscious I can be perceived to exist.) Sexual activity nicely illustrates these different "I" senses: you can "make love to" someone else, you can be "made love to" by someone else, or you and the other person can "make love." Whether you are experiencing the sense of I or me (or both) at any given point in time depends on whether or not you are in an active relationship with the physical activity, "willing" or "intending" certain events or outcomes, or merely experiencing whatever is "happening" to you. But, as we have seen, the sense of a separate I/me very often disappears altogether from waking consciousness, as when you are "concentrating" or "just being." Even during these times, however, there may be an implicit (unconscious?) "I" who is goal-oriented or who is "trying to accomplish something."

Self-conscious splintering can be especially dysfunctional when you are "performing." Most often this kind of splintering occurs when you are attempting to perform in the presence of others—for example, when you participate in an athletic contest before a crowd or are giving a talk or a musical or artistic performance before an audience—but it can also occur when you taking a test or carrying out some other kind of competitive activity under pressure of time. What happens in these cases is that your fear of not performing well activates your Analyst ("How am I doing?) and/or your Judge ("I'm not doing as well as I should."), thereby splintering your consciousness and preventing you from devoting your full conscious attention to the task you are attempting to perform. Splintering can be especially dysfunctional when you are doing something under pressure of time, like taking a test: the Analyst: "How much more time do I have?"; the Judge: "I wasted too much time on that question!" This kind of self-conscious splintering tends to create a vicious cycle, where your critical evaluations of your performance during your performance simply exacerbate your anxiety about performing well, which tends to further impair your performance by making you even more self-conscious. In extreme cases the anxiety can reach a level where you lose complete track of what you are trying to do: "My mind went blank."

In attempting to minimize the possible negative effects of such self-conscious splintering, it is important to realize that negative <u>beliefs</u> are at the root of the problem: if you believe that you are capable of excellent performance and that you will give your best performance, then in all likelihood you will. But if you believe that you will "screw up," or if you have set performance standards for yourself that you believe you cannot meet, then you will most likely experience a high level of self-conscious splintering which will detract from your performance. Note that the likelihood that such splintering will occur has little to do with your "true" level of competence; rather, it has to do with your <u>beliefs</u> about your competence and about your ability to perform at a certain level. (Later in this chapter we will consider the question of how professional athletes or performers are able to avoid splintering; see "Performance Anxiety," below)

"Goal-Oriented" Splintering

One of the most common forms of splintering occurs when you are carrying out a task that has a specific purpose or defined goal: repairing something that is broken, writing a letter or e-mail message, taking a shower or bath, driving your car to a specific destination, and so on. Very often when you are engaged in such an activity your mind begins to focus more on the final goal—finishing the task—and less on the task itself. This kind of splintering—not being fully "mindful" of the task itself—is particularly likely to happen when the task is very routine or when you are in a hurry to finish it (see chapter 11). There can be at least two negative consequences when you splinter your consciousness in this way: (1) you may not perform the task well because you are not devoting your full attention to it, and (2) you may make it difficult for yourself to get any pleasure or enjoyment from the task. And even if the task is difficult and challenging, focusing too much on getting it finished, rather than on merely <u>doing</u> it, can interfere with effective performance.

We can illustrate this process with an example. Let us say that your motorcycle needs some maintenance work, so you decide to spend some time putting it in good working condition. There are at least three related matters that you can "think" about as you set to work:

1. The maintenance activity itself.
2. Finishing the activity (realizing your intent: to "fix" the motorcycle)
3. The "you" who is performing the activity

If your conscious attention is fully devoted fully to #1, you are being "mindful" of what you are doing and you will most likely perform at a high level. And while there is no way you can perform the motorcycle maintenance work properly without at least <u>some</u> sensory awareness of the task (i.e., vision and touch), you may still be able to carry out the work while you think about other things. For example, if you are impatient with the motorcycle maintenance work because you are "in a hurry" to go on to other things, your consciousness will be split between the work and the immediate goal of "finishing" it (#2). Similarly, your consciousness may be split because you are aware (#3) of the "you" who is performing the activity: "Here I am tinkering with my motorcycle again." In theory, the presence of either or both of these forms of splintering—the "I" who is acting or the "goal" of the activity—could interfere with effective performance by diverting a part of your conscious focus away from the maintenance activity itself. In effect, you are being "distracted" from the activity by thoughts such as "I am performing this activity" or "I need to finish the maintenance as soon as possible so I can go on to other things." Further, when such splintering occurs, it becomes easy for your Moral Judge to make an appearance: "If you weren't in such a rush you could do a much better job."

In short, being fully mindful would mean that you became sufficiently involved in the maintenance task that you were no longer consciously aware of the fact that "I" initially embarked upon this activity because the motorcycle needed maintenance or that the "purpose" of the activity ("my" intent) is to maintain the machine in proper working order. Rather, the doing of the act itself would preoccupy your waking consciousness to the extent that your sense of purpose or intent would disappear from conscious awareness along with the self-conscious "I" or "me" who is doing it. In reflecting later on such an experience, you might say "I became so absorbed in what I was doing that I forgot why I was doing it," or "I was so absorbed that I lost track of the time."

In fact, your ability to enjoy motorcycle maintenance or any other activity that might be regarded as "work" may depend to a large extent on whether or not you can drive the intent or "goal" of the activity, or concerns about much time it is taking, out of your conscious awareness. However, if you focus your consciousness primarily on the goal—to "finish" the maintenance task—the task becomes more like "work" that seems to have no value unless and until it is done: "I became so focused on reaching my destination that I couldn't enjoy the trip." This preoccupation with reaching the end or goal can also cause you to become impatient and to overreact to delays (see below). This particular kind of splintering of consciousness is what eastern philosophical traditions call "desire" or "attachment" (i.e., to the goal).

Splintering and "Work"

The workplace can provide many opportunities for people to splinter their consciousness. Whether such splintering turns out to be functional or dysfunctional often depends on the nature of the work task you are trying to perform. For example, if the task involves very difficult or unfamiliar elements, or if it requires that you learn certain new skills, the importance of being able to focus your consciousness fully on the <u>doing</u> of it, rather than on its intent or ultimate purpose, can hardly be overestimated. In short: **when you are learning a new skill or performing an unfamiliar task, the quality of your work is likely to suffer in direct proportion to the extent that your conscious attention is focused on something else.**

On the other hand, there are many types of jobs where a voluntary splintering of consciousness is not only possible, but probably necessary to make the work bearable. This is especially true of jobs that are boring and repetitive such as clerical work or working on an assembly line. Most jobs, in fact, involve at least some tasks that can become routine and uninteresting, once they have been mastered. Perhaps the most common form of splintering is by way of conversation: one commonly sees workers in fields such as construction, manufacturing, and farming conversing with each other while they work. Workers in personal service fields such as taxi driving and hair care frequently carry on conversations with their clients that have nothing to do with the work being performed. One important function of these nonwork-related conversations is to make a job that may otherwise be tedious and boring more tolerable and possibly even enjoyable. Thus, if such industries were to prevent their employees from conversing with each other while they work, they might well experience a substantial decline in the quality of performance, a lowering of morale, and increased turnover rates.

Splintering on the job can take many other forms: daydreaming, listening to music, knitting, and even reading. In some work situations such splintering may actually serve to <u>enhance</u> productivity. Note that activities like reading and conversing necessarily become the primary focus of consciousness, while most of the "brain work" required by the job is performed by the unconscious with the assistance of one or more sense modalities (most often vision and hearing). Other types of splintering (e.g., listening to music) may require only a minimal involvement from waking consciousness, leading the workers free to devote their main attention to the job task. Some workers in highly creative fields such as painting and writing, where the work may require a major focus of consciousness, are nevertheless able to perform their work effectively while music is playing in the background. Indeed, many artists and writers believe that their creativity is actually enhanced by the music. What is not entirely clear, of course, is how much of these artists' attention is actually being devoted to <u>listening</u> to the music.

Some of the most difficult jobs are those where the basic task is repetitive and boring, but where it is necessary to maintain a high degree of attention and vigilance to the task at hand. Typical examples of such jobs would be a night watchman, a Secret Service agent, a radar operator, or any assembly line job that involves operating potentially dangerous equipment such as a lathe or circular saw.

The real question with splintering your consciousness while you are carrying out some physical activity, of course, is <u>whether your performance might be impaired</u>. Take driving on a freeway as an example. Does daydreaming or having a conversation with a passenger have any effect on the quality of your driving? What difference does it make if the passenger is sitting in the back seat? Do such activities interfere with your ability to respond to emergencies? While answers to such questions might well depend on the driver and the nature of the conversation or the daydreaming, it is important to understand what happens in your consciousness when a potential emergency arises. Consider the following: if you see anything unusual or potentially threatening while you are driving on a freeway—a vehicle just ahead of you that comes to an abrupt stop, for example—your entire conscious attention will immediately be mobilized around the driving task, and no more conversation or daydreaming is likely to occur until the threat is removed. What happens here is that your unconscious, which has been doing most of the "analysis" of the incoming visual information (while your conscious attention is focused on something else), "decides" that there is a threatening situation that requires your full conscious attention. Your conscious mind obviously does not make such decisions, since it does not rationally assess the situation before deciding to take action: "Hmm, since suddenly I'm gaining rapidly on that car ahead, I'd better slow down." On the contrary, you focus your entire attention on the driving and hit the brakes <u>all at the same time,</u> without first "thinking" about what to do. In other words, these "choices" are being made by your nonconscious mind.

In short, this discussion suggests an important principle about splintering: **Whenever you encounter a situation that your nonconscious mind determines to be potentially dangerous or threatening, all splintering ends and your full conscious attention becomes focused on that situation.**

SPLINTERING AND "LEARNING"

This remarkable ability to perform a complex physical activity like driving while you simultaneously focus most of your conscious attention on a completely different mental activity is possible only because most of the processing of the incoming sensory information (mostly vision and touch) is being done by the unconscious. The unconscious is not only analyzing the sensory data, but is also instructing the muscles in your arms and legs to make appropriate adjustments in the steering and foot pedals. The unconscious thus "frees up" the rest of your normal waking consciousness to do other things. Thus, **when you say that you have "learned" a "perceptual-motor" task like driving a car or riding a bicycle, what you really mean is that the unconscious part of your mind is able do most of the brainwork.** Moreover, the unconscious has also been trained to recognize abrupt changes in that incoming sensory information—for example, an obstacle in the road ahead—that require your full conscious attention.

"DISTRACTIONS"

When you say that something is "distracting," you usually mean that it is threatening to splinter your consciousness at a time when you want to focus all of your attention on something else. Another way to say this is that your "attention is being diverted" away from whatever it is that you want to focus on. The distraction can be sensory (e.g., something you see or hear) or mental (an "unwanted" thought or feeling). For example, when you are attempting to learn a complex skill like driving a car, you usually resist splintering your consciousness because you believe that the learning process requires your full concentration. Under these conditions, you would be inclined to regard anything that interferes with your ability to concentrate fully on the learning task as a distraction. To return to our example of driving a car: most novice drivers would regard loud music or a talkative passenger as distracting because they have not yet reached the point where they can rely primarily on their unconscious mind to do the driving. Driving and most other perceptual-motor tasks thus require the novice's full conscious attention until the task becomes familiar and routine (i.e., until it has been "learned" by the unconscious). However, even if you have learned well a particular skill like driving a car, there are many circumstances where you still might consider any competing stimulus to be distracting you from the task at hand. For example, if you are driving at night on unfamiliar roads or if the driving conditions are especially hazardous, you may not want your consciousness to be splintered by conversation or any other distraction. In other words, if you believe that the task involves a significant potential for risk (or believe that the "stakes" involved in performing it competently are high), having "learned" it may not be sufficient for you to trust your unconscious to take over most of the work.

Another important factor in whether or not you will regard competing stimuli as distracting is your beliefs about your own competence. For example, regardless of your driving experience or your "true" driving ability, you also need to <u>believe</u> that you have achieved a certain level of mastery over the task. Thus, there are some experienced and competent drivers (i.e., those whose unconscious <u>is</u> able to carry out most of the work) who still feel insecure about their driving skills—that is, <u>believe</u> that their unconscious mind cannot be trusted to do most of the driving—who would become irritated when a passenger tries to carry on a complex conversation with them while they are driving, because they feel threatened by the realization that part of their conscious attention is being drawn away from the driving task. In fact, a very insecure driver may be so focused on the driving task that she does not even "hear" the would-be conversationalist.

DISTRACTIONS, BELIEFS, AND EMOTIONS

Most of us at one time or another have experienced feelings of frustration or irritation under the following conditions: when you are trying to focus ("concentrate") all of your normal waking consciousness on a particular task (driving, reading, meditating, problem-solving) while someone or something else is distracting your attention away from the task. The external source may simply be a sound or other annoying sensory stimulus, or it may be another person who is competing for your attention. We resist having our consciousness splintered when we feel that the task in which we are engaged requires our full attention. If there is an accompanying feeling of irritation, it probably emerges from competing or conflicting beliefs.

Let us see how all this works using a concrete example. Suppose that you are absorbed in reading some complex prose when your young child tries to engage you in conversation. You can (a) tell the child to go away and continue devoting your full consciousness to reading; (b) put the reading material down and devote full attention to the child; or (c) try to splinter your consciousness and do both things simultaneously. The feelings of irritation or frustration, however, may emerge regardless of which behavioral choice you make! You may blame the child ("the kid bothered me while I was trying to read"), but the feelings actually emerge from your beliefs. Let us see how this might happen.

While your full conscious attention is focused on the reading task, the child begins to ask you questions. You immediately feel irritated. How has the "child stimulus" been interpreted by your unconscious to generate this emotional state? In all likelihood, the child's presence has activated either (a) negative, emotionally loaded beliefs, and/or (b) contradictory or mutually incompatible beliefs. "Contradictory" beliefs are those that cannot be satisfied simultaneously, that is, where <u>any</u> response that you may make to the child in an effort to satisfy one belief will necessarily contradict the other. There are literally dozens of different beliefs that might come into play here, so let us look at several possible examples:

1. "I've had a busy day, and I deserve to have some quite reading time to myself."
2. "I should be a good parent."
3. "Good parents should always be responsive to their kid's requests for attention."
4. "I'm such a versatile person that I should be able to read and respond to my kid's questions at the same time."
5. "I've been neglecting my kid lately."
6. "My kid is spoiled."
7. "I need to do this reading, <u>now</u>!"

What is remarkable about the human mind is that it is possible to hold all of these beliefs at the same time. Let us now look at their implications. If belief #4 is activated by the child's questions, you might try to splinter your attention by continuing to read while simultaneously giving cursory answers to the child's questions. Your primary attention would remain focused on the reading material, while your perfunctory (and partially unconscious) answers to the questions would hopefully satisfy the child. This splintering of consciousness might even "work"—that is, satisfy belief #4—if it were not for the other beliefs. Your unconscious knows full well, however, that you are basically trying the brush off this kid, which (a) triggers #5, which is a negative belief about yourself, and which (b) runs directly contrary to belief #2 and especially belief #3. Your unconscious now recognizes that your behavior either contradicts your beliefs or has activated contradictory beliefs, so it signals your conscious mind accordingly. The signal can come in various emotional forms: irritation, anxiety, guilt, resentment, anger, or a sense of frustration. The frustration might come from the unconscious realization that belief #4 is really not being validated: you find you cannot really splinter your consciousness effectively. The triggering of negative belief #5 and the unconscious realization that beliefs 2 and 3 are being contradicted might also produce a feeling of guilt. If this guilt feeling leads you in turn to put down the reading material and spend some "quality time" with the child, your unconscious will recognize that belief #1 or #7 is being contradicted and may therefore signal your conscious mind with a feeling of irritation or resentment. Belief #6 may also be triggered, which would reinforce the feeling of resentment and possibly even contradict belief #2.

Before continuing with this example, it is important to point out that we have just encountered one of the "rules" by which the mind works: **it is important to our psychological well-being that our experience be consistent with our beliefs.**[1] This is perhaps most obvious in the case of beliefs about what is true or what is real, but it also applies to beliefs about goodness or rightness. When our experience (including our own behavior) contradicts such beliefs, the unconscious sends a "signal" to the conscious mind in the form of a negative emotion (anxiety, irritation, guilt, depression, etc.).

In short, **there are at least two ways in which beliefs can be involved in generating negative emotional states: when our experience either (a) contradicts our beliefs or (b) confirms negative beliefs about ourselves or others.**

Let us illustrate these mechanisms by exploring another possible scenario involving belief #6, the idea that your kid is spoiled. The child's questions might well trigger this belief initially, which could lead you to scold the child or simply to ignore the child's questions. Such behavior would certainly be consistent with beliefs #1 and # 6, but would almost certainly trigger negative belief #5 and be interpreted by the unconscious as contradicting both beliefs 2 and 3. It could also activate negative belief #5 and contradict belief #2. Accordingly, your unconscious might well signal these problems by producing strong feelings of guilt or possibly anxiety in your waking consciousness. As long as you continue reading and ignoring the child, the guilt will persist, which may ultimately make it difficult for you to concentrate on your reading. Your inability to derive any further pleasure from the reading may well lead to a feeling of irritation (i.e., belief #1 is being contradicted) and, if belief # 6 is triggered, a strong feeling of resentment or anger toward the "spoiled" child who has "prevented" you from reading. Your normal waking consciousness may well be able to experience feelings of mild guilt and mild irritation simultaneously, but it ordinarily has difficulty experiencing anger together with much of anything else. Anger, in short, tends to "swamp" your conscious awareness (see the next chapter). Since anger tends to drive most other emotional states out of your conscious experience, it is also a very convenient "cover up" emotion (we will expand on this idea in the next chapter).

The point to keep in mind here is that a negative emotional state can be a conscious signal that certain beliefs are being contradicted by your experience. The "wisdom" of the unconscious has detected a contradiction between what you are experiencing and what you hold to be true. The nature of the emotion(s) being experienced will vary according to the belief(s) involved (another important issue to be explored in the next chapter). In the same way, the "wisdom" of the unconscious can cause it to send an emotional signal that you are harboring contradictory beliefs. Whatever the intended "message" might be, **negative emotional reactions should be taken as signals to explore your relevant beliefs.**

Self-help guides and "parenting" manuals might well have some advice to offer on how to handle dilemmas like the one we have been discussing. Such advice may often prove to be of little value, however, if it ignores the belief systems that are inevitably involved. You might be advised, for example, to incorporate the child into the reading, perhaps by inviting the child to sit in your lap or simply to snuggle up while you continue reading. Even if the child is content with such passive attention, your belief systems may not be so content! (e.g., belief #5, that you have been neglecting the child). But in the more likely event that the child is not satisfied by such action, other beliefs (e.g., 1 and 7—that you "deserve" to finish your reading, or 2 and 3—that you "should" be a good parent) may end up being frustrated. Similar challenges to your beliefs may be associated with other types of advice, such as "patiently explain to your child that this is your time to read in privacy and that you will be glad to talk at some later appointed time" (e.g., belief 5—that you have been neglecting your child) or "set aside your reading until the child goes to bed so that the two of you can spend quality time together" (beliefs 1 and 7—that you "deserve" to read in peace—or belief 6—that your child is "spoiled.").

While there may be no ideal solution to this particular dilemma, one compromise approach is to apply the principle of mindfulness: instead of splintering your consiousness, do "one thing at a time." Specifically, you can set aside the reading completely and to devote your full attention to the child for a period of time, after which you can attempt to get back to your reading. Depending on what it is that the child wants, the transition from conversation to reading may or may not be easy, but if it proves to be difficult you can probably imagine several possible strategies that might smooth that transition. In any event, this "solution" has at least one sure advantage: the child receives your undivided (unsplintered, mindful) attention for a period of time.

In a sense, any sort of splintering that interferes with your efforts to perform a task well could be viewed as a "distraction." Recall our earlier discussion about the "self-conscious" splintering of consciousness, where one part of consciousness is aware of a personal "I" or "me" and the other part is aware of the work I am trying to carry out: "I" am trying to write these words. "I" try to comprehend these words as I read them over. It is, in fact, very hard for me to write well or creatively as long as my consciousness is splintered in this way, because the self-conscious awareness of the "I" who is doing the work serves as a distraction, making it impossible for me to devote the full creative potential of my consciousness to the writing task. In the same way, the child's questions would tend to distract my attention in such a way that it becomes difficult to read. Intense emotional states can do the same thing: distract all or a portion of your waking consciousness so as to limit your creativity, problem-solving ability, and capacity for concentration. (See the next section for more on this.)

Our earlier discussion of motorcycle maintenance highlights still another type of distraction: by focusing a major part of your attention on the intent behind any activity (i.e., the goal or end product of that activity), you may make it difficult to focus fully on the task at hand, and thereby to perform it competently or creatively. In other words, **focusing too much attention on a goal can actually make it more difficult to attain that goal.** This is not to say that planning or goal setting is a poor idea, but simply that, once you commit yourself to a particular goal-directed activity, it may be desirable or even necessary to submerge your conscious intent and your awareness of the goal into the unconscious so that you can devote your full waking consciousness to the performance of that activity. The unconscious "knows" what your intent or ultimate goal is, and will guide you accordingly.

TIME PRESSURE

Focusing your consciousness fully on what you are doing in the present moment is easier said than done. One type of distraction that can make it especially difficult to focus your consciousness in this way is the pressure of time (see chapter 11). Once again, beliefs play an important part in the process. To begin with, it is important to realize that "deadlines" can be either externally imposed by others or self-imposed, and that there are several different beliefs about time pressures that you might hold, each of which can have unique consequences in terms of your ability to devote your full waking consciousness to any task:

1. "It is essential to complete this task in the shortest possible time."
2. "This task must be completed by a certain time."

3. "I will have to cut corners and/or take risks to complete this task on time."
4. "There is not enough time to complete this task."

There are also many personal beliefs about yourself and others that can be brought into play when you perform any task under perceived time pressures:

5. "It is important for me to be punctual."
6. "Others will think less of me if I'm late."
7. "It is important that others think well of me."
8. "I'm late with things too often. I never allow enough time to do things well."
9. "I've got to clean up my act when it comes to being on time."
10. "Haste makes waste."
11. "My work should always be of the highest quality."
12. "Others will think less of me if my work is not of the highest quality."

Belief #1 may actually help to focus your attention on the task at hand, because it really sets no limits; it merely challenges you to perform the task as quickly as possible. In your haste to accelerate completion of the task, however, you will trigger beliefs #3 and #10, which can easily set up a conflict: acting on beliefs #3 and #10 will necessarily contradict beliefs #11 and #12. The resulting concern could well trigger a feeling of anxiety about whether your work will be of acceptable quality, thereby splintering your consciousness and limiting your ability to focus your full attention of the task itself.

We could go on with dozens of other even more complicated examples of how trying to perform tasks under pressure of time can either contradict certain beliefs or activate negative beliefs, thereby generating emotional states which splinter consciousness in such a way as to interfere with effective task performance.

"VOLUNTARY" AND "INVOLUNTARY" SPLINTERING

Note that we have now discussed three different examples of a splintering of consciousness that produce very different results. In the "talking-while-driving-on-the-freeway" example, the splintering can make the driving task less boring and presumably more pleasurable. (Whether it affects the quality of task performance is perhaps debatable; while it could be argued that driving would be improved if the driver's "full attention" were on the task, there is no guarantee that, in the absence of the conversation with the passenger, the driver's consciousness would not be splintered in some other way, e.g., by daydreaming). It is also important to realize that the splintering in this example is voluntary: the driver chooses to engage in conversation with the passengers, and can consciously choose to disengage, for example, "hold on a minute, there's a flashing light up ahead."

In contrast to the driving example, in the "child distracts me while I'm reading" example the splintering could impair performance (reading), depending on how the child responds to your invitation to sit on your lap while you continue reading. Finally, in the "performing-a-task-under-time-pressure" example, the splintering not only has a negative effect on task performance but is also involuntary. All of us have experienced this kind of splintering: where our anxiety or worry about performing a task under time pressure actually interferes with our ability to do it. Taking a test that has a time limit is a common experience for many students where time pressure can interfere with effective performance.

"PERFORMANCE ANXIETY"

Does a conscious sense of anxiety or concern always interfere with task performance? Are there not circumstances under which such an affective state can actually improve performance? For some students, anxiety about doing well on a timed test might actually serve as a motivator to perform better. And what about professional athletes, musicians, or entertainers, many of whom admit to feeling "nervous" prior to a performance, but subsequently perform brilliantly? Why does the anxiety in these cases seem not to impair performance? Can such anxiety even enhance performance?

Once again, it would appear that beliefs play a central role in this process. If you believe that anxiety will impair your performance, then it might well do so. But anxiety is less likely to be a negative factor when you experience it in connection with tasks that are highly familiar and with which you believe that you have achieved a certain level of mastery. The key to successful performance, then, is to believe that you are capable and able to perform the task well. "Nervousness" under these conditions poses an interesting question: Since you believe that you have mastery over the task and are capable of excellent performance, what is the nervousness all about?

Let us examine this question in a bit more depth. Most accomplished professionals—regardless of their particular field of endeavor—harbor deeply ingrained beliefs about their work. Following are a few typical examples:

- I am capable of performing at a high level of excellence.
- In order to maintain and develop my skills, I should always strive to excel.
- Excellence in performance requires that I focus my full attention and that I devote all of my physical and psychic energies to the task.

When the time to perform approaches, these beliefs obviously come into play. The professional realizes (perhaps unconsciously) that the validation and satisfaction of these beliefs will require her to mobilize and concentrate her psychic and physical energy. But notice—and this is a key issue—this realization occurs prior to the actual performance in anticipation of that performance. In all likelihood the "nervousness" that some professionals consciously experience prior to a performance is not so much a concern about poor performance (which would contradict their belief in mastery), but rather a manifestation of the tremendous mobilization of energy and intense focus of attention that they believe will be required for excellent performance. Since the performance has not yet started, there is no natural outlet or release for this energy, so it takes the form of "nervousness." Performers describe this affective state in various ways: "excitement," "butterflies in the stomach," "the jitters," and so on. Some performers may actually manifest this energy build-up physically by pacing back and forth, sweating profusely, getting "the shakes," or even vomiting.

That there are significant beliefs at play here is revealed in statements such as, "I'd worry if I didn't get nervous before a performance." The "nervousness," in this case, constitutes conscious evidence of the energy build-up that is believed to be necessary for excellent performance.

Most important of all, however, is that **with professionals, conscious awareness of the anxiety or tension usually disappears once the performance begins**. In other words, excellent performance usually requires that there be no splintering of consciousness <u>during</u> the performance, i.e., that the professional's waking consciousness be entirely focused on the task at hand. Indeed, if an athlete or entertainer makes mistakes early in a performance but subsequently performs excellently, a sympathetic critic might say, "after getting over an early case of the jitters, she did very well." In this case, there are several possible beliefs that might be involved in causing the jitters:

"I didn't go through a sufficient energy build up prior to the performance."

"The performance standards I've set for myself today may be too high."

"My level of performance may not be up to the standards of this particular audience (or opponent, if the field is athletics)."

Most professionals are able to "get over" affective states that may interfere initially with their early performance because their basic belief that they are competent permits them to discard beliefs that are basically situationally determined (like those listed immediately above), especially when they realize (usually unconsciously) that these beliefs are creating affective states that interfere with performance. Beliefs about one's professional competency, in other words, are usually core beliefs (see chapter 10) that can cause the professional to discard more superficial (e.g., situationally determined) beliefs when these latter beliefs produce experiences that threaten the core beliefs. In other words, if you believe in your basic competence as an athlete, and you find yourself performing below your capabilities because of "nervousness" about the perceived superior competence of your opponent or the perceived "importance" of the contest, your basic core belief about your level of competence is not threatened: "I don't have to play 'above my head' just because my opponent is so good or because the game is so important, not if my uncertainty ("nervousness") about being able to do so makes me play worse than usual. Sure, my opponent is better and/or the game is important, but what I should do is to concentrate on what I know I can do." Here we should recognize a subtle but critical distinction: it is not your beliefs about the opponent or the game that are so important, but rather what you believe that you should or must do under the circumstances, and whether you really believe that you <u>can</u> do it. In fact, in our society there are even widely-shared cultural beliefs about such matters: "True professionals always do their best, regardless of the circumstances."

ATTENTION AND MENTAL HEALTH

All of us have experienced times when we have not been able to focus our conscious attention fully on some task because of thoughts or feelings that are both "uninvited" and "unwanted." You might describe such a state by saying you are "having difficulty concentrating." A common example of this phenomenon occurs when you are trying to read something: your eyes scan the words on the page, but the words have little or no meaning for you because your consciousness is otherwise preoccupied with unrelated thoughts and/or feelings. You suddenly become aware (mindful) of what has been happening when you realize that you have no comprehension ("no idea") of what you just "read." If the distracting thoughts or feelings are powerful enough, you can go back and reread the same passage one or more times and still not understand what you have read! It is even possible to read the passage out loud and not comprehend it! This sort of splintering is most likely to occur when the reading material is either complicated or of little intrinsic interest, but it can and does occur with any kind of written material if the "distracting" thoughts or feelings are sufficiently strong.

All of us have experienced such times when it is difficult to concentrate, but when your waking consciousness is repeatedly visited by the same "unwanted" thoughts, we call it "obsessive" thinking. And when you regularly experience the same negative emotional states, we might call it "depression" or "anxiety." Often obsessive thinking is accompanied by negative emotions, for example, when you worry constantly about some possible future illness or catastrophe. People who regularly have difficulty functioning in their work or personal life because of such thoughts or feelings are sometimes labeled as "neurotic." Neuroses can have behavioral manifestations—obsessive thinking is often accompanied by compulsive behavior (e.g., frequent hand washing or "superstitious" behavior) and anxiety and depression are often accompanied by physiological symptoms or sleep disorders—but the underlying psychological state is one of an "involuntary" splitting of consciousness. In other words, a "neurotic" person is one who feels he has to some extent "lost control" of his conscious experience. Since we all experience uninvited and unwanted thoughts and feelings from time to time, the question of who is and is not "neurotic" is to some extent an arbitrary judgment.

It is easy to see why Freud was so interested in the role of the "unconscious" in neurosis: these unwanted thoughts and feelings must come from somewhere, and the unconscious is the logical place to look. However, it is perhaps unfortunate that the early popularization of the concept of the unconscious occurred in the context of the study of emotional distress or mental illness, since it encouraged people to look at the unconscious primarily as the source of psychological problems. The unconscious was thus seen primarily as the repository of dark and sinister memories, fantasies, and impulses that had been repressed because they caused us too much psychological pain. If the unconscious is thus "responsible" for inflicting so much discomfort on our conscious experience, then surely it is to be feared. The Freudian concept of "repression" (the "motivated forgetting" of unpleasant or threatening thoughts or feelings) tended to reinforce this negative and foreboding view of the unconscious as the "repository" for such memories and feelings.

While the nonconscious mind no doubt houses such memories and feelings, if we embrace the much broader concept of the unconscious set forth in chapter 1—as a very intelligent, versatile, and wise part of our mind that also maintains our physiological functioning, protects us from danger, interprets much of our daily experience, allows us to carry on several complex tasks at the same time, and is the source of our creativity—the Freudian view of the unconscious seems very narrow and distorted. In fact, this larger and more positive view of the unconscious would lead us to look at "neurosis" is a very different way. Perhaps our unconscious is instead trying to "send us a message" in the form of "unwanted" thoughts and feelings. This "message" can be interpreted as follows: if these obsessive thoughts and negative feeling states arise as a result of beliefs that are either incompatible or negative, then perhaps it is time to begin examining in some depth any beliefs that might be associated either with these unwanted thoughts or with the events that lead to such negative feeling states. What do we believe to be true about ourselves? About others? About the nature of our relationships with others? About the events of our daily life? How might these beliefs be involved in generating these unwanted thoughts or feelings? In exploring such beliefs it is important to keep in mind that "unwanted" thoughts and feelings are often serving some psychological purpose: for example, to protect us from experiencing other (usually painful) memories, feelings, or thoughts.

ATTENTION AND "MINDFULNESS"

In chapter 3 it was pointed out that being "mindful" means focusing your attention fully on what is currently happening around you and what you are doing, feeling, and thinking in the present moment. Mindfulness thus means being fully aware and conscious of your ongoing sensory experience (sights, sounds, smells, etc.), of your current thoughts and feelings, and of the state of your body. There are many ways to describe mindfulness: being "focused in the now," "being in the moment," "just being," or—as the title of a classic book on the subject advises—Be Here Now.[2]

One likely reason for the growing popularity during recent decades of meditation and eastern spiritual practice in general is a growing recognition that modern technological living has caused many of us to splinter our consciousness so thoroughly and continuously that we are seldom fully mindful of what we are doing and feeling in the present moment. Eating is a prime example of such splintering. How often do you eat while your primary focus of attention is on something else: talking, arguing, watching TV or a movie, or just thinking about a topic that has no connection to eating? When you eat in this way, how aware are you of how your food actually looks, how it feels in your mouth, or how it really tastes? Are you really aware of how it feels when you chew and swallow and when the food moves down your esophagus to your stomach? How often do you find yourself reaching for the next bite before you have really tasted, chewed, and swallowed the food that is already in your mouth? How can you ever fully appreciate and enjoy your food if you eat in this fashion? Like many other physical activities, the task of eating—picking up food, putting it into your mouth, chewing, and swallowing—has been sufficiently well "learned" that the unconscious can carry it out with little involvement of the conscious mind.

Modern society has created innumerable devices for splintering our consciousness while eating. Basically what happens is that we are encouraged to eat while being primarily preoccupied with something else. Eating is thus subordinated to semi-conscious status through TV dinners, snack foods sold in movies and at public events, and "fast food" in general. Fast food is often consumed while the person is driving, walking, reading, or otherwise focused on something else. We have become so habituated to eating in this fashion that we automatically create mental distractions for ourselves even when there is no external stimulus such as the TV or a sporting event. How many times have you eaten breakfast while reading the morning paper? How often do you eat while your normal waking consciousness is primarily focused on what happened yesterday or what you plan to do during the day?

The fact that the average American is overweight and that diet programs have become such big business can be at least partially explained by this splintering of consciousness that occurs when we eat. We have become relatively unconscious—"*un*mindful"—of how our food looks, smells, feels, and tastes while we eat, and we are equally unconscious of when we are full or whether we are still hungry.

Let us compare these modern eating habits with the more traditional style where a family or group of friends sits down and "breaks bread together." Now you might argue that consciousness is also splintered in this more traditional scenario, since people normally engage in conversation when they eat in this manner. The main difference, I think, is that the conversation that occurs as a family eats together is often focused on the food and the eating process—who prepared it, how it looks and smells, how it tastes, and so on. Communal meals also afford the opportunity to say grace or give thanks before eating. In other words, eating in the traditional fashion at a dining table tends to be more mindful.

There are many other situations in modern life besides eating where the quality of our experience is diminished by a splintering of consciousness. For example, our increasingly fast-paced existence tempts us to cram more and more activities into our day, which in turn forces us to rush through each activity so we can go on to the next one. Basically, hurrying is a process where we try to accelerate the pace of an activity in the interest of finishing it as soon as possible. The net result is that we are less mindful of each activity because we are doing it "with one eye on the clock." Our ability to be mindful of what is happening in the moment is similarly impaired by an ever-increasing number of technological devices that can distract our attention: pagers, cell phones, faxes, portable TV or stereo, voice mail, e-mail, and so on.

This discussion should not be interpreted to mean that splintering of consciousness is <u>necessarily</u> negative or dysfunctional. Indeed, there may be many situations where splintering has real value—for example, to help make tedious or boring work more bearable or possibly even enjoyable. The main point to keep in mind is that **it is useful to develop the habit of being <u>mindful</u> of those situations when you are splintering your consciousness so that you can determine what consequences it might be having in your life.**

CONCLUSION

You can make a big improvement in the quality of your conscious experience simply by changing what you pay attention to. However, the quality of your experience from moment to moment also depends on <u>how</u> you focus your attention. To experience anything fully, or to perform certain activities at the optimal level, it is necessary to be able to devote your full attention to it. However, when it comes to many of the things we do during a typical day, we often find ourselves "splintering" our attention, where we carry out one activity while simultaneously directing the main focus of our consciousness to something else. Splintering can be a voluntary act—as when you choose to watch a TV show while you eat—or "involuntary," as when you get distracted either by external stimuli (telephones, pagers, others who want your attention, etc.) or by internal thoughts or feelings that are "uninvited." The key to controlling such internal distractions is to understand the underlying <u>beliefs</u> that give rise to these unwanted thoughts and feelings.

NOTES

1. This principle is central to Leon Festinger's much-cited theory of "cognitive dissonance" (see *A Theory of Cognitive Dissonance*, Wiley, 1959).
2. Ram Dass, Lama Foundation, 1971.

CHAPTER 5

FEELINGS AND EMOTIONS

"People … would rather have one good, soul-satisfying emotion than a dozen facts."
—Robert Keith Leavitt (2007)

How do you feel right now? Even if your response is "no particular way," or "I'm not really feeling anything right now because I'm just reading," try the following exercise: **close your eyes for 30 seconds, focus your full attention on your mind and body, and ask yourself, "what is my feeling state right now?"** Go ahead. Try it.

Most of the time when you perform this little exercise and you really pay attention to your feeling tone, you will be able to detect one or more feeling states like the following:

calm
content
alert
relaxed
tired
intrigued
curious
sleepy
bored

Mindworks: Becoming More Conscious in an Unconscious World, pp. 101–124
Copyright © 2007 by Information Age Publishing
All rights of reproduction in any form reserved.

comfortable
uncomfortable
bland

Do any of these apply? Most people will check several of them. But if you are still convinced that you are not feeling anything right now, ask yourself if any of the following might apply:

impatient
dubious
skeptical
irritated
doubtful

Since these are all feeling states, it is very difficult ever to argue that you are feeling nothing. That "bed" of feeling is always there, although it is often very subtle and many of us often fail to recognize—to be "mindful" of—what our current feeling state is at any moment. Since so much of your behavior and experience is based on how you happen to be feeling at any moment, cultivating the habit of regularly recognizing and reflecting on your current feeling state can be an extremely useful way of gaining more control over your life. One of the major purposes of this and the next four chapters is thus to encourage you to become more mindful of your various feeling states and to suggest some specific techniques for doing it.

WHAT <u>ARE</u> FEELINGS?

The term "feeling" is a very broad umbrella which covers a large portion of what we experience in our normal waking consciousness. And as I have already suggested, regardless of what you might be "thinking" about and regardless of whatever sights, sounds, or other information might be coming into your consciousness through your sense organs, you are almost always feeling <u>something</u>. Often these feelings are very subtle and difficult to identify and to label, but some feeling state is almost always present in consciousness. This "bed" of feeling, in turn, provides the subjective context for your thoughts and sense impressions. And your thoughts and sense impressions can, of course, interact with and change your feeling state from moment to moment.

Feelings can vary a lot in terms of their <u>intensity</u>. Some of your most intense feeling states—sexual feelings and anger, for example—have a strong physical basis, while other intense feelings include your more powerful negative emotions like fear, guilt, or shame. However, it is important to recognize that the term "emotion" is a more limited term that we usually reserve for some of our more intense feeling states. Although I will often use the terms "feeling" and "emotion" interchangeably, keep in mind that "feeling" is a somewhat broader term that can also include physical sensations like hunger, thirst, and pain. These physical feelings can, of course, be associated with many different types of emotions.

Still other feeling states are closely connected to your sense organs, for example, the feeling of being warm or cold, the feeling of being "startled" by a sudden loud sound, or the many varieties of feelings connected with the sense of touch. I will refrain from equating all sensory impressions with "feelings," however, since much of the visual and auditory information you get is more appropriately called "sense impressions" rather than "feelings." Thus, you can "see" the words in this sentence, but you can hardly call these visual images "feelings." You might well <u>respond</u> to something you are reading with a feeling state—curiosity, interest, satisfaction, doubt, confusion, boredom—but that feeling is not the same thing as the visual impression you get from the words printed on the page.

We will pay special attention in this chapter to your more <u>subtle</u> feeling states. When psychologists talk about "feelings" or "emotions," they usually mean the more powerful ones like fear and anger. However, for every one of these powerful states that you can name, there are literally dozens of much less obvious, but nevertheless very important, feeling states that you can experience. Most of the time you are experiencing one or more of <u>these</u> more subtle feeling states, and it can be very useful to become more adept at identifying them as they emerge in your consciousness.

FEELING "VERSUS" THINKING

Psychologists like to make a distinction between "cognitive" aspects of consciousness, which involve thinking and reasoning, and "affective" aspects, which involve feeling and emotion. This distinction is reflected in most dictionaries, where "feeling" is typically defined in part by using phrases such as "an absence of reasoning" (*Webster's New World Dictionary*, p. 532). Most of us are taught to believe that "rational thought" and "logic" are "higher level" mental activities than "base" feelings or emotions. This belief is supported by several "obvious" facts: humans are supposed to differ from lower animals, and adult humans are supposed to differ from small children, primarily in terms of their ability to "reason." In contrast to the "reasoning" adult human, small children and animals are supposedly driven more by "primitive" impulses, feelings, and "instincts." In other words, our society has been conditioned to believe that feeling is something inferior to thinking because it is a "lower level" or more "primitive" aspect of consciousness.

Among other things, this denigration of feelings has to do with the issue of <u>control</u>: whereas thinking and reasoning tend to be associated with having control over one's life, emotionality is typically associated with a lack of control. These negative views about feelings and emotions are misleading, for at least three reasons: (1) since thinking almost always takes place in a "bed" of (often quite subtle) feeling, the two are basically inseparable (see chapter 8); (2) it is extremely unlikely that the consciousness of any "lower" animal or any very young child is even remotely capable of experiencing the range and variety of subtle feeling states of which the adult human is capable; and (3) many emotions, as we have already seen, are <u>caused</u> by "thinking," that is, the (largely unconscious) interpretation of events that is governed by your beliefs. Beliefs, of course, <u>are</u> thoughts—ideas or propositions about what is true, good, important, and possible.

One reason why our culture tends to see thinking as "higher" or "better" than feeling and emotionality is that we often confuse feelings with "impulses" and "instincts." For this reason, I have included as a postscript to this chapter a brief discussion of the distinctions among these concepts.

WHY ARE FEELINGS IMPORTANT?

What would life be like if human beings were just thinking machines—rational, logical beings with no capacity to experience feelings or emotions? Would life be worth living? Since no one would "care" (a feeling!) about such questions, they would obviously never be asked. In fact, if you do not "care" about anything, if nothing "matters," then there is little point in living, no "desire" to live, and no "fear" of dying.

If you take a few moments to reflect on the meaning and purpose of your own existence and try to put it into words, it is difficult to avoid using feeling terms such as love, contentment, happiness, satisfaction, compassion, and fulfillment. Feelings, in short, are fundamental to life and to living. While love, caring, and compassion are feelings that make it possible for human beings to live together and survive, feelings such as hatred, fear, greed, and vengeance are at the root of most of the behaviors that threaten our welfare and survival: violence, dishonesty, terrorism, and war. For all of these reasons, this book devotes fully five chapters—this one and the next four—to a detailed consideration of feelings and emotions.

VARIETIES OF FEELING STATES

The English language is replete with words and phrases that can be used to describe how you feel at any moment. Few of us appreciate how extensive and elaborate this part of our language really is, which is another way of saying that few of us realize how rich and varied the "affective" part of our conscious experience can be.

To get a better sense of the entire spectrum of affective states that you can experience, I decided to examine all the words in a medium-sized English dictionary in order to identify all the different words or phrases that you can use to describe how you are feeling at any moment. In trying to decide whether a particular word qualified as a "feeling descriptor," I had to be able to answer "yes" to the following question: could I use the word or phrase to describe my mood or how I am feeling? Using this test, I found that I had to exclude several hundred "affective" words that you might use to describe or judge someone's <u>behavior</u>, as opposed to the way that they actually <u>feel</u>. Examples of such words would be outgoing, deceptive, talkative, demanding, sullen, selfish, and so on. While you might mean to <u>imply</u> that someone feels a certain way when you use such words to describe that person or his effect on another person, you would not ordinarily use words like these when your main intent is to describe how the person is actually <u>feeling</u>. However, I did include words that could be used both ways, that is, to describe behavior <u>or</u> feeling states. Examples of such words would be sleepy, mad, determined, and jealous.

This rather tedious exercise—reading every word in the dictionary and writing down the ones that could be used to describe feeling states—proved to be well worth the effort. I was able to identify more than a <u>thousand</u> different words or phrases that most of us use at one time or another to describe the way we feel. When you realize that your feeling state at any given time often involves <u>combinations</u> of such feelings—a for example, if you are feeling "satisfied" about something you might also be feeling "proud" or "happy"—the number of different feeling states that are possible numbers in the hundreds of thousands.

A more intriguing outcome of this dictionary exercise was the discovery that the hundreds of different words and phrases fell nicely into five groupings:

- Feelings having to do with your <u>intent</u> or <u>motivation</u> (compelled, aimless, yearning);
- Feelings having to do with <u>bodily</u> states or that involve <u>physical</u> sensations (excited, tired, dizzy, "got the jitters");

- <u>Cognitive</u> feelings relating to your thought processes (sure, skeptical, confused);
- <u>Interpersonal</u> feelings having to do with your <u>relationships</u> with other people (loving, trusting, embarrassed); and
- <u>General</u> feeling states that are not limited to one of the other four categories (happy, sad, carefree, worried, confident).

The first four groups of feeling states—those that involve motivation, physical sensations, cognition, and interpersonal relationships, respectively—will be reviewed in chapter 6 ("Motivation and Intent"), chapter 7 ("Body and Mind"), chapter 8 ("Thinking and Feeling"), and chapter 9 ("Consciousness and Community"). In this chapter we will review in some detail those "general" feeling states that are not readily classifiable into one of the other four categories. A number of these general feeling states, in fact, could actually apply to <u>several</u> of the other categories.

GENERAL FEELING STATES

The analysis of the more than 100 "feeling" words and phrases in this category revealed 27 identifiable general feeling states. When you realize that there are usually several different words or phrases that can be used to describe each of these states—if I feel "calm" I could also say I feel "peaceful"—there are really a lot more than 27 states. However, to keep the total number of different feeling states within reasonable bounds, I have grouped together words that seem to describe very similar states.

"Positive" and "Negative" Feelings

One of the most remarkable features of these general feeling states is that nearly all of them can be classified as either positive or negative. I use the word "positive" simply to mean that <u>the feeling is one that most people would seek out or try to maximize</u>. And I use the term "negative" not as a value judgement—that the feeling is "bad"—but rather to indicate that <u>the feeling (a) is one that most people try to minimize or avoid or (b) is likely to be judged negatively by others</u>. One reason why it is important to be able to distinguish among different feelings in this way is that **many of the choices that shape your daily behavior are intended either to generate positive feeling states or to avoid experiencing negative feeling states**. (In chapter 6, "Motivation, Intent, and Desire," we will examine the implications of this principle in detail.) This is not to suggest either (1) that negative feelings will necessarily go away just because you suppress or otherwise avoid them, or (2) that negative feeling states should always be avoided; for example, it is usually important to be able to experience grief or to mourn when a loved one dies. Also, it is important be *mindful* of negative feeling states when they arise, especially those that can lead to actions that you might later regret.

What is perhaps most interesting about these general feeling states is that, for almost every positive feeling, there is one or more corresponding negative or "opposite" feeling states. An obvious example would be "happy" versus "sad." Such "bipolar opposites" can be conceived of as anchoring the poles of a continuum:

Happy .... **Sad**

If I were to ask you to "locate" yourself on this continuum in terms of how happy or sad you feel right now, you would most likely put yourself somewhere near the middle, meaning that you were neither particularly happy nor particularly sad at the present moment.

Imagine, then, a number of different feeling continua, each with a positive feeling state at one extreme (e.g., "relaxed") and its negative counterpart at the other extreme ("tense").

"Reactive" Feelings

It is possible, of course, to feel "happy" without any particular reason. But if your feeling of happiness arises in reaction to some specific event, it takes on a somewhat different flavor, and we have developed a different set of terms to describe such "reactive" feelings. The important point about such reactive feelings is that, in your mind, the feeling is associated with a particular event. Let us say that you are in a positive mood because you have just successfully completed a very difficult project. You could, of course, say that you feel "happy" about your achievement, but in all likelihood you would instead say that you felt "pleased." Similarly, if you are experiencing a negative feeling state because something has not gone the way you expected, you could say that you are "unhappy," but you would probably be more likely to express your "reactive unhappiness" by saying that you feel "disappointed." And, as we shall see shortly, several of the other general feeling continua like "**happy.............sad**" have a corresponding "reactive" continuum like "**pleased.............disappointed**."

As it turns out, the various continua of general feeling states (both reactive and nonreactive) form two large groups:

- Feelings related to happiness
- Feelings related to ease and contentment.

Let us now look at each of the different bipolar pairs that fall within each of these two broad categories.

Happiness

The happiness continuum—with <u>happy</u> at the positive end and <u>sad</u> or <u>unhappy</u> at the negative end—is certainly one of the most basic and important of all the feeling continua. Indeed, **many if not most of the motivational states described in the next chapter are in one way or another concerned either with achieving happiness or with avoiding sadness or suffering.** In one of his recent books, *Ethics for the New Millenium* (1999), the Dalai Lama expresses this basic truth about human consciousness simply and directly:

> The desire or inclination to be happy and to avoid suffering knows no boundaries. It is in our nature. (p. 5)

Since a happy state, like most other feeling states that we will describe, can vary somewhat in how it actually <u>feels</u> to you, there are several other terms that you can use to capture these subtle variations. Variations on feeling happy would include feeling merry, jolly, cheery, gay, cheerful, or jovial. Alternative terms for describing the opposite pole of this continuum—when you feel unhappy—would include sad, gloomy, downcast, and glum. We can thus "enrich" the happy-unhappy continuum by including some of these alternative feeling terms:

Happy	**Unhappy**
jolly	sad
merry	gloomy
cheerful	downcast
jovial	glum

There are also several alternative terms for describing the "reactive" version of this continuum, **Pleased** versus **Disappointed**. Instead of saying that you feel "pleased" about something that has happened, you might prefer to say that you feel glad or satisfied. On the negative end of this continuum, if something has not gone the way you expected, you could feel "disappointed," but you might instead prefer to say that you feel displeased or sorry. Here is the "enriched" pleased-disappointed continuum:

Happy	....	**Disappointed**
satisfied		displeased
glad		sorry

Since there are <u>degrees</u> of happiness and unhappiness, how do you describe your feeling state when you are <u>very</u> happy or unhappy? We do indeed have a several ways of labeling such extreme feeling states. For example, if you are feeling very happy, you can communicate that feeling by saying that you feel joyful, ebullient, exuberant, buoyant, exhilarated, or joyous. On the opposite end of this continuum, when you are feeling very <u>un</u>happy, you have even more ways to express such a feeling: depressed, miserable, melancholy, morose, down, low, dismal, rotten, or "in the doldrums." By adding "joyful" (and its alternatives) at the positive end and "depressed" (and its alternatives) at the negative end of the continuum, we can extend or "stretch" the "happiness" continuum at both ends: at the positive end from happy to joyful, and at the negative end from unhappy to depressed. Here is the "enriched" version of this extended continuum:

Joyful..................	**Happy**..................	**Unhappy**..................	**Depressed**
exhuberant	jolly	sad	miserable
ebullient	merry	gloomy	melancholy
bouyant	cheerful	downcast	down
joyous	jovial	glum	dismal

Like happiness, joyfulness has a "reactive" counterpart, so if you are feeling joyful <u>in response</u> to something wonderful that has happened—for example, the birth of a child or grandchild—you might say instead that you feel "thrilled." Variations on feeling thrilled would include feeling elated, delighted, or jubilant. Thus, while it is possible to be in a joyful mood without any particular "cause," you are ordinarily "thrilled" or "delighted" in <u>response</u> to something positive that has happened. On the negative end of this "reactive" continuum, when something really impor-

---

EXERCISE

(a) Think of a recent time when you felt very pleased about something. What happened to make you feel that way? (b) Repeat this process using a recent time that you felt disappointed about something. (c) Can you think of a recent time when you felt happy without any particular reason? What were you doing at the time?

tant has not gone your way or when something terrible has happened, you might feel "despondent." And, as we found with depression, there are many variations on feeling despondent: grief-stricken, downhearted, saddened, disheartened, dejected, distraught, heartsick, and disconsolate. While despondence and depression obviously have much in common, despondence ordinarily represents a reaction to some event (e.g., the death of a loved one), while depression or unhappiness may or may not occur in direct response to some event.

In short, while you can spontaneously experience happiness and joy (or their negative counterparts, unhappiness and depression) without necessarily associating them with specific life events, feeling pleased or thrilled is usually a response to some positive event, and feelings of disappointment or despondency usually occur in response to a perceived failure or "loss." Here, then, is the "enriched" version of the extended "reactive" continuum of happiness:

Thrilled...............	Pleased..................	Disappointed...................	Despondent
elated, jubilant	satisfied, glad	displeased, sorry	dejected, heartsick

And here are the short versions of the two "happiness" continua:

joyful....................	happy...................	unhappy....................	depressed
thrilled................	pleased.................	disappointed.............	despondent

The final "happiness" continuum, which will be labeled <u>transcendence</u>, refers to extraordinary feeling states that are generally less familiar and more difficult to describe than the feelings we have discussed up to now. I am using the word "transcendent" here in the sense of "surpassing" or "going beyond" ordinary experience. Other ways of describing a transcendent state would be to say that you feel blissful, ecstatic, or rapturous. For many people a transcendent feeling state has a spiritual quality about it.

It may be easier to get a sense of what I mean by "transcendent" if you take a moment to consider what other terms you might use if you were to experience a transcendent feeling <u>in response</u> to some specific experience

---

EXERCISE

(a) Examine each of the eight feeling states that make up the two happiness continua above and see if you can recall a time that you felt that way; (b) for the four "reactive" feelings, can you identify the event(s) in each instance that triggered that feeling?

or event. Thus, if such a feeling emerged in your consciousness as a reaction to something like extraordinarily beautiful music, a spectacular sunset, prayer or deep meditation, being in love, or a very moving speech or sermon, you might instead say that you were uplifted, transported, enraptured, carried away, moved, or inspired.

There is probably no real "opposite" feeling to transcendence (other than a lack of transcendence!). However, if I were forced to define an opposite pole to this feeling continuum, I would probably pick either of two very similar states: outrage and anger. Outrage, of course, represents a "reactive" emotional response, since you are usually outraged about something that has happened. Variations on outrage would include feeling appalled, aghast, and horrified. Anger, a more complex feeling that may or may not occur in response to some specific event, will be discussed in detail in the chapter on physical or bodily feelings (chapter 7, "Body and Mind").

In sum: just as transcendent feelings can arise either spontaneously ("I am in a state of bliss") or in response to some event ("I have been uplifted by..."), so can the negative polar opposite feelings be either spontaneous ("I feel angry") or reactive ("I am outraged by..."). Here are these two sets of feelings arranged first on a "non-reactive" and then on a "reactive" continuum:

Transcendent .... **Angry**
blissful, ecstatic   furious, mad

Uplifted .... **Outraged**
blissful, ecstatic   furious, mad

It goes without saying that the various states of "happiness" discussed so far are very closely related. Thus, it is much easier to feel transcendent or blissful if you also feel either happy or joyful, and it is much easier to feel angry or outraged if you also feel either unhappy or depressed. And

EXERCISE

(a) Try to recall a time you reached a transcendent or blissful feeling state (or came close to being in such a state). What were you doing at the time? If other people were involved, how important was their presence? (If you are not sure you have ever experienced such a state, what do you think are the most likely circumstances under which you could?) (b) Make a list of all the situations or circumstances you can think of where you would be most likely to reach a transcendent state.

the same goes for "reactive" feelings: it is much easier to be uplifted or inspired by something if it also pleases or thrills you, and it is much easier to be outraged by something if it either disappoints you or makes you feel despondent.

Contentment

The various feeling continua discussed in this section have to do with the extent to which you are feeling content or at ease, as opposed to upset or distressed. While there are a number of different feelings that can be found at the positive (content) poles of these continua, we find an even larger number at the negative (distressed) poles. There are at least five different feeling states that reflect varieties of emotional contentment (or a <u>lack</u> of distress): <u>safe</u>, <u>serene</u>, <u>confident</u>, <u>carefree</u>, and <u>playful</u>. Each of these positive states, in turn, has one or more corresponding negative states that indicate various forms of emotional distress.

Let us start with the <u>safety</u> continuum. When we speak of "emotions," we seldom imply states as subtle as a feeling of safety, yet when people say things such as "I feel safe" or "She felt safe" they are really describing a subtle and potentially very important feeling state. Other words that we sometimes use to convey such a feeling would include secure, protected, comfortable, and possibly "at home." The importance of feeling safe or secure becomes much clearer when we contrast it with the much more familiar emotion that anchors the opposite end of this continuum: <u>fear</u>. Since intense fear—as in "frightened" or "terrified"— usually involves physiological changes such as increased respiration and heart rate, fear will be discussed in detail in the chapter on physical feelings (chapter 7, "Body and Mind"). However, when you use the word "fearful" to mean that you feel "unsafe," there are a number of alternative forms that such a feeling can take: afraid, threatened, vulnerable, unsafe, unprotected, apprehensive, in danger, at risk, or "in harm's way." Following is the enriched safety continuum:

Safe	Fearful
secure,	vulnerable,
comfortable,	in danger,
protected	unsafe

A feeling state that is closely related to safety is <u>serenity</u>. You are most likely to experience this feeling when you are in a beautiful environment, when you are quiet and undisturbed, and when you are not thinking about all the unfinished tasks you have yet to complete. Other words that

EXERCISE

(a) Think of the last time you felt fearful. What happened to make you eventually feel safe? Then, (b) finish the following sentences: "One of my biggest fears is…" and "I feel safe and secure when…"

you could use to describe this kind of feeling include calm, content, peaceful, mellow, untroubled, and unworried. (Chapter 7, "Body and Mind," discusses two "positive, low energy" states—relaxed and comfortable—that are very much like serenity, except that they also involve some sort of bodily feeling).

Since there are many different reasons why you might <u>not</u> be able to feel serene, the opposite (negative) pole of the serenity continuum includes at least three different feeling states: <u>irritable</u>, <u>frustrated</u>, and <u>anxious</u>. Irritability is one of those feeling states that can have a long life, in the sense that you can sometimes be in an irritable mood for most of the day! Irritability is a particularly common feeling state in contemporary urban society, in part because of noise, overcrowding, and the automobile. (While the automobile is obviously a very useful tool, there are few things in modern society that can rival the automobile as a potential source of irritability!) Alternative ways to say you feel irritable include feeling moody, grumpy, cross, disgruntled, negative, or annoyed.

<u>Frustration</u> is, of course, a close cousin of irritability, but it usually does not persist for such a long time and it is more often focused on a particular situation or event: "I'm frustrated because the traffic isn't moving!" Variations on saying you feel <u>frustrated</u> include feeling stuck, trapped, restrained, restricted, fettered, or hamstrung.

Since the third feeling occupying the negative pole of the serenity continuum—<u>anxiety</u>—typically includes physical components, it will be discussed in detail later in "Body and Mind" chapter 7.

Drawing a continuum for the feeling of serenity is a bit more complicated, since it actually has <u>three</u> different negative poles

Serene	⋯⋯⋯⋯	**Anxious**
calm,		agitated,
content		tense

Serene	⋯⋯⋯⋯	**Frustrated**
untroubled		stuck

Serene	⋯⋯⋯⋯	**Irritable**
peaceful,		annoyed,
mellow		cross

EXERCISE

(a) Think of a recent time when you felt really peaceful or serene. Where were you and what was happening? (b) Can you recall what happened to make the feeling go away? (c) Do you have enough peace and serenity in your current life? What would you need to do to have more?

A close cousin of feeling safe or serene is feeling <u>confident</u>. There are few affective states that have received as much attention in the psychological literature (both popular and academic) as confidence, which is also often referred to as "self-confidence" or "self-assurance" (or, somewhat less accurately, as "self-esteem" or "ego-strength"). Keep in mind, however, that we are referring here not to actions that make you <u>appear</u> "self-confident" in the eyes of others, but rather to a personal <u>feeling</u> of confidence. There are any number of other ways that you can describe your state of mind when you are feeling confident: assured, certain, adequate, upbeat, optimistic, or worthy. And if your feeling of confidence relates to some task or challenge that lies ahead, you might also say that you feel well-prepared or well-qualified. It comes as no surprise to find <u>insecurity</u> at the opposite (negative) pole of the confidence continuum. Other ways of communicating a feeling of insecurity would be to say that you feel unsure, uncertain, inadequate, unprepared, unqualified, or possibly awkward. Here, then, is the enriched confidence continuum:

Confident	Insecure
adequate,	inadequate,
assured,	unsure,
certain,	uncertain,
well-prepared,	unprepared,
well-qualified	unqualified

The two final positive feeling states relating to feelings of ease or contentment are feeling <u>carefree</u> and feeling <u>playful</u>. I must admit that "carefree" is a word that I seldom hear people use to describe their feelings. Given the many responsibilities that most of us have taken on in our adult lives, there are very few moments when we can honestly say that "I haven't a care in the world." And other than "lighthearted," about the only other way to express such a feeling would be to say that feelings of distress are <u>absent</u> from your consciousness, that is, to say that you feel unconcerned, nonanxious, or unworried. <u>Playfulness</u> is, of course, closely related to feeling carefree, but there are many more ways to describe your feelings when

EXERCISE

Complete the following sentences:
"What really irritates me..."
"The most frustrating..."

you feel playful: you can say that you feel silly, frolicsome, mischievous, devilish, frisky, rowdy, or rambunctious.

The opposite (negative) pole of the carefree continuum includes at least four different states: <u>obligated</u>, <u>on guard</u>, <u>conflicted</u>, and <u>worried</u>. A feeling of <u>obligation</u> often involves others, but it can also arise in connection with personal standards you have set for yourself. For example, when you feel personally obligated, say, to complete some important task you are working on before you start doing something else for your own pleasure, you could also say you feel "responsible." Thus, since I promised myself that I would try to finish this chapter today, I will continue working on it rather than stopping to watch a sporting event that is coming up in a few minutes on television. In other words, my sense of obligation to myself prevents me from "playing" until I have fulfilled that obligation. (The sense of obligation you feel when someone else is involved, as in feeling "indebted to" or "beholden to" someone, is an "interpersonal" feeling which will be discussed in chapter 9, "Consciousness and Community.")

<u>Guardedness</u> presents a different kind of contrast to feeling carefree. Rather than acting from a felt sense of responsibility or obligation, people who feel guarded somehow need to "protect" themselves, either from others or from themselves. (Again, feelings of guardedness that are directed toward other people will be discussed in chapter 9.) When you feel guarded, you tend to be overly careful of what you say and so. There are several alternative ways to express feelings of guardedness: cautious, careful, wary, cagey, and vigilant.

The third contrasting state to feeling carefree is to feel <u>conflicted</u>. This kind of feeling arises when you are confronted with a dilemma and you "don't know which way to turn." In such a situation you could also say you have "mixed feelings" or that you feel "ambivalent." (Since ambivalence is really a motivational state, it is discussed at length in chapter 6, Motivation, Intent, and Desire).

The final contrasting state to feeling carefree is <u>worried</u>, a negative feeling state that we all experience from time to time, and that some of us experience chronically. This feeling is a close cousin to feeling anxious, although is it is less likely than anxiety to be accompanied by bodily feelings (see chapter 7). When you worry, it is almost always connected to beliefs about possible future events (see chapter 11, "The Experience of Time").

In short, if we were to display the "enriched" continuum that has carefree at the positive end, it might look something like Figure 5.1.

The <u>playfulness</u> continuum also has two closely related feeling states at its opposite pole: <u>serious</u> and <u>somber</u>. Thus, if you feel that someone is feeling too playful or rowdy, you might say, "c'mon, get serious!" The word "serious" can have several other meanings, but in the context of this discussion to say you feel "serious" suggests that you are <u>concerned</u> about something that you regard as important. On the other hand, to feel "somber" is to feel "dark" or "gloomy." Clearly, it is very difficult to feel playful if you feel either serious or somber! Figure 5.2 shows this "enriched" continuum.

In sum, the first three positive states signifying feelings of ease or contentment—safe, serene, and confident—can easily "go together," and the same is true of the five opposing feelings that signify distress: fearful, irritable, frustrated, anxious, and insecure. Similarly, the final two positive states in this category—carefree and playful—easily go together, as do their six opposing feelings: obligated, guarded, conflicted, worried, serious, and somber. These four feeling clusters, in turn, "go together" with the various states signifying happiness and unhappiness. Thus, if you are feeling happy or joyful you are also much more likely to be feeling either safe, serene, confident, carefree, or even playful, whereas if you are feeling unhappy or depressed you are also much more likely to be feeling either fearful, irritable, frustrated, anxious, insecure, guarded, obligated, conflicted, worried, serious, or somber.

One final type of general feeling state that really does not form a continuum or have a negative "opposite" state is when you feel "**reflective**" or "**meditative**." (We could also include this type of feeling under "cognitive" feeling states—see chapter 8—since it usually involves some kind of thought process; indeed, another word for this feeling might be "thoughtful.") There are many different "ways" that you can be in a reflective or

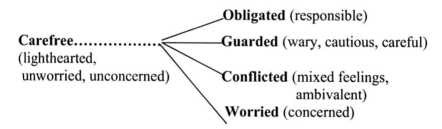

Figure 5.1.   "Enriched" continuum that has carefree at the positive end.

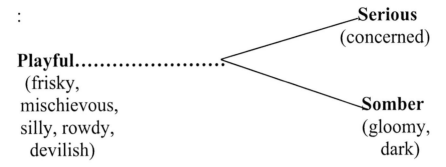

Figure 5.2.   The playfulness continuum with its serious and somber opposite poles.

meditative state: when you are going over some past event in your mind, planning for some future event, trying to solve a problem, thinking more generally about yourself or your life, or simply daydreaming without any particular purpose or intent. Reflective or meditative states would also include the way you feel when you engage in one of the more formal or disciplined kinds of meditative practice such as "mindfulness" meditation (see chapter 3). You are most likely to find yourself in a meditative or reflective state when you are by yourself in a relatively quiet place, and when you are feeling calm, safe, relaxed, and content.

THE ROLE OF BELIEFS

As pointed out in chapter 2, many feelings are based on your beliefs. This is particularly true of negative feelings, which almost always can be traced to one or more negative or limiting beliefs. For example, if you feel

EXERCISE

Complete the following sentences:
"I have a feeling of obligation..."
"To feel carefree I..."
"I am very conflicted...
"Playfulness..."
"I worry most..."
"I am on my guard..."

unhappy or disappointed, it is usually because you have failed to attain (or lost) something that you believe is important. If you feel fearful, it is almost always because you believe that something or someone represents a potential threat. Similarly, if you get angry at someone, it is because you believe that that person has harmed you or otherwise done you wrong. And if you feel insecure, it is usually because you believe that you are lacking something.

While positive feelings can sometimes also emerge from your beliefs—you might feel happy or pleased because you achieved or attained something that you believe to be important—very often it is difficult to pinpoint any particular beliefs that have given rise to such feelings. Thus, feelings like serenity, playfulness, joy, or transcendence frequently arise without the obvious involvement of associated beliefs.

ASSESSING YOUR OWN GENERAL FEELING STATES

Table 5.1 lists each of the different general feeling states that we have discussed in this chapter. Next to each feeling are two rating scales. (a) **Indicate how frequently you experience each feeling.** Then, (b) **Indicate whether, in the future, you would prefer to experience each feeling <u>more</u> frequently, <u>less</u> frequently, or at about the <u>same</u> frequency.**

Once you complete this exercise, it would be useful to take a few moments to reflect on those feeling states that you would like to experience either <u>more</u> frequently or <u>less</u> frequently, with the following questions in mind:

- What implications do these feeling "imbalances" have for those things that I tend to focus my attention on? Can I affect the frequency with which I experience various states by changing what I focus my attention on (e.g., the people I associate with, what I read, what I do in my leisure time, etc.; see the chapter 4)?
- What do these feeling "imbalances" tell me about my beliefs? Do I want to form an intention to bring my general feeling states more in line with my desires (see the chapter 6)? What beliefs do I need to reexamine?

Perhaps we can make all of this a bit more concrete by means of an illustration that uses one of these states, the feeling of *peacefulness* or *serenity*, as an example. For many of us who live and work in today's fast-paced technological society, feeling serene or peaceful is not a very common experience; it seems that there are just too many stresses and pressures and too many things that we have to do. For purposes of this illustration

Table 5.1. Self-Rated General Feeling States

Date:___/___/___
Time___a.m./p.m.

Choose a time period to rate yourself (right now, past week, past month, etc.).

During the period being rated, how often did you feel each of the following ways? (Circle the appropriate number.)					In the future, how frequently would you *prefer* to experience this feeling?		
	Most of the time	*Frequently*	*Occasionally*	*Seldom*	*Never*	*More*	*About the same*	*Less*
Joyful	5	4	3	2	1	3	2	1
Unhappy/sad	5	4	3	2	1	3	2	1
Depressed	5	4	3	2	1	3	2	1
Thrilled/elated	5	4	3	2	1	3	2	1
Disappointed	5	4	3	2	1	3	2	1
Happy	5	4	3	2	1	3	2	1
Pleased	5	4	3	2	1	3	2	1
Despondent/dejected	5	4	3	2	1	3	2	1
Transcendant/ecstatic	5	4	3	2	1	3	2	1
Angry	5	4	3	2	1	3	2	1
Uplifted/inspired	5	4	3	2	1	3	2	1
Outraged	5	4	3	2	1	3	2	1
Safe/secure	5	4	3	2	1	3	2	1
Refective/meditative	5	4	3	2	1	3	2	1
Serene/peaceful	5	4	3	2	1	3	2	1
Irritable/annoyed	5	4	3	2	1	3	2	1
Frustrated/trapped	5	4	3	2	1	3	2	1
Fearful	5	4	3	2	1	3	2	1
Anxious	5	4	3	2	1	3	2	1
Confident/assured	5	4	3	2	1	3	2	1
Somber	5	4	3	2	1	3	2	1
Carefree/lighthearted	5	4	3	2	1	3	2	1
Obligated/responsible	5	4	3	2	1	3	2	1
Insecure/uncertain	5	4	3	2	1	3	2	1
On guard/wary	5	4	3	2	1	3	2	1
Conflicted/mixed feelings	5	4	3	2	1	3	2	1
Playful/frisky	5	4	3	2	1	3	2	1
Serious	5	4	3	2	1	3	2	1

Any comments

let us assume that you indicated that you would ike to feel **serene** or **peaceful** "more" often than you currently do. One way to begin to experience such a feeling more often is to engage in a simple exercise where you ask yourself a brief series of questions (note that the phrasing of some of the questions can easily be modified to address feeling states that you would prefer to experience <u>less</u> often):

- **In what types of situations am I most likely to feel this way?**
  In the case of feeling peaceful or serene, you might include those times when you are alone, without interruptions, and without something that has to be done or taken care of right away. You might also include times when you are in beautiful surroundings (e.g., by the sea, in the mountains, out in the country), when you are listening to beautiful music, when you are reading and relaxing, or when you are praying, meditating, or in a place of worship. If you have children, it might also include those times when you and your partner are alone and the children are asleep.

- **What are some of the things I am likely to <u>do</u> when I feel this way?**
  During those times when you are feeling peaceful or serene, perhaps you are also more likely listen to certain kinds of music, read certain types of literature, drink or eat certain things, tend the garden, pursue hobbies, engage in creative activities (art, music, writing, etc.), take leisurely walks, daydream, or think about particular people or subjects. Perhaps you are also more likely to act certain ways in the presence of others (e.g., be more patient, considerate, generous, and empathic).

- **What <u>other</u> feelings are likely to arise when I feel this way?**
  Whenever you feel peaceful and serene, are you also more likely to feel happy, pleased, safe, secure, reflective, carefree, or confident? And when it comes to your relationships with others, are you more likely to feel connected, caring, trusting, loving, forgiving, or appreciative?

- **Have I structured my life in certain ways that make it less likely that I will feel this way? What are some of the patterns that I have established?**
  For most of us, feelings of serenity and peacefulness are not very likely to arise when we fill our days with lots of "things to do," whether these things have to do with work, family, home, or community. The same kind of frenetic existence can also characterize our "vacations." In our modern society these problems of "busyness" are exacerbated by technologies that bombard us constantly

with stimulation of all sorts, making it increasingly difficult for us to create the conditions (above) where we are most likely to feel peaceful and serene: being alone without external stimulation and interruptions, reading for pleasure or listening to relaxing music, finding an appropriate time and place for quiet prayer, mediation, or worship, and so on.

While it is easy to "blame" our modern technological society for these problems, it is important to realize that, in most instances, we <u>choose</u> to over-schedule ourselves and to fill our lives with gadgets that consume more and more of our time. The point of this question, in short, is to encourage you to explore in some detail the extent to which you have <u>chosen</u> to structure your daily experience in such a way that the feeling in question is less likely to arise in your consciousness.

- **What is a recent time when I felt this way? What did I do? What other feelings did I experience?**
  The idea behind these questions is to get you to think in some depth about a recent time when you experienced the feeling in question so you can address the next questions as fully as possible. For example, perhaps you last experienced real feelings of serenity and peacefulness early one morning while you were sitting quietly by yourself watching the sunrise.

- **What are some of my relevant beliefs that were involved in that situation?**
  The point of this question is to encourage you to seek a deeper understanding of the problem that goes beyond simplistic "solutions" of the type that you have probably already considered: "I need to simplify my life." "Perhaps I should take more time off for myself." "I need to learn how to relax." The issue is not that there are such obvious ways for you to experience greater peace and serenity in your life, but rather <u>why you have not embraced them</u>. And here is where beliefs come in. The relevant belief topics in this situation could cover a wide range of issues: Do you believe that you really "deserve" to take time off for yourself? Do you believe that you have to achieve at the highest possible level, no matter what the cost? If you choose to be by yourself in a pleasant environment without anything to "do," do you believe that you are "wasting time?" Do you believe that others will think will think less of you if you are not working around the clock? And so on. And such beliefs may be closely connected to other beliefs (about your own capabilities, about competing with others, etc.). Since each person and each situation is unique, your own intuition is the best guide in identifying the most relevant beliefs.

- **Is it in my best interests to continue acting on all these beliefs? If I really want to change how often I experience the feeling in question (and the other feelings and actions that tend accompany it), should I consider suspending or altering some of my beliefs?** For example, if you have a pretty clear idea about the places and situations that tend to bring about feelings of serenity and peacefulness (above), do you want to consider challenging some of the beliefs that <u>prevent</u> you from putting yourself in such places and situations more often? (See chapter 10 for strategies for changing dysfunctional beliefs.)

  A final strategy would be to identify some of your beliefs about (a) the relevant feelings (e.g., serenity, peacefulness) and (b) the key concepts that might be involved in such beliefs (e.g., "responsibility," "laziness," "success," etc.). (For detailed suggestions on how to conduct such critical analyses, see chapter 10.)

POSTSCRIPT: ON DISTINGUISHING FEELINGS FROM INSTINCTS AND IMPULSES

"Feelings" and "emotions," as referred to in this book, are by no means the same thing as "impulses" and "instincts." Let us first look at instincts. When people use the term "instinct" they are usually referring to tendencies or inclinations to do certain things or behave in certain ways that are biological in origin and therefore "built in" to the organism at birth (and, since most instincts are assumed to be genetically-based, at conception). Instincts like hunger and thirst, for example, serve an important survival function because they can cause you to seek something to eat or drink when your body needs nourishment or water. While you sometimes act upon your instincts without much conscious thought, they can certainly "cause" you to have particular thoughts: wondering where the nearest fast food restaurant or drinking fountain is, for example. Instincts can also "cause" you to <u>feel</u> a certain way (e.g., hungry or thirsty). The hunger <u>instinct</u>, in other words, differs from the <u>feeling</u> of hunger: you can feel hungry or feel thirsty, but you cannot "feel" your hunger instinct. Instincts, in other words, are behavioral <u>tendencies</u> that can give rise to thoughts and feelings. Instincts can (and usually do) cause certain feelings to arise in consciousness—feeling hungry or feeling thirsty—and the feelings can in turn can give rise to thoughts: When I feel hungry I might think about going to the refrigerator. But I can still "feel" hungry even when my stomach is full, that is, when I do not "need" food in the biological sense (as is apparently the case with many obese people and others with eating disorders). Your instincts, in other words, are built-in tendencies for you to behave in certain ways that can, in turn, cause you to experience feelings and thoughts, but the instinct is not the same thing as the feeling or thought.

An <u>impulse</u> is a tendency or inclination to act that comes on very suddenly. However, we can use the word in two very different ways: To describe someone's <u>behavior</u> ("she did it on impulse," "he acted impulsively"), or to describe a <u>state of consciousness</u> ("I felt the impulse to..."). In the latter instance we are speaking of a mental state that incorporates both <u>thought</u>—whatever it is that you feel an impulse to <u>do</u>—as well as <u>feeling</u>, that is, the sudden urge or <u>impulse</u> to act.

The first meaning, where we <u>describe</u> someone's behavior as "impulsive," is <u>not</u> necessarily a description of that person's state of consciousness, but it often involves an <u>inference</u> about the person's consciousness that may or may not be true. Sometimes we mean to imply that the person "acted without thinking of the consequences," but such inferences can easily be wrong. Thus, I can suddenly feel the urge to act in a certain way, briefly consider ("think about") the consequences, and then decide to act anyway. Someone else may observe my behavior and still conclude that I "acted impulsively." What has really happened here is that I <u>have</u> indeed "thought" before acting, but the other person would probably consider my thinking to be faulty!

Using the word "impulsive" to characterize someone else's behavior often carries with it a negative judgment, as in "irresponsible." By contrast, when you want to characterize "impulsive" behavior in a more favorable light, you would be more likely to call it "spontaneous." (We also use this word to describe behavior that is "natural" or that is not coerced or solicited by "outside" forces.) Both terms, however, can be used to suggest that the person acted without first "thinking" much about the action or its likely consequences.

When we try to use the term "impulse" to describe the state of someone's consciousness, we usually mean that they acted "without thinking." This could imply that the person acted without "considering the consequences," but it could also mean that the urge or impulse to act came into consciousness suddenly, rather than being the outcome of a lot of rational thought. (The notion of "intuition" also comes to mind here; see chapter 12.) However, it may well be that much of what we call "impulsive" behavior involves neither prior thought <u>nor</u> prior feeling. If a valuable piece of delicate pottery slips out of your hand, you may well grab for it "impulsively" without <u>first</u> experiencing a conscious feeling of anxiety or fear that it might break if it hits the floor.

In short, when it comes to characterizing the state of someone's waking consciousness, the term "impulse" simply describes a "felt urge" to do something that emerges suddenly into consciousness. The impulse usually involves some thought (i.e., whatever "it" is you feel the urge to do), but it is not just a thought; there is also a feeling of pressure or intense energy <u>behind</u> the thought that is "pushing" you to act: "I feel a sudden urge to..." In other words, there is a big difference between merely thinking about doing something, on the one hand, and experiencing a sudden strong urge ("impulse") to do it, on the other.

To summarize: "feelings" are not the same thing as either instincts or impulses. Your instincts can indeed give rise to certain feelings (and thoughts), and you can certainly <u>feel</u> an impulse to do something. But to describe someone else's behavior as either instinctual or impulsive is <u>not</u> necessarily to describe anything about their conscious experience.

CHAPTER 6

MOTIVATION, INTENT, AND DESIRE

Why are you reading this book? Why do you find yourself in the particular place where you happen to be located today? What do you expect to be doing tomorrow? How about next week? Answers to such questions inevitably require you to look at your <u>motives</u> and <u>intents</u>: you make your life choices from moment to moment in order to fulfill certain aims and objectives that you have set for yourself. Your motives and intents, in other words, give <u>meaning</u> to your actions. Clearly, if you want to gain a fuller understanding of why you do the things that you do, you need to become better acquainted with your motives, intents, desires, and purposes. And if you are not entirely happy with how your life has been affected by some of the choices you made, then it may be useful to reexamine and perhaps consider changing some of these motives and intents.

Your intentions are basic to almost everything you do. Perhaps the only exception to this rule would be (1) "reflexive" behavior—raising your knee when the doctor taps your patellar tendon or withdrawing your hand from a hot stove—actions which are pretty much "wired in" by your physiology and your genetics, and (2) actions which are coerced by others—for example, at the point of a gun. However, even most coerced behavior could be viewed as motivated, in the sense that you do what the person with the gun tells you to do because your intent is to avoid being shot!

Mindworks: Becoming More Conscious in an Unconscious World, pp. 125–141

Motives, desires, and intentions serve at least two critical and closely connected functions in your conscious experience: they give <u>meaning</u> to the things that you do, and they supply the psychic <u>energy</u> or "juice" that causes you to act. In other words, in the absence of intentions, desires, and motives, you probably would not "do" much of anything (you might not even survive!) and your thoughts, feelings, and actions—indeed, your life—would not mean much to you.

Since intentions are usually focused on the <u>future</u>, it is not surprising that our language is replete with "motivational" verbs that signify something that has not yet occurred: intend, seek, desire, try, hope, strive, wish, and so on. In other words, most of us believe that we do much of what we do in the present moment <u>in order</u> to accomplish certain future ends. We go to school <u>so that</u> we can get a good job later on. We work <u>so that</u> we can have enough money to live comfortably. We groom and dress ourselves <u>so that</u> we will look attractive. We diet and exercise and eat well <u>so that</u> we will live a long and healthy life. When you stop to think about it, there are literally thousands of such motives that govern much of our behavior. A few of the more common ones:

- To be loved
- To be financially comfortable
- To feel useful
- To be happy
- To be respected
- To be joyful
- To learn and to feel competent
- To experience adventure
- To create
- To serve others
- To please our parents
- To have self-respect
- To be healthy
- To do the right thing
- To enjoy good friends
- To avoid pain and discomfort
- To experience pleasure

Like your beliefs, your intents and desires are so numerous that you cannot be consciously aware of most of them most of the time. Instead, you "store" them in your nonconscious mind, where—just like your beliefs—they continue to influence your conscious experience and your behavior.

INTENTS, DESIRES, AND BELIEFS

Your intents and desires are closely connected to your beliefs, since you usually desire or strive for something because you believe that:

- it is the "right" thing to do;
- you are lacking something without it;
- it will give you pleasure
- it will allow you to avoid (or relieve) some pain or discomfort;
- it will bring you happiness (or help you avoid unhappiness)
- something dire will happen without it;
- it is expected of you; or
- it will help you gain the approval of others.

Your beliefs thus provide a kind of "breeding ground" for your intents and desires. More specifically:

- **Your intents, motives, and desires are intimately connected to your beliefs about what is good, what is important, and what is possible.**

Desires, in particular, are most closely connected to beliefs about goodness and importance: you may desire to have great wealth, for example, because you believe that being rich is both important and good. In other words:

- **You desire something because you believe it is either good or important (or both).**

But your beliefs about what is <u>possible</u> highlight an important difference between merely desiring, on the one hand, and actually intending, on the other: even if you desire to be rich, you are not likely to make much of an effort to attain great wealth—be "motivated" or "intend" to attain it—unless you also believe that it is possible for you. At the same time, even if you desire something <u>and</u> believe that it is attainable, you still may not form an intention to attain it if you also believe that it is <u>bad </u>(either bad for you physically or bad in moral terms). You may, for example, desire to have a sexual encounter with someone and even believe that such an encounter is attainable, but not try to make the encounter happen because you believe that it would be morally wrong. In other words:

- **When you desire something because you believe that it is important, whether or not you will actually form an intention to attain it will depend in part on your beliefs about its attainability <u>and</u> goodness.**

VARIETIES OF MOTIVATIONAL STATES

My dictionary search for feeling words turned up more than 100 different words and phrases that you can use to describe your desires, motives, and intents, and these can be organized into at least 29 different motivational feeling "states." These 29, in turn, can be used to form at least seven different motivational feeling continua: **attraction, engagement, commitment, desire, intent, willingness, and acquiescence.**

Attraction (Versus Repulsion)

Let us first look at the positive (attraction) pole of this bipolar continuum. Probably the mildest form of attraction to something is to feel merely that you are "interested" in it: "I'm interested in what Antarctica is like, but I doubt that I will ever make any effort to go there." Next would come the feeling that you are "attracted" to it, which implies that you might <u>consider</u> doing something about your interest (another way to express such a feeling would be to say that you are "drawn to" something). And the most intense feeling of attraction—the end point on the continuum—would be to feel "obsessed" or "consumed" by it. On the negative (repulsion) end of this continuum, the mildest form would be captured by words like "disinclined" and "disinterested," and the strongest by the word "repulsion." Finally, if you were neither attracted nor repelled by

---

EXERCISE

(a) Think of at least two recent occasions when you "desired" something, but did not make an effort to attain it. (b) For each of these occasions, identify the relevant belief(s) that were involved in your decision not to pursue what you were desiring.

something, you would probably say that you are "neutral" or "indifferent." The full "attraction" continuum would thus look like this:

Obsessed......	Attracted......	Interested....	Neutral........	Disinclined..	Repelled
consumed	drawn to	inclined	indifferent	disinterested	

Engagement (Versus Disengagement)

To say that you are "attracted" suggests that you <u>might</u> do something about whatever attracts you, but it is entirely possible for you to feel attracted to something (or even obsessed with it) and still maintain some personal distance from it. You can, for example, be very attracted to another person but never form any specific intention to get to know that person. Or, you could be obsessed with money or with the idea of being wealthy but never develop any concrete plans that would enable you to make more money. To feel "engaged," on the other hand, is to feel directly <u>connected</u> to whatever it is that attracts or interests you (or, in the case of disengagement, to feel <u>dis</u>connected): for example, you develop specific plans for meeting the person or for making a lot more money. Thus, in contrast to a feeling of mere interest, a feeling of engagement implies that you are also taking <u>action</u>. Acting on such a feeling can, in turn, also strengthen your feeling of engagement.

The continuum of engagement is also more complex than the attraction continuum, in the sense that you can feel that your engagement is either "proactive"—you became engaged pretty much on your own initiative—or "reactive"—your engagement is in <u>response</u> to something. A feeling of proactive engagement would be captured by words such as "involved" and "engaged" or, in the extreme, by phrases like "absorbed in," "driven," "pumped up," "worked up," "caught up in," or "have a zest for." A feeling of reactive engagement would be signified by words like "challenged," "provoked," and "drawn in by" or, at the extreme, by phrases like "captivated by," "inspired by," and "compelled by." Thus,

---

EXERCISE

(a) Think of a time when you felt "obsessed" with, or very strongly attracted to, something (the "something" could be another person, a recent experience, an idea, or some personal goal). What beliefs about importance and/or goodness were involved? (b) Repeat the exercise with somebody or something that repelled you.

you could become "involved" or "engaged" proactively in a candidate's political campaign because you are a loyal member of their party, or you could become a supporter reactively because you were "captivated" by their personality or "inspired" either by their platform or by their rhetoric.

The negative (disengaged) pole of this continuum also has both proactive and reactive feeling terms. The proactive version includes feeling words like detached, diffident, uninvolved, and disengaged, while the reactive version would include phrases like put off by, uninspired by, repelled by, and turned off by. Thus, you might become "uninvolved" or "disengage" from politics because of other demands in your life that have higher priority, or you might avoid political involvement because you are "turned off" or "repelled" by a candidate's negative campaigning. Here, then, are the two engagement continua:

Proactive

Absorbed............................ **Engaged**............................ **Uninvolved**
caught up in,   involved   detached,
driven   disengaged

Reactive

Captivated............................ **Challenged**............................ **Turned off**
compelled,   provoked,   put off,
inspired   drawn in   uninspired

Commitment

Commitment is, of course, a close cousin of engagement, in the sense that (a) feeling engaged is often accompanied by a feeling of commitment, and (b) you are much more likely to become <u>disengaged</u> from something if you are not committed to it. It is possible, however, to <u>feel</u> committed but not engaged ("I feel very committed to my partner, but we

EXERCISE

Complete the following sentences:
"**What really turns me off…**"
"**I am easily captivated…**"
"**I need to get more involved…**"

spend very little time together"), or to be engaged without a strong commitment ("I'm spending a lot of time on my work, but my heart's not really in it"). It is also possible to find yourself in an ambivalent or "wavering" state of mind where you cannot decide whether or not to commit yourself. The continuum of commitment thus has three principal points:

Committed............................	Wavering.............................	Uncommitted
determined,	ambivalent,	unmotivated,
resolved,	tentative	lackadaisical,
unwavering,		aimless
resolute		

Some of our major life dilemmas involve a "mismatch" between our levels of involvement and commitment:

- Feeling very committed to someone—a parent, child, partner, or friend—but not being very engaged with them (or even <u>avoiding</u> much engagement)
- Being very engaged or spending a lot of time with something—work, childcare, school—without a strong sense of commitment.

Desire and Intent

Your desires and intentions share one important attribute in common: they are <u>future</u>-oriented, and almost all of the words that describe such feelings are verb forms (in contrast to adjectives, which describe most other types of feeling states). When you say you "desire" something, you are looking ahead in time to the possibility that you will have something that you currently feel that you lack. Similarly, when you "intend" to do something, you are again looking ahead in time with the aim of changing your present circumstances in some way. Desiring (and to a lesser extent, intending) also implies a belief either that you currently <u>lack</u> something or that you are somehow <u>dissatisfied</u> with you current situation. There are,

---

EXERCISE

Think of some aspect of your life where there is a "mismatch" between your level of involvement and your degree of commitment. What beliefs underlie (1) your current level of involvement (or disengagement) and (2) your current degree of commitment (or lack thereof)?

however, important differences between these two motivational states. Intending, for example, implies that you <u>will</u> take some form of action, whereas desiring tends to be more passive: you may or may not act on your desire. And while intending usually implies that you desire something, desiring something does not necessarily mean that you will actually form an intention to make it happen. In fact:

- **Desiring something without forming an intention to make it happen implies a conflict in beliefs.**[2]

Desiring and intending also form quite different kinds of continua. Let us look at each in turn.

The high end of the continuum of desiring would be to <u>crave</u> something. Other terms that you might use to describe such a feeling—which implies a sense of desperation—would be to "long for," "need," "hunger for," "ache for," or "yearn for." Next in line on the continuum would be to say that you <u>desire</u> something. Other ways of expressing such a feeling would be to say that you "fancy," "want," "relish," "have an appetite for," or "have a hankering for." A weaker form of desire would be to say that you <u>hope</u> for something, and the weakest of all would be to say that you <u>wish</u> for something. As it turns out, there are few, if any, alternative words for expressing the feelings of hoping and wishing. In sum, the "enriched" continuum of desiring looks like this:

Craving....................	Desiring....................	Hoping....................	Wishing
long for,	want,		
yearn for,	fancy,		
have a need,	relish,		
hunger for	have a hankering for		

At first glance, the continuum of Intent appears to have only two points—**intent** and **lack of intent**—that is, you either intend or do not intend to do something. A closer look, however, reveals that there can be a sort of intermediate state where you are "considering" doing something,

EXERCISE

Think of something that you desire, but that you are not currently intending to pursue. What beliefs about goodness, importance, and possibility are involved in (1) your desire, and (2) your current lack of intention to pursue it.

EXERCISE

(a) Take each of the four points on the continuum shown on the previous page and identify something that you have recently craved, something you have recently desired, something you have recently wished for, and something you have recently hoped for; (b) for each of these, identify some of the relevant beliefs concerning what is important (or necessary), what is good (or bad), and what is possible (or impossible).

but have not yet formed a clear intention to do it. We can thus conceive of a continuum of intent with three points:

Intend................................. Considering......................... No Intention

Note also that there are many ways to express the feeling that you intend to do something:

- Intend
- Endeavor
- Try
- Aim to
- Attempt
- Take pains to
- Strive
- Aspire

When you use either of these last two—striving and aspiring—to describe your feeling, you probably believe that whatever you are attempting to do is of great value or has high status.

When it comes to your intentions, it is important to keep two basic principles in mind:

- **Of all your different motivational feeling states, your intentions are usually of the greatest significance because they form the basis for most of your <u>actions</u>.**
- **Your intentions reflect your beliefs about what is <u>important</u> and what is <u>possible</u>.**

We can illustrate these two principles with a simple diagram:

Beliefs → Intents → Actions

In short, your beliefs help to form your intentions which, in turn, give rise to your actions.

Willingness and Acquiescence

These two motivational states are "reactive," in the sense that they usually imply a reaction to some external request, requirement, or demand. (Since these external requests often come from other people, similar feeling states will also be discussed in the chapter on interpersonal feelings; see chapter 9, "Consciousness and Community.") While the two feeling continua have much in common, to be "willing" suggests that your reaction is pretty much voluntary or freely given, whereas to "acquiesce" suggests that you are responding to pressure. That acquiescence is also more of a reaction to pressure is suggested by the fact that all the "acquiescence" states are described by verbs, while most "willingness" states are described by adjectives.

The willingness continuum includes at least five different states:

Eager...............	Willing..............	On the Fence....	Reluctant..........	Unwilling
enthusiastic	agreeable, accepting	undecided, hesitant	disinclined, resistant, averse to	refuse to, decline, reject, turn a deaf ear

In contrast to the Willingness continuum, the Acquiescence continuum includes only two states:

Acquiesce	Object
yield, give in, concede, comply	disagree, protest, dissent, oppose

EXERCISE

(a) For each of the five points on the willingness continuum, think of a time when you felt that way (at work, in school, or at home) in response to a request to do something. (b) In each case, what does your response tell you about your beliefs?

EXERCISE

(a) Think of a recent time when you have initially felt reluctant about some external pressure or demand, but eventually acquiesced or "gave in." What beliefs were at the basis of your initial reluctance? What beliefs led you to acquiesce? (b) Repeat the exercise with a situation when you did not acquiesce.

TAKING STOCK OF YOUR DESIRES AND INTENTS

We will conclude this chapter with a substantial personal exercise involving some of your current intents and desires. The purpose of this exercise is twofold: to reflect on some of the intents and desires that govern your daily actions, and to understand the beliefs that underlie these intents and desires. To give you an idea of what the exercise entails, we shall begin with a hypothetical example: let us say that one of your current goals is to lose weight. How important is this goal to you? What effect, if any, does it have on your actions? What beliefs underlie this goal?

The first step in answering such questions would be to assess the degree of <u>attractiveness</u> of the goal, which can be done using the continuum of Attractiveness discussed earlier:

Obsessed......	Attracted......	Interested....	Neutral........	Disinclined..	Repelled
consumed	drawn to	inclined	indifferent	disinterested	

Which point on the continuum best describes how attracted you are to the goal of losing weight? Since you have already indicated that losing weight is a personal goal, we would expect you to say that you are at least "interested" in losing weight (the neutral, disinclined, and repelled alternatives would come into play only when you are rating the degree of attractiveness of a goal that you have not personally embraced). Let us say that you pick "interested" as the best descriptor. The next step is to assess your level of <u>desire</u>. Here is that continuum:

Craving.................	Desiring..................	Hoping....................	Wishing
long for,	want,		
yearn for,	fancy,		
have a need,	relish,		
hunger for	have a hankering for		

If you only "wish" that you could lose weight, it is probably not going to happen. "Hoping" is a little stronger, since it implies that you <u>might</u> exert some effort on behalf of the goal. "Desiring" and "craving" imply even stronger levels of motivation.

The next question is whether you have formed a clear <u>intention</u> to act on your desire to lose weight. Here again is the relevant continuum:

Intend.................................. Considering......................... No Intention

By "intention to act" I mean that there are specific <u>actions</u>—diet or exercise plans, timetables, etc.—that you are already taking or plan ("intend") to follow in an effort to lose weight. Note that it is not really possible to act on your desire to lose weight if your "intent" is not coupled with such specific plans. In other words, simply <u>saying</u> that "I intend to lose weight" is not enough. Thus, in the absence of any concrete action (or of a recognition of the necessity to develop a specific plan of action that includes implementation timetables), it would be more accurate to say either that you are "considering" losing weight, or that as of now you have "no plans" (i.e., have not yet formed an intention) to lose weight.

The next motivational stage is actual <u>engagement</u>. To assess your level of engagement, you can once again use one of the continua already discussed:

Absorbed............................ Engaged.............................. Uninvolved
caught up in,   involved   detached,
driven   disengaged

Of course, if you have not as yet taken any concrete action to lose weight, you would still be "uninvolved." If you have taken some action, whether you are "absorbed" or merely "engaged" would depend on how much conscious attention, time, and effort you are devoting to that action.

The final aspect of your motivation that can be assessed is your level of <u>commitment</u>:

Committed........................... Wavering.............................. Uncommitted
determined,   ambivalent,   unmotivated,
resolved,   tentative   lackadaisical,
unwavering,   aimless
resolute

When it comes to actually realizing your goal, this is probably the most important motivational state. Thus, if you are completely committed to losing weight, then there is a very good chance that you eventually will. Commitment is most effective, of course, when it is accompanied by engagement or <u>action</u>. In the case of a desire to lose weight, you might <u>feel</u> very committed before there is actually any engagement (dieting, exercising, etc.), but that commitment could waver once you begin to act. At the same time, if you begin to act (i.e., start a diet) when you are "uncommitted," you will be very unlikely to realize your goal of losing weight because you are basically "going through the motions." This latter phrase describes a situation where there is <u>engagement without commitment</u>. (Being uncommitted, of course, may also constitute a form of <u>resistance</u>!)

Let us pause briefly to summarize these initial steps in assessing your motivational state with respect to any goal or objective:

- Specify the goal or objective;
- Assess its degree of <u>attraction</u> for you;
- Determine your level of <u>desire</u> for the goal;
- Assess your level of <u>intent</u> to realize the goal;
- Assess how <u>engaged</u> you are in trying to realize the goal; and
- Determine how <u>committed</u> you are to realizing the goal.
- Identify any <u>conflicts</u> or <u>ambivalence</u> in your intents and desires.

When you examine the various continua that can be used in making these assessments, it is obvious that certain alternatives will generally tend to "go together." Thus, if you are "attracted" to the goal and "desire" it, then you will be likely to "intend" to attain it, to get "engaged" in efforts to attain it, and be "committed" to attaining it. Or, if you are "obsessed" with the goal and "crave" it, you are likely to become "absorbed" in attempting to attain it. Similarly, if you are only "interested" in the goal and only "wish" or "hope" to attain it, your level of intent is more likely to be "considering" and your level of commitment is more likely to be "wavering." Finally, if you are "disinclined" toward or "repelled" by the goal, you are most likely to have a "lack of intent" and to be "uninvolved."

Ambivalence and Conflict

These parallels suggest that the next step in assessing your motivation with respect to any goal or objective is to identify any conflicts or ambivalence in your various desires and intentions. One of the realities of modern life is that we periodically experience conflicts or contradictions in our motives and intents. In fact, one clue that you might be experiencing such conflicts is that you find yourself near the midpoint of one or more of these motivational continua: **on the fence, considering, neutral, wavering,** and so on. Obviously, if you are experiencing such conflicts, it is important to understand the underlying beliefs that are involved.

Another approach is to assess how <u>consistent</u> your various motivational states are. I have already suggested, for example, that it is possible to be "engaged" but not "committed." **Whenever you find an inconsistency in your motivation toward a particular goal, you can be sure that you harbor inconsistent or contradictory beliefs about the importance, goodness, or attainability of that goal.** Following are some of the most common motivational inconsistencies, together with the belief configurations that typically accompany such inconsistencies:

Motivational Inconsistency	Associated Beliefs
• Attracted (Desire) + No Intention	"Goal is very important;" "Goal is not good and/or unattainable."
• Attracted (Desire) + Wavering	"Goal is very important;" "Goal is of dubious goodness and/or difficult to attain."
• Engaged + Uncommitted (Indifferent)	"I have to do this, but it is either unimportant and/or compromises other goals or beliefs."
• Engaged + Wavering	"Goal is of questionable importance/goodness and/or difficult to pursue."
• Intend + Uninvolved	"Goal is important and attainable, but pursuit will be very difficult."

There are many illustrations of such inconsistencies that we could cite from almost any area of daily life. For example, in the area of personal relationships, here is typical example of each inconsistency:

- **Attracted + Wavering:** You would like to have an affair with a certain person, but that person is much younger (or much older, or married, or a subordinate employee, or going out with your best friend, etc.).

- **Engaged + Uncommitted:** You go out on a date with someone you are not attracted to and do not particularly like to please a friend or relative (or for business reasons, or to repay a debt, etc.)

- **Engaged + Wavering:** You agreed to move in with someone but now find that the relationship did not turn out the way you expected.

- **Intend + Uninvolved:** You intend to pursue another person who has already expressed an interest in you, but you have not yet made any effort to do so because you are too busy with your career or schoolwork.

Whenever you detect such an inconsistency in your motivation, it is useful to identify and examine critically the relevant beliefs that underlie it. Thus, in the first example shown above, where you desire something but have no intention of pursuing it, you can ask yourself questions such as the following:

- Why do I desire something that I believe to be wrong (or unattainable)? What do I feel I am lacking without it? In what sense would I be better off with it? And if I would not be better off, then <u>why</u> do I still desire it?
- <u>Why</u> is it wrong? What beliefs are involved here? (Or: Why do I feel that it is unattainable? What beliefs about "possibility" are involved here?)

In trying to apply this kind of analysis to your own motivation, it is first necessary to decide <u>which</u> of the many hundreds of motives and intents that govern your current life you want to examine. There would ordinarily be little point, for example, in investigating the sorts of intentions that underlie everyday routines like sleeping, eating breakfast, brushing your teeth, getting dressed, and going to work. Such behavior is obviously "motivated," but since the underlying intentions are usually self-evident and typically do not pose any kind of "problem" for you, it would not be of much value to invest a lot time or energy reflecting on or "analyzing" them. The same would generally be true of what we might call "general" or "background" motives, by which I mean those intents and desires that apply to most of us most of the time and that we therefore tend to take for granted: the desires to stay alive, to remain healthy, to experience pleasure, and to avoid pain or discomfort would be good examples. I must qualify this exemption, of course, in the case of those relatively rare situations where a person's desire to avoid <u>any</u> kind of pain or discomfort becomes dysfunctional, or where a person intentionally <u>seeks out</u> pain or discomfort (i.e., masochism). In such cases, the underlying beliefs are clearly well worth investigating. Also, while most of us tend to take the "pleasure principle" for granted, there are instances where our pleasure-seeking can cause us a lot of trouble. Further, to remind ourselves about the pervasiveness of the pleasure-seeking motive, it might be a useful exercise for each of us periodically reflect on the many manifestations of this motive in everyday life: our attraction to good food, sex, music, art, poetry, fragrant flowers, bird songs, beautiful scenery, humor, fresh air, cool breezes, wood fires, sunsets, hugs, caresses, and so forth.

The motives and intents that usually provide the richest material for the kind of "belief analysis" outlined above are those that deal with your personal relationships, money and possessions, work and career, avocations and leisure, and personal development. A good way to begin the analysis is simply to take an inventory of your desires and intentions in each area by asking yourself, "what do I <u>desire</u> and what are my <u>intentions</u> with respect to…":

- *Personal Relationships* (parents, spouse or partner, children, friends, coworkers, neighbors, adversaries, sex, marriage, family)
- *Money and Possessions* (wealth, investments, economic lifestyle, retirement, house, car, clothes, other personal possessions)
- *Work and Career* (further education, professional accomplishment and achievement, short and long term job and career goals)
- *Leisure/Avocations* (vacations, rest, recreation, hobbies)
- *Personal Development*: <u>physical</u> (body, health, diet, exercise, motor skill development); <u>cognitive</u> (knowledge, self-understanding, language competency, technical skills, creative/artistic development); <u>affective</u> (emotional control, emotional expression, emotional maturity, self-image/esteem, peace of mind, wisdom, spiritual practice and development, tolerance, empathy, interpersonal skill development)

To do a comprehensive inventory and belief analysis in all of these areas is obviously a major undertaking. An easy way to begin is simply to identify two or three of your <u>strongest</u> desires, hopes, wishes, and intentions in each area. For most people, this beginning exercise will make one thing clear: **when it comes to our motives and intents, most of us have a lot on our plates.** If this applies to you, then it is clear that <u>prioritizing</u> your various desires and intentions is of major importance. Prioritizing is especially important in light of the fact that your time and energy is finite and your conscious mind is not capable of focusing on much more than one thing at a time. In fact, you can get a rough idea of what your <u>current</u> priorities are simply by asking yourself the following questions:

- **"What activities do I spend most of my time and energy on right now?**
- **When I am just thinking, daydreaming, or reflecting, what are the things that I am most likely to focus on?**
- **What wishes, desires, and intentions are <u>implied</u> by my answers to the first two questions?**

An obvious next set of questions to ask yourself is,

- Are these "implicit" priorities consistent with my most important life goals? If not, why not?
- What beliefs about importance, goodness, and possibility are at the root of these implicit priorities? If there are inconsistencies between these and my "stated" priorities (i.e., my current or "actual" priorities and my "ideal" priorities), what underlying belief issues are involved?
- Do I need to consider reordering my priorities?

CONCLUSION

In this chapter we have looked at your different motivational states: your wishes, desires, and intentions. The dictionary analysis of feeling terms reveals that there are at least seven different continua of motivational states: attraction, engagement, commitment, desire, intent, willingness, and acquiescence. While your various desires and motives are "stored" in the nonconscious part of your mind most of the time, they continuously influence your thoughts, feelings, and actions and—with a little effort—you can make yourself consciously aware of most of your desires and intents most of the time.

Your intentions are of particular importance, primarily because (a) they form the basis for your actions and (b) they reveal some of your beliefs about future events that are both possible <u>and</u> important. Desires are also important, in the sense that they reveal some of your beliefs about what is <u>lacking</u> in your current life.

Periodically "taking stock" of your different motivational states can be an extremely useful exercise, not only because of what you can learn about your belief systems, but also because of what it can reveal about the priorities that govern your current life.

NOTES

1. One might say that it could also imply a conflict in needs or wants, but needs and wants are really based on beliefs about what is important or what is good.
2. One might say that it could also imply a conflict in needs or wants, but needs and wants are really based on beliefs about what is important or what is good.

CHAPTER 7

BODY AND MIND

Mind versus body. Mental versus physical. Sprititual versus material. Subjective versus objective. Thought versus action. These and many other
similar distinctions or "dualisms" have their origins in the fact that your
consciousness is capable of seeing itself as containing two very different
kinds of content: the physical sensations that seem to come either from
outside stimulation of your five senses or from inside your body, and the
thoughts and emotions that seem to come from "somewhere else." The
"bodily" feelings that will be the subject of this chapter are of special
interest because they represent one aspect of consciousness where "mind"
and "body" intersect. Thus, when you feel very angry, fearful, or sexual,
you are not just thinking about something (an enemy, a threat, a lover);
rather, you are also experiencing something in your body: your heart
beating faster, your breathing becoming more rapid, your muscles tens-
ing, and so on. Since these bodily sensations and their associated
thoughts are fully integrated—for example, fear involves both muscular
tension and thought (i.e., about whatever it is that you are fearful of)—the
mind-body dualism clearly breaks down in the case of bodily feelings. In
other words, when it comes to bodily feeling states, the "mental" and the
"physical" come together in a single "package."

The exercises that opened the first chapter of this book were designed
in part to demonstrate that, barring a sudden pain or other abrupt
change in the condition of your body, you are not mindful of your bodily

Mindworks: Becoming More Conscious in an Unconscious World, pp. 143–159
Copyright © 2007 by Information Age Publishing

sensations most of the time. The body-mind relationship is, of course, a two-way street: Just as a sudden pain or loud noise can cause certain thoughts to arise in your consciousness, so can your conscious thoughts and feelings cause your body to feel different. The dictionary search for feeling terms (see chapter 5) revealed an entire class of feeling states whose emergence in consciousness is usually accompanied by bodily sensations associated with changes in respiration, accelerated pulse or heart rate, perspiration, flushing, muscular tension, and the like. (Many of these bodily changes, of course, can be traced to changes in hormonal secretions and alterations in brain chemistry.) While the systematic study of mind-body relationships is an important and rapidly growing field of inquiry in its own right, this chapter—like the rest of the book—will focus specifically on the phenomenological aspects of these relationships: feeling states that involve bodily sensations.

"SENSATIONS"

Since the "feelings" that most obviously involve bodily sensations also tend to be the simplest and, from the point of view of understanding how your consciousness works, least interesting ones, we shall mention them only briefly. I am speaking here, of course, of hunger, thirst, pain, and other specific sensory impressions having to so with tastes, smells, sights, heat and cold, and the sense of touch: soft, hard, smooth, rough, clammy, sticky so on. Strictly speaking, these are more appropriately called "sensations" rather than "feelings." Certainly it would make little sense to call them "emotions" (although they can obviously give rise to emotions). Notice, however, that our language uses many of these same sensations metaphorically to describe emotional or feeling states:

- "I have a soft spot in my heart for her."
- "I had a rough day."
- "It pains me to say this."
- "The experience left a bad taste in my mouth."
- "I want to savor this moment."
- "He was embittered by the experience."
- "He was green with envy."
- "I'm feeling kind of blue today."
- "It warms my heart."
- "I gave a lukewarm response."
- "I got hot under the collar."

- "The whole thing <u>stinks</u>!"
- "I <u>smell</u> a rat."

We have developed an especially large number of these physical metaphors that refer to alimentary or gastrointestinal functions:

- "He has no <u>guts</u>."
- "She <u>hungered</u> for his affection."
- "You make me sick to my <u>stomach</u>."
- "I couldn't <u>swallow</u> his explanation."
- "I got all <u>choked</u> up."
- "I had a sinking feeling <u>in the pit of my stomach.</u>"

Even our profanity frequently relies on gastrointestinal metaphors:

- "Don't be an <u>asshole</u>."
- "You're full of <u>shit</u>."
- "He's an old <u>fart</u>."

Consider the tremendous variety of emotions and feelings implied in these fairly commonly-used metaphors: anger, fear, envy, skepticism, disgust, sadness, contempt, desire, frustration, anxiety, depression, suspicion, caring, etc. In short, we frequently associate many different kinds of emotional states with bodily sensations.

In chapter 5 we mentioned that the dictionary search identified four types of feeling states that typically involve physical sensations: feelings having to do with your <u>general sense of well being</u>, feelings having to do with your <u>energy level</u>, <u>sexual</u> feelings, and feelings having to do with <u>clarity of consciousness</u>. Let us consider each of these types of feeling states separately.

GENERAL SENSE OF PHYSICAL WELL-BEING

Whenever someone greets you with a traditional "How're you doing" or "How's it going," they are basically asking you about your general sense of well-being. The analysis of feeling self-descriptors discussed in chapter 5 revealed that there are at least two different approaches that you can use to describe your general sense of physical well being: <u>Normalcy</u> and <u>Wellness</u>. Let us start with Wellness. Most of us have learned to describe our general sense of physical well-being in terms of the <u>degree</u> of wellness that we feel. Since there are clearly many different degrees of general well-being that we can experience, we have developed at least five different sets of terms to use, each corresponding to a different point on the continuum of Wellness. At the "positive" extreme we use words like "terrific" and "great." You cannot really feel any better than that! At the other extreme we use terms like terrible, awful, sick, ill, crummy, and lousy. If your bad feeling state is a little less extreme, you might instead say that you are feeling out of sorts, out of whack, or funky, or say "I've felt better." If you are not feeling your best, but you are not really feeling sick, you might use descriptors like "fair," "not bad," "so so," or "tolerable." Finally, if you are feeling better than "fair" but not "terrific," you might say you feel "good," "well," "fine," or "OK." In other words, the continuum of wellness ranges across at least five different levels:

Terrific	Good	Fair	Out of Sorts	Lousy
great	well, fine	not bad, tolerable	funky, I have felt better	awful, sick

The continuum of "Normalcy" is much simpler than the Wellness continuum, although it can utilize some of the same words. Thus, to communicate that you feel "normal," you might use words like "fine" and "OK." (Sometimes you also use these same words in response to an inquiry from a concerned friend or companion who wonders if you might be sick or injured: When you respond "I'm fine" or "I'm OK," you mean "it's not serious" or "I've recovered.") On the opposite pole of this continuum—when you are not feeling normal—you might describe yourself as feeling funny, strange, odd, weird, or unnatural. The continuum of Normalcy thus looks like this:

Normal	Strange
fine, OK	odd, weird, funny

EXERCISE

(a) Using the 5-point continuum of general well-being shown above, how would you rate the way you feel right now? When was the last time you felt very different from now? Do you know why you felt that way? How long did it last? (b) When was the last time you felt strange or weird? Can you remember what happened to make you feel that way?

Wellness and Normalcy are, of course, related—if you are feeling lousy, you are obviously not "normal" or "OK"—but there are still important differences. For example, just because you are feeling "strange" or "odd" does not necessarily mean that you feel "sick" or "lousy." And just because you are feeling "normal" or "OK" does not mean that you are feeling "great" or "terrific."

ENERGY LEVEL

Certain bodily feeling states are associated with either very high or very low levels of energy (psychologists sometimes refer to your energy level as your "arousal level"). "High energy" states are often accompanied by an urge to <u>do</u> something and by physical changes such as more rapid breathing or increased heart rate, while "low energy" states are typically associated with decreased levels of metabolic functioning and a <u>lack</u> of interest in "doing" anything. We have developed a long list of words to identify feeling states that have to do with different energy levels, and the feelings described by most of these words can be looked at in two different ways: in terms of the energy <u>level</u> (high or low), and in terms of the energy <u>quality</u> (positive or negative). If we combine energy quality with energy level, we end up with four types of bodily feeling states: positive-high energy, positive-low energy, negative-high energy, and negative-low energy. Let us look at each of these combinations separately.

Positive-High Energy Feelings

When you feel good and full of energy, there are at least two different ways that this good feeling can be manifest: <u>vigor</u> and <u>exhilaration</u>. When you feel <u>vigorous</u> or "energetic," you often want to express that high energy in some way, for example, by talking to someone or by engaging in physical activity such as exercise, sports, taking a walk or a hike, doing chores around the house, and so on. Other words besides vigorous and energetic that you might use to describe such a feeling would include full of zip, lively, frisky, fresh, spry, or invigorated. <u>Exhilaration</u> is also a high energy state that leads you to want to express it in some form of physical activity, but it has an added dimension of happiness or cheerfulness that usually accompanies it. Sometimes when you feel this way you might be inclined to hug someone or sing or dance. Other words that you might use instead of exhilaration would include elated, euphoric, enthusiastic, fired up, tingly, or excited. And if the excitement has come on in <u>response</u>

to something good that has happened, you might say you feel enthralled, electrified, exultant, or thrilled.

POSITIVE-LOW ENERGY FEELINGS

Positive feelings that are accompanied by <u>low</u> energy levels also occur in two basic forms: <u>relaxed</u> and <u>comfortable</u>. Other terms that you might use to describe a feeling of relaxation would include calm, mellow, and laid back. Alternative terms for feeling comfortable might include snug and cozy. In contrast to the high energy states, which are often accompanied by an urge to do something very physical, feeling relaxed or comfortable might "motivate" you to daydream or meditate or possibly even to go to sleep.

Negative-High Energy Feelings

When it comes to bodily feeling states, negative feelings tend to be much more complex than positive feelings, regardless of whether they involve high or low levels of energy. Some of the highest levels of negative energy are associated with being <u>angry</u>. Just like feeling exhilarated, feeling angry is usually accompanied by rapid breathing and increased heart rate and an urge to <u>do</u> something: yell or scream, attack another person, break something, and so on. Consider all the different ways you have to describe such feelings: angry, hostile, outraged, mad, and—if you are <u>very</u> angry: apopleptic, inflamed, furious, enraged, livid, or crazed.

In addition to anger, there are at least two other "negative high energy" states that you can experience: <u>fear</u> and <u>anxiety</u>. Like anger, fear typically is accompanied by accelerated metabolic functioning and often leads you to want to <u>do</u> something: run away, hide, call 911, or even attack

---

EXERCISE

(a) Think of a recent time when you were in a positive-high energy state, that is, when you were feeling vigorous or exhilarated. Can you explain how you got into that state? Can you recall some of the things you most wanted to do? (b) Can you describe some of the conditions or circumstances under which you would be most likely to find yourself in a positive-low energy state (i.e., feeling relaxed and comfortable)?

or attempt to drive away whatever it is that you fear (another person, animal, etc.). Alternatives to "fearful" would include "scared" and "frightened." An extremely fearful, very high energy state would be "panicked" or "terrified."

There is, of course, an intimate connection between fear and anger, in the sense that you are likely to get most angry at the things you fear the most. While we commonly think of fear and anger as "primitive" feelings, the fact is that these feelings almost always arise in your consciousness because of your <u>beliefs</u>: You fear something because you <u>believe</u> that it is a threat, and you get angry at someone because you <u>believe</u> either that they have wronged you or that they represent some kind of threat.

<u>Anxiety</u> is a somewhat more subtle and complex feeling state. While anger and fear frequently involve specific objects—you fear or get angry at a particular person or thing—it is possible to experience fear, anger, and especially anxiety as a general condition without any specific external "cause." (Some people, in fact, carry a perpetual "readiness" to experience fear or anger.) And while anxiety does not usually involve the same urge to <u>act</u> that normally accompanies anger and fear, the feeling <u>itself</u> tends to be very "physical": sweating, fidgeting, more rapid breathing, etc. This interesting physical quality of anxiety is revealed in most of the alternative terms that are available to describe anxious feelings: tense, agitated, jittery, jumpy, edgy, restless, and "got the willies." A very common and unique kind of anxiety occurs when you believe that you do not have enough <u>time</u> to do something you want to do or believe you should do. When this happens, you might say that you feel hurried, rushed, pressured, harried, flustered, hassled, stressed, frenetic, or overwhelmed. (The issue of how you deal with your sense of time will be discussed in detail in chapter 11.)

In short, there are at least four different types of negative feelings that involve high levels of energy: anger, fear, anxiety, and the feeling of being rushed or hurried.

Negative-Low Energy Feelings

The low energy side of negative feelings is equally complex, involving at least three different types of feeling states. The first two—<u>fatigue</u> and <u>weakness</u>—are the most obviously "physical" states in this category. There are many ways to say you are tired: fatigued, exhausted, bushed, tired, wiped out, worn out, zonked, overtired, and dead tired. Variations on feeling weak are fewer: feeble, run down, and perhaps impotent (meant in the nonsexual sense). The third negative, low energy state is probably best captured by the word "listless." Here again we have several possible varia-

EXERCISE

(a) **When you are feeling really angry, how does your body feel? What are some of the things that you are most likely to do? (b) List two of your biggest fears. For each one, indicate some of the belief(s) that are involved.**

tions: flat, droopy, sluggish, leaden, lifeless, limp, dead, and languid. We might also want to include "depression" here, but there are several different "ways" that you can be depressed. You can be depressed and droopy, for example, but you can also be depressed and anxious or depressed and agitated. For this reason I have included depression under general feeling states (see chapter 5) rather than bodily feeling states.

It should be pointed out here that fatigue does not always have to be a "negative" feeling state, given that you can feel tired or worn out while also feeling happy or content—for example, after you have successfully completed something that required you to expend a great deal of energy. Typical examples of "good feeling fatigue" would be how you might feel after having good sex or successfully completing a challenging physical task.

Another important point to remember about the relationship between energy and feeling is that <u>the same energy level can be associated with wildly different "physical" feeling states</u>. Thus, if your energy level is very low, you can be feeling relaxed, calm, and mellow, or you can be feeling weak, tired, and listless! Similarly, if you are functioning at a very high energy level, you can be feeling exhilarated and enthusiastic, or you can be feeling furious, terrified. anxious, or rushed!

A particularly interesting characteristic of these "energy level" feelings is that they can be used to form eight "positive-negative" continua where, for each positive state, there is a corresponding negative state <u>at the opposite energy level:</u>

Positive	Negative
Relaxed	Tense
Laid back	Hurried
Calm ....Fearful..............	Terrified
Mellow ....Angry.................	Enraged
Energetic	Weak
Invigorated	Tired
Excited	Listless
Exhilarated	Depressed

SEXUAL FEELINGS

For each of the eight feeling continua shown above, <u>it is not possible to experience feelings at opposite ends of the continuum at the same time.</u> Thus, when you feel tense, it is not possible to feel relaxed; or, when you are feeling listless, there is no way you can also be feeling excited. The same would be true of the two "well-being" continua discussed earlier: if you are feeling "lousy" you cannot also be feeling "terrific," and feeling "strange" precludes feeling "normal."

Sexual feelings, on the other hand, really have no polar opposite other than "lack of sexual feelings," the extreme case being when you feel "turned off," "repelled," or "repulsed." Another unique characteristic of sexual feelings is that they are very complex, in the sense that they could also be classified under general feeling states (chapter 5), motivational feeling states (chapter 6), or feeling states having to do with other people (chapter 9). However, since sexual feelings do not <u>necessarily</u> involve other people and since they clearly involve physical sensations and have a biological basis, I have included them here under "bodily" feelings. While the bodily sensations that accompany sexual feelings are typically associated with swelling and increased blood flow in the sexual organs, sexual feelings also usually involve a general sense of excitation that is often accompanied by other sensations that arise from general flushing, perspiration, accelerated respiration and heart rate, and tactile stimulation. Moreover, these bodily sensations can also be accompanied by sexual thoughts and mental images.

Despite the power and diversity of sexual feelings, there are only a limited number of words to draw upon in describing how you feel when you feel "sexual": sexy, aroused, excited, lustful, horny, sensual, and turned on. Our language contains a number of other terms for describing <u>behavior</u> that appears to involve sexuality—lewd, lascivious, prurient, flirtatious, seductive, "coming on," "hitting on," "putting a move on"—but we have developed only a few terms for describing sexual <u>feelings</u>.

But what is perhaps most interesting about sexual feelings is their complexity and the variety of affective contexts in which they can arise: sexual feelings can be, and usually are, accompanied by one or more <u>other</u> feeling states. As a matter of fact, sexual feelings can be accompanied by feelings from <u>any</u> of the other categories of feeling states: general, motivational, interpersonal, and cognitive. Moreover, sexual feelings are often accompanied by <u>other</u> "bodily" feelings, both positive and negative. Thus, you can feel sexy <u>and</u> either energetic or exhilarated, but you can also feel sexy and anxious, sexy and fearful, sexy and rushed, or even sexy and angry!

Let us now look at how sexual feelings can be accompanied by feelings from the other general categories. In the general feeling area, you might feel sexy and happy, sexy and joyful, sexual and playful, or even sexual and transcendent. On the other hand, you might feel sexy and unhappy, or sexy and frustrated (a common combination for many adults without sexual partners, and especially for adolescents!). You might feel sexy and confident, but you could also feel sexy and insecure! And while you might feel sexy and pleased, you could also feel sexy and disappointed! Finally, your feeling of sexiness could be combined with a feeling of confidence, but it could just as easily be accompanied by feelings of insecurity. In short, feelings of sexiness can, and frequently do, combine with almost any other kind of general feeling state.

Since sexual feelings frequently involve other people, it should come as no surprise that they can also occur in combination with several positive interpersonal feeling states that will be discussed in chapter 9: trusting, loving, liking, charmed, flattered, admiring, or grateful. On the negative side, sexual feelings can occur in conjunction with feeling self-conscious, guilty, or embarrassed, feeling that you have been offended or taken advantage of, feeling disdainful or contemptuous, or even feeling resentful.

In the same vein, sexual feelings can be, and usually are, combined with one or more of the <u>motivational</u> states described in chapter 6: wishing/yearning, interested/inclined toward, aspiring/striving, feeling engaged/absorbed, and even feeling compelled. On the negative motivational side, sexual feelings can also be accompanied by feeling detached/ disengaged, ambivalent/hesitant, or even blocked (i.e., the feeling of being thwarted or hindered).

Finally, sexual feelings can be accompanied by feeling states that have to do with <u>cognitive</u> processes (see chapter 8). Perhaps the most common cognitive state that accompanies sexual feelings, especially in your younger years or when you are thinking about, or about to have sex with, a new partner, is <u>curiosity</u>. You can also feel sexual while you are also feeling amazed or astonished, or be sexual while you are focused and mindful. On the other hand, sexual feelings can also occur together with feelings of skepticism, doubt, confusion, or even boredom!

This discussion suggests that sexual feelings are among the most complex and probably the most "versatile" of all of our feeling states. Perhaps more than any other feeling we can identify, sexual feelings can occur in combination with a number of other feelings states that are, themselves, contradictory or opposite: exhilaration or anger, enthusiasm or anxiety, trust or suspicion, confidence or embarassment, liking or resentment, certainty or doubt, contentment or frustration, and so on.

EXERCISE

(a) If something were to happen to make you feel sexual right now, what would it be? (b) Think back over your recent sexual life and write down as many other feelings that you experienced at different times when you were feeling sexual. Did the circumstances—the situation, your state of mind, and so forth,—have anything to do with the appearance of these other feelings?

This discussion suggests that a key challenge in understanding your own sexuality is to be aware of the <u>other</u> feeling states that arise when you are feeling sexually aroused, thinking about sex, or engaging in sexual activity.

FEELINGS RELATING TO CLARITY OF CONSCIOUSNESS

We do not usually think of "consciousness" in bodily or physical terms, and yet our language contains a number of terms suggesting that subtle physical processes can affect the overall state of your consciousness. Most of these terms suggest varying degrees of what we might call <u>clear-headedness</u>. When your consciousness and your physical state are well synchronized and in tune, you will most likely describe the state of your consciousness with words like clear-headed, clear, alert, aware, and awake. On the other hand, when your bodily state is interfering with your ability to perceive and think clearly, there are at least four different ways you can describe your state of mind: "faint," "sleepy," "disoriented," or "intoxicated." There are, in turn, several different words available to describe each of these states of "nonclarity."

<u>Faintness</u> is a very diverse category, where you can feel either faint, light-headed, unsteady, dizzy, giddy, or dreamy. Variations on feeling <u>sleepy</u> would include feeling semiconscious, somnolent, groggy, dopey, half-asleep, or half-awake. Alternatives to feeling <u>disoriented</u> would include feeling hazy, dazed, foggy, fuzzy, or "in a trance." Finally, there are many ways to say that you feel <u>intoxicated</u>: stoned, drunk, high, wrecked, wasted, ripped, fried, tipsy, and loaded. These four ways of <u>not</u> being clear-headed can, and often do, go together, as when you might feel both drunk and sleepy at the same time, or simultaneously stoned and disoriented.

Figure 7.1 shows the full "clarity of consciousness" continuum.

I could also have included some of these states under "cognitive" feeling states (chapter 8) rather than bodily feeling states, but they are

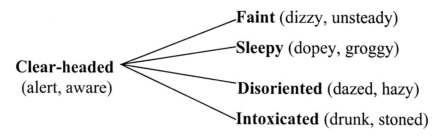

Figure 7.1.   Full "clarity of consciousness" continuum.

included here because they are describing the conscious <u>context</u> in which thought can occur rather than a <u>type</u> of thinking or a thinking <u>process</u> per se (see chapter 8). Even so, there are several different ways that the cognitive feeling states described in the next chapter (chapter 8) might be combined with these Physical/Cognitive feeling states. For example, you will find it easier to be either <u>mindful</u> or <u>focused</u> in your thinking when you feel "clear-headed." On the other hand, feeling either "faint" or "intoxicated" makes it more likely that you will also feel <u>confused</u>, <u>unknowing</u>, or <u>unaware.</u>

Feelings related to clear-headedness can also occur in combination with other physical feeling states. Obviously, feeling clear-headed tends to go along with feeling <u>normal</u>, <u>energetic</u>, and even <u>terrific</u>. By contrast, feeling drunk can be combined with such diverse feelings as <u>angry,</u> <u>relaxed</u>, <u>fatigued</u>, <u>lousy</u>, or <u>sexy</u>. Other feelings of intoxication—especially those associated with the use of "mind-altering" drugs—can be accompanied by an even wider range of other physical feeling states: <u>exhilarated</u>, <u>great</u>, <u>sexy</u>, <u>relaxed</u>, <u>strange</u>, <u>spaced out</u>, <u>terrible</u>, <u>anxious.</u> or <u>terrified</u>. Although people do not ordinarily take mind-altering substances to feel to feel anxious or terrified, the diversity of feeling states that can be brought on by such substances may well be part of their appeal.

If you feel "not clear" in the sense of "sleepy" or "dreamy," that feeling would often be combined with other physical feeling states such as <u>relaxed</u> or <u>fatigued</u>, but if you feel either faint or dizzy, you might well also feel <u>strange</u>, <u>lousy</u>, <u>weak,</u> or even <u>anxious</u>.

TAKING STOCK OF YOUR PHYSICAL FEELING STATES

This final section includes a major exercise similar to the one already suggested for general feeling states (chapter 5). Table 7.1 lists each of the different physical feeling states that we have discussed in this chapter. Next to each feeling are two rating scales. (a) Indicate how fre-

Table 7.1. "Bodily" Feelings

Date:___/___/___
Time___a.m./p.m.

Please specify the time being rated: past hour   past 24 hours   past week   past month   past year

Situation (Where are you and what are you doing now?_____

For each feeling state, please circle the number that corresponds to how frequently you experience that feeling during that time period.					In the future, how frequently would you *prefer* to experience this feeling?		
	All of the time	Most of the time	Some of the time	Seldom	Never	More	*About* the Same	Less
Terrific (great)	5	4	3	2	1	3	2	1
Lousy (sick, awful)	5	4	3	2	1	3	2	1
Normal ("OK")	5	4	3	2	1	3	2	1
Strange (funny, odd)	5	4	3	2	1	3	2	1
Energetic (full of zip)	5	4	3	2	1	3	2	1
Listless (flat, droopy, lifeless	5	4	3	2	1	3	2	1
Relaxed (calm, mellow)	5	4	3	2	1	3	2	1
Tense (anxious, jittery, edgy)	5	4	3	2	1	3	2	1
Comfortable (cozy, snug)	5	4	3	2	1	3	2	1
Uncomfortable	5	4	3	2	1	3	2	1
Exhilarated (elated, euphoric)	5	4	3	2	1	3	2	1
Depressed (down)	5	4	3	2	1	3	2	1
Wide awake	5	4	3	2	1	3	2	1
Sleepy (drowsy)	5	4	3	2	1	3	2	1
Clear-headed (alert, aware)	5	4	3	2	1	3	2	1
Faint (dizzy, light-headed)	5	4	3	2	1	3	2	1
Tired (fatigued, exhausted)	5	4	3	2	1	3	2	1
Weak (feeble)	5	4	3	2	1	3	2	1
Intoxicated (drunk, stoned, high)	5	4	3	2	1	3	2	1
Disoriented (dazed, hazy)	5	4	3	2	1	3	2	1
Angry (furious, mad)	5	4	3	2	1	3	2	1
Fearful (scared, frightened)	5	4	3	2	1	3	2	1
Sexual (turned-on, aroused, horny)	5	4	3	2	1	3	2	1
Hurried (rushed, pressured)	5	4	3	2	1	3	2	1

Any comments

quently you experience each feeling. **Then, (b)** Indicate whether, in the future, you would prefer to experience each feeling <u>more</u> frequently, <u>less</u> frequently, or at about the <u>same</u> frequency.

Once you complete this first part of the exercise, it would be useful to take a few moments to reflect on each of those feeling states that you would like to experience either <u>more</u> frequently or <u>less</u> frequently. Let me try to illustrate how this reflective process might go using one of these states, the feeling of being **hurried**. Feeling hurried or rushed is a very common experience for many of us who live and work in today's fast-paced technological society. It seems that there are just too many things to do and too little time to do them. For purposes of this illustration let us assume that you indicated that you'd like to feel hurried/rushed/pressured "less" often than you currently do. One way to begin to change this unwanted pattern is to engage in a simple exercise where you ask yourself a brief series of questions:

- **In what types of situations am I most likely to feel this way?**
  In the case of feeling rushed or hurried, you might include those times when you have a scheduled appointment, engagement, reservation, or other commitment and you feel you have barely enough (or not enough) time to be on time. You might be traveling to get to your appointment, or you might be trying to finish some other task so that you can be ready for the appointment.

- **What are some of the things I am likely to <u>do</u> when I feel this way?**
  If you are feeling rushed while you are, say, driving your car on the way to work or to an appointment, perhaps you are more likely to take chances or drive recklessly. Similarly, if you are hurrying to finish a task so you can be ready for your next appointment on time, you may get sloppy or careless and not do a good job with the task at hand.

- **What <u>other</u> feelings are likely to arise when I feel this way?**
  If you happen to be in a hurry when you are driving your car to work or to get to an appointment, you may also experience feelings of tension, impatience, or irritation, especially if you encounter heavy traffic or other delays. You may also be more inclined to get angry with other drivers. Or, if you are hurrying to finish a task so you can get to your appointment, you may be more likely to experience feelings of frustration or anxiety if you encounter interruptions, delays, or other obstacles to completing that task. And, if you believe that getting to work on time or being on time for your appointment is very important, you may also experience feelings of anxiety or worry.

- **Have I structured my life in such a way that I am especially likely to feel this way? What are some of the patterns that I have established?**

In the case of feeling hurried, it is often the case that such feelings are especially likely to arise because we have crammed most of our waking hours full with all sorts of obligations and commitments. These commitments might involve your work or profession, family members, neighbors, friends, or simply maintaining your home, car, and other possessions. This tendency to "over-schedule" gets reinforced by technologies such as desk calendars, Blackberries, and Palm Pilots which, in effect, encourage us to fill up the "blank spaces" in our days with commitments. With such a full schedule, it is easy to become rushed or hurried because there is no "room" for any kind of interruption or delay.

These problems are also exacerbated by our modern "consumer society" and especially by the burgeoning "technology revolution." By acquiring more electronic gadgets such as cell phones and pagers, we invite almost nonstop interruptions in our daily lives. Modern electronic devices also tend to make more and more demands on our time, whether it be reading and responding to e-mail, listening to and answering voicemail, or simply maintaining each device in working order. These same technologies are also designed to lure us into devoting substantial amounts of our daily lives to such diverse and potentially time-consuming things as playing video games, "surfing the net," participating in internet chat rooms, text messaging, listening to stereos, or watching videos, DVDs, or the hundreds of channels of television that are now becoming available. Finally, by continually creating new electronic devices and regularly "upgrading" all of our existing ones, the purveyors of technology tempt us to spend increasing amounts of our time shopping or simply learning how to use each new gadget or each "new and improved" version of our "old" gadgets.

While it is easy to "blame" these technologies and those who profit from their sale and use for the ever-expanding demands they make on our time, it is important to realize that, in most instances, we <u>choose</u> to acquire such devices and <u>decide</u> how much time we will devote to using and maintaining them

In short, the point of this question is to encourage you to explore in some detail the extent to which you have <u>chosen</u> to structure your daily experience in such a way that the "unwanted" feeling is likely to arise in your consciousness.

- **What is a recent time when I felt this way? What did I do? What other feelings did I experience?**
  The idea behind these questions is to get you to think in some depth about a recent time when you experienced the feeling in question so you can address the next questions as fully as possible.

Let us say, for example, that you recently worked late and arrived home in a big rush to dress for an important social engagement that same evening. After dressing, you noticed that your jacket had a bad stain on the front, which required you to change your shirt and slacks because you did not have another jacket that matched what you initially put on. Since you left yourself no leeway for such a minor delay, you began to add feelings of irritation and frustration to your feeling of being rushed. Your partner, who was ready to go when you arrived home from work, started getting impatient and chided you for being late, which only intensified your feelings of rushing, frustration, and irritation. Then, as you were driving to your engagement, you encountered unexpectedly heavy traffic, which contributed still more to these same feelings. You can probably elaborate on this familiar scenario with further developments that could well have evoked even more intense feelings (e.g., anger), resulting in behavior that you might well have ended up regretting.

- **What are some of my relevant beliefs that were involved in that situation?**

  The point of this question is to get beyond a simplistic understanding of your tendency to feel rushed or hurried. You could tell yourself (and, on occasion, probably have), "I need to allow more time for things" or "I've taken on too many things, and I need to cut back." The issue is not that there are such obvious "solutions" to your problem, but rather <u>why you have not embraced them</u>. And here is where beliefs come in. The relevant belief topics in this situation could cover a wide range of issues: responsibility, punctuality, staying "up-to-date," and so forth. Do you believe that you must schedule yourself every minute of every day? Do you believe that you must always possess the latest technology? What <u>other</u> beliefs might be involved in such beliefs (e.g., about needing to achieve at the highest possible level, about your own capabilities, about competing with others, etc.). Since each person and each situation is unique, your own intuition is the best guide in identifying the most relevant beliefs.

- **Is it in my best interests to continue acting on all these beliefs? If I really want to change how often I experience the feeling in question (and the other feelings and actions that tend accompany it), should I consider suspending or altering some of the beliefs that lead me to feel and act this way?**

  Take, for example, the belief that you need to achieve at the highest possible level. A common behavioral consequence of embracing such a belief is that you will do everything possible to enhance your career development by cramming as much achievement-related work as you can into each day. Your work will inevitably spill over into your evenings, weekends, and "vacations." Moreover, to make sure that you do not "waste" any time, you may also acquire the latest cellular telephone which you can use to make business calls during "down" times in airline lounges or waiting rooms, while commuting or traveling, or simply while walking from one place to another. Since your daily calendar will always be full, and since you will tend to allocate the absolute minimum amount of time required for each scheduled task, you will regularly find yourself hurrying to complete each task. And when something takes longer than expected to complete, you'll find yourself hurrying even more to "catch up."

To scrutinize the beliefs that lead you to embrace such a pattern, you may want to start asking yourself a series of questions: What other beliefs might be behind my wanting to devote so much of my time and energy to achieving? What will happen to me—my lifestyle, my self-esteem, my sense of worth, my relationships with others, my happiness, the quality of my life—if I devote less time and energy to my work? How much less "successful" will I be? What difference will that make in my life? What does success really mean to me? If I choose to devote more time to pursuits that will allow me to feel less rushed and hurried, what effects will that have on my life?

Another strategy is to examine critically some of the key concepts that characterize the belief in question (e.g., "achievement," "success," etc.) For detailed suggestions on how to examine such concepts, see chapter 10.

CHAPTER 8

THINKING AND FEELING

"... thoughts are not just cold ideas existing in a vacuum, but they are rich with blood, so to speak, engorged in a halo of emotions that flow onward with the thoughts."

—Eugene Taylor, *A Psychology of Spiritual Healing* (1997)

One of the most interesting outcomes of my dictionary search for "feeling words" was the realization that there are a substantial number of feeling states that have to do with thinking. Like the mind-body "dualism" discussed in the last chapter, our western culture has led most of us to think that there is a sharp division between thinking and feeling, that thoughts and feelings are completely separate components of our conscious experience. Indeed, it is sometimes suggested that thinking and feeling act in opposition to each other. In the same vein, some of our metaphors even suggest that thoughts and emotions exist in different parts of the body, as, for example, when we speak of "the head" (meaning thinking and reasoning) versus "the heart" (meaning feeling and emotions).

Many psychologists and educators have reinforced this dualistic view by emphasizing the distinction between "cognitive" and "affective" human traits.[1] And in recent years our educational system has come to see itself as primarily concerned with developing students' "cognitive" abilities (reading, computing, analytical or critical thinking, etc.), to the near-exclusion of affective qualities. This narrowing of our educational focus is

Mindworks: Becoming More Conscious in an Unconscious World, pp. 161–171
Copyright © 2007 by Information Age Publishing

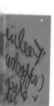

unfortunate, not only because "affective" qualities such as motivation and honesty contribute to effective learning, but also because our capacity to solve many of our society's problems depends heavily on affective "talents" such as empathy, leadership, commitment, and social responsibility. In this connection, as you read below about the various affective states that have to do with thinking, ask yourself the following questions: How important would it be to take this feeling into account in designing an effective educational program? Does the feeling have anything to do with being an effective physician, lawyer, scientist, artist, teacher, or public official?

FEELINGS THAT HAVE TO DO WITH THINKING

My dictionary search turned up 85 different feeling words that relate to thinking. These words can, in turn, be organized into at least 15 different "thinking-feeling" states: curiosity, amazement, understanding, certainty, familiarity, mindfulness, reflectiveness, absorption, puzzlement, skepticism, haziness, boredom, distraction, doubt, and confusion. Some, but not all, of these states form bipolar opposites.

Curiosity and Amazement

Curiosity is in many ways one of our most "alive" feeling states, since it is intimately connected with creativity and the quest for knowledge. Alternate feeling terms describing states that are very similar to curiosity would include intrigued, fascinated, tantalized, and interested. Compared to being merely "interested" in something, being "curious" implies that you are more likely to <u>do</u> something about (i.e., act on) your feeling. It is probably not much of an exaggeration to say that, without human curiosity, there would be no science, no art, and little human exploration. The great motivating power of curiosity becomes obvious when we realize that curiosity can cause us to temporarily forget some of our basic human needs (food, sleep, etc) and can even lead some people to undertake challenges that put their very lives at risk.

A "reactive" feeling state that is closely related to curiosity is **Amazement.** In fact, one might argue that some people indulge their curiosity in order to experience the feeling of amazement which often accompanies discovery. The richness of this feeling state is reflected in the large number of alternative words that can be used to describe feelings of amazement: awed, agog, astonished, astounded, agape (at), blown away, dazzled, flabbergasted, stunned, and thunderstruck.

The feeling that comes closest to being the opposite of curiosity, interest, or amazement is **boredom.** Boredom is a state of consciousness where you have difficulty paying attention, concentrating, or sustaining your interest in something (about the only alternative feeling term for "bored" is "disinterested"). We might regard boredom as a kind of "avoidance" feeling, in the sense that when you feel bored you would rather <u>not</u> be doing whatever it is that is "making" you feel bored. You may also feel that you should instead be doing something else, but that "something else" is either ill-defined or seen by you as presently unattainable.

Whether or not boredom constitutes a serious problem depends on the circumstances. For example, most of us have had the experience of being bored by a speaker, performer, book, film, play, or television show. In these circumstances the feeling usually lasts only a brief time and can often be relieved by direct action (e.g., walking out of the theater). By contrast, boredom can be much more debilitating when there seems to be "no way out," that is, when you believe that the situation that leads to boredom will persist indefinitely (or extend over a substantial period of time) and is something you "can't avoid." Such problems are most likely to arise when you are feeling bored with your partner or other family member, a close friend, school, or your job. Boredom can occur in almost any line of work, but it is especially relevant to the field of education. For the student, boredom can make education seem like a "waste of time" and can be a primary reason for dropping out of school. If you happen to be the teacher, there are few things that pose a greater challenge than students who are bored with your class, with the subject matter, with studying, or with school in general. In other words, both teaching and learning become much more difficult when the student is bored.

Comprehension

One of the most important "cognitive feelings" is comprehension or understanding, the feeling that you "know" or are "clear" about some-

---

EXERCISE

(a) Complete the following sentences:
  • I'm really curious about…
  • What amazes me…
  • The most boring…
(b) Identify some of the beliefs that are implied in each of the sentences.

thing, that you can "make sense of" or "make meaning" out of it. While you are most likely to experience such a feeling in the context of language or speech—"I understand what he just said," "I'm not sure I know what she means," "Can you make sense out of this poem?"—the feeling of understanding or making meaning can also apply to abstractions such as an idea or a theory or to "nonverbal" phenomena such as music or art ("What does this painting mean to you?"). And when it comes to our relationships with other people (or even pets or other animals), "understanding" can also imply <u>empathy</u>, the sense that you know what another being is thinking or understand how they are feeling (see also chapter 9).

The opposite pole of comprehension or understanding—when you <u>do</u> <u>not</u> understand something—can take several forms. The most obvious is simply <u>not</u> knowing or understanding something: "I don't know what that word means," "I have no idea what he's talking about." A more disconcerting state of not knowing would be **confusion,** a cognitive feeling for which we have several different terms: confused, puzzled, bewildered, mystified, befuddled, bemused, and confounded. If you are actively <u>trying</u> to understand something but not succeeding, you could also feel **stuck** or **stymied**, and if you believe that it is something that you <u>should</u> be able to learn or understand, you might also feel "dumb" or "stupid."

Figure 8.1 shows the positive and four negative poles of the continuum of comprehension.

Certainty

Closely related to the feeling of comprehension is the feeling of being certain or "sure" about something. Generally speaking, if you feel you really know or understand something, you will also tend to feel "certain" that you know it (other terms that you might use to label such a feeling

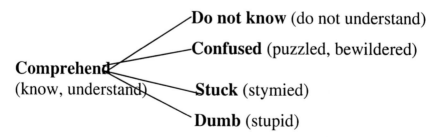

Figure 8.1.   The positive and four negative poles of the continuum of comprehension.

would include "sure," "convinced," "believe," "persuaded," and "cock-sure"). But a feeling of certainty can apply to things other than facts or knowledge. You can, for example, feel "certain" in your moral beliefs or values, or about your tastes and preferences. The feeling of certainty, of course, defines one end of a continuum which has **doubt** ("uncertain," "unsure") at the opposite end.

The continuum of certainty has a great deal of significance for your beliefs. Since beliefs are really ideas or propositions (about what is true, good, important, or possible; see chapter 2), **the more certain you are about any belief, (a) the greater its effect on your experience and (b) the more difficulty you will experience in trying to change or suspend it.**

Attentiveness and Focus

Chapter 4 was devoted to a consideration of how your conscious experience can be shaped merely by the things that you pay attention to. Here we look at "attentiveness" as a subjective quality of consciousness. "Paying attention," of course, is something that most parents and teachers emphasize a good deal with their children and students, in part because of a principle that was presented earlier in chapter 4: **your success in learning anything new is directly related to the extent to which you can focus your conscious attention on the material to be learned.** There are several other ways that you can describe your state of mind when you are being attentive: observant, alert, watchful, conscious, aware, or mindful. (When you are paying close attention to what is happening in the moment, you are being "mindful" in the sense of what was described in chapter 3.) By contrast, when you are not being attentive, you might describe your state of mind with terms like distracted, unaware, inattentive, mindless, "mind wandering," "daydreaming," or possibly "spaced out."

It is important to realize that attentiveness is somewhat of a relative term, in the sense that you ordinarily "pay attention" to something in particular. So when you realize that you are being "inattentive," what you usually mean is that you are not paying attention to whatever it is that you believe you "should" be paying attention to. (At such times, you may well be "paying attention" to something else!) In other words, **whether or not you see yourself as being "attentive" depends in part on your beliefs about what you "should" be paying attention to.**

A cognitive feeling state that is very close to being attentive is **focused**. The major distinction is that, while you can try to "pay attention to" or "be aware of" several things at once, being "focused" implies a narrowing of your attention. Your entire attention, in other words, is devoted to a

---

EXERCISE

Think of a recent time when you thought you
were not "paying attention." (a) What beliefs (e.g., about the goodness or importance of the thing you were not paying attention to)
were involved? (b)What were you thinking about at the time? Can
you identify any relevant beliefs?

---

single object. This feeling of being focused is also captured by terms such
as absorbed, engrossed, fixated (on), and concentrating (on). A "reactive"
and intense kind of focusing of your conscious attention is captured by
terms such as "captivated" and "spellbound." There are several different
ways to describe the opposite end of this feeling continuum, i.e., when
you feel that your conscious attention is <u>not</u> focused: hazy, unclear, unfocused, divided, vague, fuzzy.

Recognition

Another cognitive feeling state occurs when you "recognize" something
familiar that arises in your consciousness. The "something" could be a
person, place, object, word, idea, or even a feeling. There are only a few
ways besides "recognize" to describe such a feeling: "acquainted with" and
"familiar with." At the opposite end of this continuum—when you <u>do not</u>
recognize something—you could also say that it is "new" to you, that you
are "unfamiliar" or "unacquainted" with it, or even that it strikes you as
"unusual" or "strange." Finally, if something falls in between these two
extremes, you might say that it is "vaguely familiar" or that it "reminds"
you of something.

Surprise

Surprise is a very distinctive cognitive feeling state that usually arises
suddenly when something unexpected occurs in your consciousness. The
"something" could be another feeling, a sensory impression, an idea or
thought, or some external event.

Skepticism

This is another very specific feeling state that almost always has to do
with a thought, idea, or proposition: "I'm skeptical about that." As it hap-

pens, there are a variety of other ways that you can express such a feeling: dubious, doubtful, leery, disbelieving, unconvinced, unpersuaded, and unswayed. Note that the word "doubtful" can be used to describe two different kinds of cognitive feelings: *skepticism* (as it is used here) and *uncertainty* (as used above under **Certainty**).

Reflectiveness

While the term "reflection" can be used to describe a way a thinking (see below), the sense in which it is used here refers to a feeling state or "mood" where you are generally quiet, relaxed, and undisturbed while you are thinking, as in "I was in a reflective mood." Other terms that you might use to describe such a feeling state would include "contemplative," "thoughtful," and "meditative." A closely related way of thinking would be "daydreaming" (see below), which is perhaps best described as a very unfocused form of reflection.

VARIETIES OF COGNITION

The dictionary search for feeling words turned up several dozen words relating to cognition that do not, strictly speaking, represent cognitive feelings, but instead describe <u>different ways of thinking</u>. The interesting thing about these "types of thinking" is that **each of them tends to be associated with one or more "cognitive feeling" states.** These feeling states can either (a) provide the <u>impetus</u> behind the thinking process, or (b) appear as an outcome or <u>consequence</u> of that thinking process. To see how this works, let us first review briefly the various types of thinking that turned up in the dictionary search.

The most generic of all the terms is, of course, **thinking.** When you want to be a bit more specific in describing your thought process, you would be likely to use one of the several dozen other more specialized "thinking terms," which can be organized into eleven different categories or subcategories:

- **Ponder** (*think over, think about, consider, muse, mull over*): "Let me think about that for a moment."
- **Reason**—a general term comprising at least three subtypes:
  Analyze (*investigate, explore, figure, figure out, look into*): "Let me see if I can come up with a solution to this problem."
  Interpret (*infer, conclude, construe, deduce*): "He must have reacted that way because you put him on the defensive."

Judge (*weigh, assess, evaluate, compare, equate*): "Henry had the best composition in the class."

- **Associate** (*connect, see similarity*): "She reminds me of her mother."
- **Imagine** (*wonder, theorize, fantasize, think up, conceive of*): "What would I do if I were to win the lottery?"
- **Daydream**: "I'm just sort of sitting here letting my mind wander."
- **Remember** (*recall*): "I was just thinking about the film I saw last night."
- **Forget**: "I can't recall his name."
- **Speculate** (*guess, predict*): "She's soon going to run out of patience."

CONNECTIONS BETWEEN THINKING AND "THINKING FEELINGS"

Let us now look at some of the connections between "thinking feelings" and various ways of thinking.

- Feeling *interested* in or *curious* about something—say, a new electronic device that just came on the market—can frequently lead you to *ponder, reason*, or *analyze* it, since you can indulge your interest or satisfy your curiosity by understanding it better, finding out "how it works" or "what it can do." Curiosity can also cause you to use your powers of *imagination:* "I wonder how I might use this?"
- By contrast, feeling *bored* can frequently give rise to *daydreaming* (is this not what students who are bored with a classroom lecture often do?). At the same time, feeling bored with something like a lecture or a TV program can make it more difficult for you to *remember* much about it or *associate* it with other things. (Boredom can sometimes also be connected to anxiety that might arise in connection with not being able to *understand* something.)
- If you *comprehend* or *understand* an idea or concept, you will be more likely to *remember* it, *speculate* about it, and *associate* it with other ideas and concepts.
- Feeling *confused* or *stuck* about something—for example, a puzzle you are trying to solve or problem you are trying to resolve—can cause you to pay close *attention* to it, *analyze* it, or *imagine* possible solutions, but it can <u>also</u> cause you to *lose interest* and to *judge* it ("It's too difficult," "There's no solution").
- Being *mindful* and *attentive* not only facilitates *analysis, interpretation*, and *judging*, but also makes it more likely that you will be able to *associate* and *remember.*

- Feeling *skeptical* about something can often lead you to *analyze* or *judge* it.
- While feeling *uncertain* or *unsure* about something can often motivate you to *ponder, analyze* or *investigate* it, such a feeling can also make you reluctant to *interpret* it or *speculate* about it.
- *Imagining, pondering,* or *analyzing* can often lead to feelings of *recognition, comprehension, certainty,* and even *amazement.*

In short, this analysis makes it clear that

- **"Cognitive feelings" can have profound effects on <u>how</u> you think; and**
- **How you think tends to generate certain types of cognitive feelings.**

So far we have been focusing strictly on different <u>ways</u> of thinking—<u>how</u> you think—and have not addressed the very important issue of <u>what</u> you think about. As it turns out, **you can learn a lot about yourself—and your beliefs—by taking a closer look at the topics or issues that tend to occupy most of your conscious attention.**

TAKING STOCK OF YOUR THINKING TENDENCIES

Table 8.1 lists 24 topics that people tend to think about a lot. If you were to pick any one of these topics that you happen to spend a good deal of

EXERCISE

(a) For each item in the "thought topic" list on the next page, indicate whether you think about it "too much," "too little," or "about the right amount." (b) Pick one or more of the topics that you think about "too much" and ask yourself the following questions: How do I usually think about it, that is, how much analysis, judging, imagining, etc. do I do? What kinds of "thinking feelings"—certainty, doubt, curiosity, skepticism, and so forth,—are typically involved when I think about it? (c) What other feelings—for example, worry, desire, and so forth,—can you associate with the topic? (d) Can you identify some of your beliefs—about truth, importance, and goodness—that might explain why you believe you think about it too much? (e) If you checked "not enough" for any topics, repeat the exercise for one or more of these.

Table 8.1.   Thinking Tendencies

(Circle the appropriate number for each topic.)   Date:___/___/___

How much do you think each of these topics?

Topic	Too much	About the right amount	Not enough
Adventure	3	2	1
Changing your life	3	2	1
Children	3	2	1
Close friends	3	2	1
Enemies/people who have done you wrong	3	2	1
Entertainment (TV, film, video, music, etc.)	3	2	1
Food	3	2	1
Getting old/dying	3	2	1
Health/sickness	3	2	1
Hobby/avocation	3	2	1
Love/romance	3	2	1
Money	3	2	1
Parents	3	2	1
Past mistakes/people you have not treated well	3	2	1
Personal appearance	3	2	1
Planning for the future	3	2	1
Politics/current events	3	2	1
Self-development/improvement	3	2	1
Sex	3	2	1
Siblings	3	2	1
Sports	3	2	1
Spouse/partner	3	2	1
Success/achievement/getting ahead	3	2	1
What others think of you	3	2	1
Work/job	3	2	1
(Add some more to the list if you like.)	3	2	1
_____			
_____			

time thinking about, there are at least two different ways to look at your thought processes: (1) <u>how</u> you tend to think about it, and (2) what kinds of "<u>thought-feelings</u>" are usually present. For example, if you tend to think a lot about your work or job, you might do a lot of analysis ("How am I going to solve that problem?") or judging ("I really screwed that up"), and you might experience both doubt ("Will I ever be able to make it right?") <u>and</u> certainty (There is no way they will ever fire me; they need me too much").

If you believe that you spend "too much time" thinking about a topic like sex, money, food, your personal appearance, or success, there is a good chance that you are harboring incompatible or contradictory motives or beliefs about that topic. For example:

- You may believe that the topic is important, but that it is "not good."
- You may believe that the topic is important, but "not attainable."
- You may believe that the topic "not important," in which case there would almost certainly be other, <u>unrecognized</u> motives, desires, or beliefs involved.

One way to begin identifying such hidden motives or desires is to complete sentences like the following: "When it comes to [*topic*], what I really want is…," or "As far as [*topic*] is concerned, my greatest desire would be…" In the case of hidden beliefs, you can similarly try to identify them by completing sentences like the following: "What [*topic*] really means to me is…," or "In my opinion, [*topic*]…"

CONCLUSION

Contrary to popular belief, thoughts and feelings are not separate and independent aspects of your conscious experience, since (1) your thoughts almost always occur in a "bed" of (sometimes very subtle) feeling; (2) many feelings—"curious," "bored," "interested"—actually describe different <u>ways</u> of thinking; and (3) certain types of "thinking feelings" tend to be associated with particular <u>types</u> of thinking: for example, feeling "confused" about something can lead you to *ponder* or *analyze* it, feeling "skeptical" about something can cause you to *judge* it, and so on.

Since you tend to experience a continuous flow of thoughts during most of your waking hours, it is useful periodically to "take stock" not only of <u>what</u> you tend to think about a lot, but also of the <u>feelings</u> that tend to accompany these thoughts. If you believe that you think about certain topics "too much" or "too little," then it is highly likely that you are holding conflicting or contradictory beliefs about these topics.

NOTE

1. An important exception would psychotherapists, most of whom appreciate the intimate connection between feelings and thoughts.

CHAPTER 9

CONSCIOUSNESS AND COMMUNITY

Up to this point we have limited our discussion of consciousness primarily to the individual: what you or I or any other person experiences "inside the head" during our waking hours. But since we are all social beings, the reality of living is that each conscious individual is necessarily part of some larger grouping—partners, spouses, friends, relatives, coworkers, family, team, club, organization, company, neighborhood, community—comprising <u>two or more</u> conscious beings. Since most of us belong to several such groups, a good deal of our conscious experience is shaped by our contacts with other group members. Our consciousness can also be substantially affected by the manner in which we experience the many other "unaffiliated" people we encounter in our daily lives. Indeed, it is probably no exaggeration to say that **the quality of your life is determined in large part by your relationships with other people.** For this reason, the main goals of this chapter are to encourage you to reflect on your typical ways of relating to others and to provide you with some tools for clarifying and understanding your relationships with the important people in your life.

As we saw briefly in the initial discussion of feeling states (chapter 5), there are certain types of feelings that are <u>uniquely</u> connected with your interactions with other people. In this chapter we will discuss these different states in some detail and explore the different types of <u>beliefs</u> about

Mindworks: Becoming More Conscious in an Unconscious World, pp. 173–204

others that can cause you to experience many of these "interpersonal" feelings. Following this we will suggest some exercises that can help you to get a clearer picture of your emotional relationships with significant people in your life. Next, in a section titled, "Getting to Know You," we will pay special attention to how your beliefs can affect the way you experience people you do not know well or people you are meeting for the first time. We will conclude the chapter with a discussion of an age-old dilemma: how to reconcile the "conflicting" needs of the individual and the community.

"INTERPERSONAL" FEELING STATES

The dictionary analysis identified more than 150 terms that can used to describe how you feel toward others. These terms can, in turn, be organized into 39 different "interpersonal" feeling states. Like most of the other feeling states already discussed, many of these interpersonal feelings can be paired together as "positive" and "negative" polar opposites of each other. However, in the case of interpersonal feelings, the negative feeling states substantially outnumber the positive states (25 to 14). Let us now examine these interpersonal states under three general headings: feelings of "relatedness," "comparative" feelings, and "reactive" feelings.

Feelings of Relatedness

Many important aspects of your conscious experience are shaped by the emotional relationships that you have with others. What are the emotional connections that you have with other people in your life? How close do you feel toward your friends, family, neighbors, and coworkers? How do you typically relate to strangers?

Probably the most fundamental of all such relatedness feelings are the polar opposites, <u>loving</u> and <u>hating</u>. Since love and hate are both complex feelings, they can assume several different forms. In the case of loving feelings, there are at least three different versions: <u>romantic</u> love, <u>nonromantic</u> love, and <u>caring</u>. For example, when you experience a feeling of <u>romantic</u> love in relation to your spouse or partner, you might say that you feel "in love with," romantic, adoring, smitten, infatuated with, or enamoured. Such feelings of romantic love are also often connected with <u>sexual</u> feelings. (Since sexual feelings are not <u>necessarily</u> interpersonal and are almost always accompanied by physical sensations, they have already been discussed under "physical" feelings in chapter 6.) On the other hand, if your loving feeling is <u>nonromantic</u>, it might be captured by words such as like, fond of, cherish, or affectionate. You can, of course, experience both romantic and nonromantic loving feelings toward the same person. (Since the word "love" has a number of different meanings and can be an emotionally loaded term, some people are uncomfortable using it to describe their feelings in friendships that are nonromantic and non-sexual; for such people the preferred term is usually "like.") Finally, <u>caring</u> refers to the way you feel when you are inclined to <u>act</u> on your loving feelings. Variations on feeling caring toward another person would include feeling kind, warm, nurturing, tender, protective, maternal, or fatherly toward that person. Note that you often combine these different types of loving feelings, since you usually "like" or feel "loving" toward those you "care about," and vise versa.

The negative or polar opposite feeling to loving is, of course, <u>hating</u>. Alternative ways to describe hateful feelings would be to say that you feel hostile or antagonistic toward the other person or that you have feelings of malice, enmity, dislike, animosity, or loathing toward that person. Closely related to hatefulness is to feel "angry" or "mad" at someone, a "bodily" feeling state that was also discussed earlier in chapter 6. Whereas angry feelings arise rapidly in your awareness and tend to last for a relatively short time, hate tends to be much longer lasting. Indeed, it is possible to carry hateful feelings toward particular people over a period of many years. These long-lasting feelings of hatred can be directed at particular individuals, but they also often involve groups, as evidenced in places such as Northern Ireland, Africa, and the Middle East, not to mention our own country (e.g., the infamous "Hatfield-McCoy" rivalry). Figure 9.1 shows the "enriched" love-hate continuum.

It should be noted that <u>caring</u> also has another negative polar opposite, feeling <u>vengeful</u>, which will be discussed below under "reactive" feelings. In a sense, "vengefulness is to hate as caring is to love," since feelings of caring and vengefulness both incline you to take <u>action</u> in relation to the other person; in the case of caring, the feeling is associated with wanting to <u>help</u>, while with vengefulness the feeling is associated with wanting to <u>hurt</u> the other person.

It goes without saying that these two bipolar continua of feelings—loving/hating and caring/vengeful—are closely related. That is, you will find it much easier to feel caring toward someone else if you also love or like them, and you are much more likely to feel vengeful toward another person if you also feel hateful toward that person.

How do your beliefs relate to feelings of love and hate? As already suggested earlier in Chapter 2, **most if not all of your negative feelings about other people are based on your beliefs**. In the case of hate, you usually feel hateful toward someone because you believe either that they have hurt or harmed you in some way or that they represent some kind of threat to you (i.e., that they <u>might</u> do harm to you.) In the latter case,

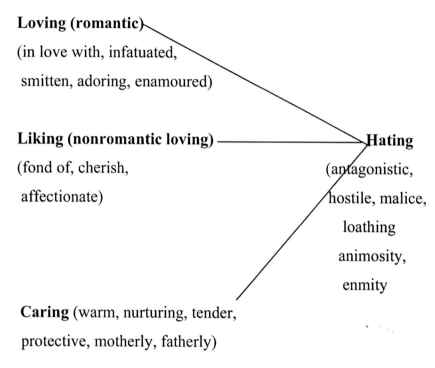

Figure 9.1.   The "enriched" love-hate continuum.

there is usually also an element of <u>fear</u> involved—which is why many psychologists contend that feelings of anger or hate are often based on fear. While this helps to explain why fear is often regarded as one of our most primitive and basic feeling states, it should also be noted that fear is <u>also</u> based on beliefs, that is, the belief that something or someone can or will do you harm. Similarly, feeling hurt—another emotion that can generate feelings of hatred—is based on a belief that someone <u>has</u> rejected you or otherwise done you harm.

In the case of positive interpersonal feelings such as loving or liking, the role of beliefs is not as clear. While it could be argued that you could come to like or love somebody because you believe that they are beautiful or good or because you believe that they have treated you well, it is usually much more difficult in any individual instance to trace the emergence of such positive feelings to particular beliefs. Most people, for example, do not like or love everyone whom they see as either good or beautiful, and most people do not necessarily love or like another person merely because they believe that person has treated them well. Romantic love, in particular, is very difficult to "explain" on the basis of particular beliefs.

EXERCISE

Think of a person for whom you have recently felt loving feelings. (a) Write down at least two related beliefs that you hold about that person. Repeat the exercise with two other people: (b) one for whom you have recently felt caring and (c) one for whom you felt hateful or vengeful.

Even though love and hate probably receive more attention in psychology and in literature than do most other feelings of relatedness, there are a great many much more subtle relatedness feelings that govern most of our emotional relationships with others. Like loving and hating, many of these more subtle feelings can be viewed as either "positive" or "negative." On the positive side, these subtle feelings of relatedness can take at least three different forms: <u>connectedness</u>, <u>trust</u>, and <u>empathy</u>. When you feel <u>connected</u> to another person—a good friend, for example—you might say that you "feel a strong connection" or "have rapport" with that person. Other ways to describe such a feeling would be to say that you feel like minded, related to, in tune with, allied with or identified with, or feel a kinship with that person. A milder version of positive connectedness would be to feel friendly or "neighborly" toward the other person. It is important to note that when you feel both strongly connected and loving toward someone else, several other feelings are likely to arise: <u>intimacy</u>, <u>trust</u>, <u>vulnerability</u>, and possibly <u>sexuality</u>.

On the negative (<u>disconnectedness</u>) end of this continuum there are two different types of feelings that we shall call "passive" and "active" disconnectedness, respectively. When you feel <u>passively</u> disconnected from others—that is, when you believe that it is not something that you have <u>chosen</u> to do—you might say that you feel alone, lonely, forlorn, left out, ignored, excluded, or like an outcast, a pariah, or an outsider. This feeling of passive disconnectedness can occur in relation to another person, but it most often arises in relation a <u>group</u>: "They make me feel like an outsider." When you feel <u>actively</u> disconnected—that is, when you believe that the disconnection is something you have chosen to do—you might say that you feel aloof, distant, isolated, separated, or alienated: "I've distanced myself from them." Note that while passive disconnectedness suggests a feeling of helplessness—"Those people don't connect with or care about me"—, active disconnectedness is to a certain extent a matter of choice: "I've disconnected myself from those people (that person)."

A close cousin of connectedness is <u>trust</u>. Here again we have a bipolar continuum with <u>trusting</u> at the positive end and <u>suspicious</u> at the negative end. Alternatives to trusting someone else would be to "believe in," "rely on," or "have faith in" them. There are even more variations on being suspicious of another person: you can also feel guarded, leery, defensive, distrustful, doubtful, unsure of, mistrustful, or "on guard" when you are around them. When it comes to your relationships with others, these negative feelings are extremely important, not only because of how they affect the way you treat other people, but also because of how their behavior toward you is affected. Obviously, people will tend to treat you one way if you trust them, and quite differently if you are suspicious of them.

A third subtle feeling state that is closely related to connectedness and trust is empathy. Empathy basically has to do with putting yourself mentally and emotionally in the other person's place, imagining how it would be to be feeling and thinking what the other person is feeling and thinking. In addition to feeling empathic toward another person, you could also feel "compassionate" or "understanding of" that person. On the negative (nonempathic) end of the empathy continuum is intolerance. Besides feeling that you have "no tolerance for" someone else's views or actions, you could also feel "unsympathetic" toward them, "offended" by them, or that you have "no use for" them. (Terms like "judgemental" and "self-righteous" might also apply, but you would ordinarily use these terms to label or judge another person's feelings or behavior rather than to describe your own feelings.) And just like suspicion and trust, empathy and intolerance are feelings that others are likely to "pick up on."

These three continua of subtle relatedness feeling states are obviously related, since you are better able to trust someone or to feel empathic if you also feel connected to them, and you are more likely to feel defensive or intolerant toward another person if you also feel disconnected or distant. These same three continua, in turn, are also related to the "loving-hating" and "caring-vengeful" continua. That is, if you have feelings of love or caring toward another person, it is much easier to establish rapport and trust and to feel empathic. At the same time, feeling disconnected from someone else or feeling suspicious or intolerant of them

EXERCISE

Complete the following sentence:
"I feel an emotional distance between myself and_____."
(b) Think of at least two other feelings that you have toward this person or group.
(c) When was the last time you felt really alone, like an outsider, like you did not belong? Can you think of any beliefs about yourself that might be associated with this feeling?

makes it easier to feel hateful or revengeful. In other words, when you are experiencing any one of these positive or negative feelings toward another person, it is easy to "slip" into one of the related feelings.

We will conclude this discussion of "relatedness" feelings by considering two additional states that, at first glance, do not appear to be particularly associated with each other: jealousy and dependency. They are, however, closely connected. Another feature of these two unique feelings is that it is difficult to find alternative terms for them. While jealousy can be used to mean "envious" (see below), the sense in which it is used here involves feelings of possessiveness directed at someone whose affections and loyalty are extremely important to you (that "someone" is frequently a spouse or lover, but he or she could also be a close relative,[1] friend, or even a child). This feeling of "jealous possessiveness" is often accompanied by a feeling of insecurity or uncertainty about the other person's affections or loyalty toward you. The feeling of jealousy is thus based on the belief that you are in competition with other people or with other circumstances in that person's life (their work or hobbies, for example). This belief (which may in turn be based on negative beliefs about your own attractiveness or desirability) gives rise to the fear that you might "lose" the affections or loyalty of that person to someone or something else. Typical situations when such feelings are particularly likely to arise are when a partner, lover, child, or close friend (a) has strong positive feelings toward people other than you or (b) invests a lot of time and energy in pursuits—job, hobby, and so forth, —that do not involve you.

Since jealousy is frequently associated with fears that arise from negative beliefs about your own adequacy or attractiveness, jealous feelings are particularly likely to appear in your consciousness when you believe that the person in question might be sexually or emotionally interested in someone else. Jealousy is thus an especially potent feeling when it is associated with sexual feelings (see chapter 6) and with two negative feelings that also carry "high energy": fear and anger. The power of jealousy, of course, is reflected in the large number of assaults and homicides involving spouses and lovers that are committed every year.

The final "relatedness" feeling state is dependency. This is a very subtle feeling that may be difficult for many people to recognize and label. Thus, while you might be able to look back on your relationship with someone else and say that you acted in a "dependent" fashion, can you describe what is it like to feel dependent? Other than a feeling of "attachment to" or the feeling of "being able to rely on" another person, I was not able to find other words for describing such a feeling. Another way to look at a feeling of dependency is that, much like jealousy, it may involve feelings of possessiveness and insecurity that are associated with a belief that you would "not be able to get along with-

EXERCISE

(a) Complete the following sentences:
  "I really feel connected..."
  "Jealousy and possessiveness...
  "I have little tolerance for..."
(b) What beliefs do you associate with your answers?

out" the other person and a consequent fear of "losing" that person.[2] In this sense, feelings of dependency can often be accompanied by feelings of jealousy.

"Comparative" Feelings

How often do you compare yourself with others? How often do you judge others in terms of your own characteristics? There are at least two different continua of feeling states that can come into play when you evaluate someone else's experiences or qualities <u>in relation to yourself</u>. The first continuum—<u>admiration</u> versus <u>envy</u>—applies to a situation where you believe that another person has something that you lack but that you value highly or that you might want for yourself: "I wish I had his money and good looks." "I'd sure like to be as successful as he is?" The "positive" end of this continuum comes into play when you respond to the person with feelings of <u>admiration</u>. Variations on admiration would include "looking up to" the other person or holding her or him in "high esteem." An extreme form of admiration would be "worshiping" or "idolizing" the other person. [It is important not to confuse "idolizing"—which is a <u>feeling</u> that you can have toward someone you admire a great deal—and "idealizing," which is a <u>judgement</u> we make when a person seems unable to see fault in ("idealizes") someone else.]

Closely related to admiration is a feeling of <u>respect</u>. While not necessarily a "comparative" feeling (it might also be listed under "connectedness"), respect is included here because it frequently accompanies admiration. The main differences are that (a) respect, in contrast to admiration, does not necessarily involve qualities that <u>you</u> would like to have or emulate and (b) while respect usually accompanies admiration, you can respect someone but not necessarily admire them: "I respect the sincerity of her religious faith." The opposite end of the continuum of respect is, of course, <u>disrespect</u>.

The "negative" pole of the admiration continuum includes two some-what different types of feelings: <u>inferiority</u> and <u>envy</u>. You feel envious or inferior when the other person's experiences, personal qualities, or pos-sessions that you might want for yourself cause you distress or discomfort. Alternatives to feeling inferior would include feeling inadequate or incompetent. About the only other word that might describe envious feel-ings is "jealousy." This word suggests not merely a sense of envy, but also a sense of <u>resentment</u> as well: "It really bugs me that he's so much more suc-cessful than I am." (In the preceeding section we also used "jealousy" to describe a very different kind of feeling having to do with possessiveness).

In short, while feelings of admiration, as well as feelings of envy and inferiority, can all arise in response to a belief that someone else has something that you lack and would like to have, admiration is usually accompanied by a feeling of <u>respect</u>, while inferiority is usually accompa-nied by a feeling of <u>discomfort</u> and envy by a feeling of <u>resentment</u>.

The second "comparative" continuum applies when someone else has experiences or personal qualities that you would <u>not</u> want for yourself. In this case the "positive" response would be to feel <u>sympathetic</u>: "I'm sure glad I'm not married to his wife!" Variations on sympathy would be to "feel compassion for" or "commiserate with" the other person. A more extreme version of sympathy, perhaps bordering on criticism, would be to "pity" or "feel sorry for" the other person. The "negative" end of the sym-pathy continuum would be to feel <u>disdainful</u> toward the other person: "When it comes to men, she sure has a knack for picking losers." Besides feeling disdainful you might also feel contemptious or scornful or "toler-ate" or "put up with" the other person.

An interesting aspect of these "comparative" feeling states is that our language has words to describe both the positive <u>and</u> negative feeling states that can arise whenever you believe that the other person has something that you lack-- admiration versus a sense of inferiority or envy-- but there are few words, if any, to describe positive feelings that might arise when the roles are reversed. That is, when you believe that you possess something desirable that the other person lacks, the only words for describing how you might feel in such a situation appear to be negative: to feel superior, smug, or haughty or "look down on" or feel that the other person is "beneath" you. If you do not feel this way ("superior") in such a situation, is there any <u>other</u> way you can feel about it? Perhaps the closest approximation to an alternative would be to feel "blessed," "privileged," "favored," "lucky," or "fortunate." Such feelings would acknowledge that you enjoy certain things that the other person lacks, but do not "put down" the other person in the process. Indeed, since feeling "blessed" or "privileged" does not really <u>require</u> a relative judgement, you can feel this way without comparing yourself to

EXERCISE

Complete the following sentences:
• "The people I most admire..."
• (What beliefs about goodness are implied in your answer?)
• "Sometimes I envy people who..."
• "I feel fortunate that I..."
(What beliefs about yourself are implied these last two answers?)

others. In short, this discussion suggests still another bipolar feeling continuum: <u>privileged</u> versus <u>superior.</u>

Once again, we find direct parallels between these "comparative" feelings and the other interpersonal feeling states already discussed. For example, if there is someone you know who has qualities that you lack but would like to have for yourself, it is much easier to have feelings of admiration or respect toward them if you also like, trust or feel identified with them. By contrast, you are much more likely to feel disrespectful, envious, or inferior if you also feel hateful toward, or distant from, them. Similarly, if you believe that you are privileged because you have some positive quality that another person lacks, you will be less likely to feel superior or disdainful if you like or feel connected to that person.

"Reactive" Feelings

There are several different types of interpersonal feeling states that can arise in <u>reaction</u> either to what others say or do ("other-oriented" reactions) or to what <u>you</u> do in relation to them ("self-oriented" reactions). Let us start with other-oriented reactions. Many of the feeling states already described also arise as reactions to others, but so far we have discussed only one such state, <u>vengeful</u> feelings that you can experience when you feel that someone has done you wrong and you want to retaliate.

In addition to feeling <u>vengeful,</u> you might also feel vindictive or revengeful. (Milder versions of feelings of vindictiveness or vengefulness would include feeling indignant, sore, or resentful, which will be discussed below under "reactive" feelings.) When it comes to reacting to <u>how others behave toward you</u>, there are basically two other sets of bipolar feelings: those that can arise when you believe someone has been "nice" to you or "done you a favor," and those that can arise when you believe you have been wronged or harmed (feelings of "victimization"). Let us now look more closely at each of these two sets of other-oriented reactions.

When you believe that someone has been nice to you or has done you a favor, you can experience at least four different kinds of emotional responses. Positive responses would be to feel either <u>appreciative</u> or <u>charmed</u>. Negative responses would be to feel either <u>obliged</u> or <u>suffocated</u>. If your reaction is to feel <u>appreciative</u>, you could also say you feel thankful or grateful:" I really appreciate what he did for me." Variations on feeling <u>charmed</u> would include feeling flattered and spoiled or, at the extreme, enchanted, enthralled, and enraptured: "I felt very flattered by all his compliments." On the other hand, if you feel <u>obligated</u> because you believe that the favors someone has done for you are either overdone or undeserved, you could also say that you feel "indebted to" or "beholden to" that person. Finally, if you believe that the positive attentions of someone else are excessive, you might feel <u>suffocated</u> or possibly "smothered." (Another possible reaction to someone else's excessive praise or attention is to feel <u>embarrassed</u>, a response which is discussed below under "self-oriented" reactions.)

There is an equally diverse set of feelings that you might have when you believe that someone else has mistreated you or harmed you. As you might expect, almost all of your possible emotional reactions in such a situation are negative. In addition to feeling <u>vengeful,</u> which we have already discussed, you might feel <u>resentful</u>, <u>hurt</u>, <u>unloved</u>, <u>threatened</u>, <u>taken advantage of</u>, or <u>frustrated</u>. As mentioned earlier in this chapter, feeling <u>resentful</u> is a "milder" version of feeling vengeful. Also, resentfulness does not necessarily include the notion of retaliating against or harming the other person that characterizes vengefulness. Variations on feeling resentful would include feeling "indignant" or "sore." Among the many variations on feeling <u>hurt</u> would be to feel "let down," "crestfallen," "wounded," or "heartbroken." In addition to feeling <u>unloved</u>, you could also feel "rejected," "uncared for," or "unlovable." If you feel <u>threatened</u> by someone, you might also say you feel "insecure" or "vulnerable." Alternatives to feeling that someone has <u>taken advantage</u> of you would be to feel "violated," "offended," "victimized," "oppressed," "ripped off," or "gypped." Variations on feeling <u>frustrated</u> would be to feel "thwarted" or "exasperated."

Other than empathy, about the only positive emotional reaction that is available to you when you believe that someone has mistreated you is to feel <u>forgiving</u>. Alternatives to feeling forgiving would be to feel "generous," "accepting," "tolerant," "understanding," or "lenient" or possibly to "condone" the other person's actions. But how can you manage to feel forgiving when you also believe the person has harmed or mistreated you? Perhaps the surest path to forgiveness in such a situation is through another interpersonal feeling state already discussed: <u>empathy</u>. The first challenge in developing some empathy for the other person is to try to put yourself in his place: what was going on in that person's consciousness that would lead him to do what he did? What motivated him? What beliefs and what feelings was he acting upon? If you were in his situation and felt the way he did, is there any chance that you might have done the same thing?

Several of these "reactive" feeling states appear to be mirror images of each other. Thus, the opposite of feeling charmed or flattered would be to feel hurt or rejected. Similarly, the opposite of feeling grateful or appreciative would be to feel that you have been taken advantage of or to feel resentful.

The converse of reacting to what others do in relation to you would be to react emotionally to what <u>you</u> do in relation to others. About the only "positive" feeling that you can experience under such circumstances is <u>proud</u>—a reaction that can arise when you realize that you have done something for others (you could also say you feel "satisfied"). On the negative side, these "self-oriented" reactions comprise at least four very important feeling states: <u>guilty</u>, <u>apologetic</u>, <u>embarrassed</u>, and <u>self-conscious</u>. Certainly the longest-lasting of the three is <u>guilt</u>. Whereas embarrassment and self-consciousness are feelings that can come and go relatively quickly (especially if you can remove yourself from the situation that initially led you to have these feelings), guilt can persist for days at a time and sometimes even for many years. Sometimes guilt can also lead you to feel angry. Alternatives to feeling guilty would be to feel "ashamed," "regretful," or "remorseful." Feeling <u>apologetic</u> is, of course, closely related to feeling guilty. The principal difference is that while both feelings involve the belief that "I did wrong," feeling apologetic also implies that you want somehow to "admit it" and possibly to "make amends." Alternatives to feeling apologetic include feeling "sorry," "contrite," or "penitent."

<u>Embarrassment</u> was mentioned above in connection with a situation where you believe that someone's else is lavishing praise or attention on you that is undeserved or overdone: "I was embarrassed by all the nice things she said." However, there is another kind of situation where you can feel embarrassed by something <u>you</u> did. While this form of embarrassment is closely related to guilt, one important difference is that embarrassment usually occurs when you feel you have done something inappropriate or wrong <u>in the presence of</u>, or <u>with the knowledge of</u>, other people: "I made a fool of myself." Moreover, embarrassment is typically a "milder" feeling than guilt and usually lasts for a much shorter period. If you feel extremely embarrassed you might say you feel "humiliated" or "mortified." While the word "sheepish" is also sometimes used to describe embarrassment, it can also be used in the sense of "apologetic."

The final feeling state in this group is <u>self-consciousness</u>. When you feel this way you might also say you feel "bashful," "shy," "conspicuous," "exposed," or "on the spot": "I felt that everyone was looking at me" Self-consciousness, of course, is closely related to feeling embarrassed or feeling apologetic, in the following sense: if you do something in the presence of others that you believe to be "wrong," you are much more likely to feel embarrassed or apologetic if you have <u>also</u> been feeling self-conscious. As a matter of fact, your feelings of embarrassment in such a situation will probably make you feel even <u>more</u> self-conscious! In other words: **self-consciousness intensifies embarrassment, and embarrassment intensifies self-consciousness!**

Summary

This taxonomy of feeling states that have to do with other people makes it clear that the emotional or feeling side of human relations can be extremely varied and complex. Figure 9.2 shows 39 of the different interpersonal states arrayed along a "positive-negative" continuum.

One very practical implication of this taxonomy is that you can use it as a guide to a fuller understanding of your own emotional relationships with the other people in your life. The taxonomy suggests, for example, that if you want to understand the emotional aspects of your interpersonal relationships, there are at least three basic sets of questions that you can ask yourself:

1. How do I <u>relate</u> to others? What kinds of feelings do I typically direct toward them? How loving or caring am I? Do I feel a close connection to them? How trusting of them am I? How much empathy do I have for them? How often do I feel suspicious, hateful, or intolerant toward others? How often do I feel lonely and disconnected from others? And when it comes to the people I care most about, how attached or dependent on them do I feel? Do their affections for other people make me feel uncomfortable or jealous?

2. How do I <u>compare</u> myself to others? Do I admire and respect their positive qualities, or do I tend to be envious of their talents and success? Am I sympathetic to their faults, or do their limitations and failures make me feel superior or disdainful?

3. How do I <u>react</u> to the way others treat me? When they do me favors, do I feel appreciative, or does it make me feel uncomfortable or obligated? When they show me a lot of attention or love, do I feel good, or do I feel suffocated? And when someone mistreats me, am I inclined to carry a grudge? Do people often take

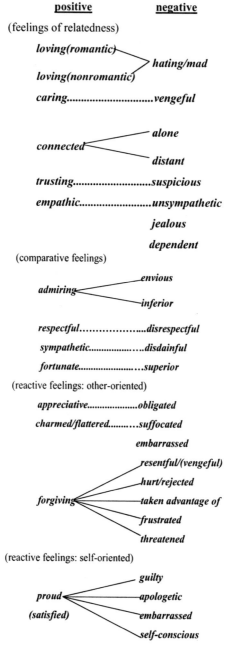

Figure 9.2.   Thirty-nine of the different interpersonal states arrayed along a "positive-negative" continuum.

advantage of me? Are my feelings easily hurt? How easy is it for me to forgive others for their mistakes? Finally, how do I react to the way I treat other people? Do I frequently find myself apologizing or feeling guilty about my actions toward others? How self-conscious am I in the presence of others? Am I easily embarrassed?

TAKING STOCK OF YOUR "FEELING RELATIONSHIPS" WITH OTHERS

In this section I will suggest some simple exercises that you can do to assess the affective relationships that you have with significant people in your life. You might find it useful to use the exercise to assess your affective relationship with people such as the following:

- Spouse or partner
- Significant relative (parent, child, uncle, etc.)
- Close friend
- Professional colleague, coworker, boss, or subordinate
- Service recipient(s) (client, student, patient, etc.)
- Service provider (physician, lawyer, therapist, teacher, contractor, etc.)
- Neighbor

Using the Feeling Rating Form (Table 9.1), there are three basic exercises that you can do:

1. **How you feel toward the other person.** In this basic exercise you simply indicate how often you experience each of the feelings by circling the appropriate number.
2. **How the other person feels toward you.** Here you record your beliefs concerning how often the other person experiences each of the 39 feelings in relation to you.
3. **What the other person thinks about how you feel toward her or him.** This is the most complicated exercise, since it requires you to record your beliefs concerning the other person's beliefs about your feelings: "She thinks I don't love her." The basic idea here is to document any beliefs you might hold about the other person's beliefs.

Table 9.1.   Self-Rated Interpersonal Feeling States

Date: ___/___/___
Time:_____a.m./p.m. (circle one)
Place:_____

Subjec person:_____   Object person:_____

How often does the subject person feel each of the following ways toward the object person? (Circle the appropriate number for each feeling.)

	All (or most) of the time	Frequently	Occasionally	Never
Connected	4	3	2	1
Caring	4	3	2	1
Guilty	4	3	2	1
Respectful	4	3	2	1
Distant	4	3	2	1
Possessive	4	3	2	1
Trusting	4	3	2	1
Sexual	4	3	2	1
Dependent	4	3	2	1
Suspicious	4	3	2	1
Angry	4	3	2	1
Intolerant	4	3	2	1
Loving (romantice)	4	3	2	1
Loving (nonromantic)	4	3	2	1
Empathic	4	3	2	1
Hateful	4	3	2	1

In comparing herself/himself with the object person, how often does the subject feel:

Admiring	4	3	2	1
Envious	4	3	2	1
Inferior	4	3	2	1
Fortunate	4	3	2	1
Disdainful	4	3	2	1
Superior	4	3	2	1

How often does the subject person experience each of the ollowing feelings in <u>reaction</u> to what the object person does?

Appreciative	4	3	2	1
Charmed/flattered	4	3	2	1
Forgiving	4	3	2	1
Respectful	4	3	2	1
Sympathetic	4	3	2	1
Suffocated	4	3	2	1
Obligated	4	3	2	1
Unsympathetic	4	3	2	1
Resentful	4	3	2	1
Hurt/rejected	4	3	2	1
Frustrated	4	3	2	1
Taken advanage of	4	3	2	1

Table continues on next page

Table 9.1.   Self-Rated Interpersonal Feeling States Continued

	All (or most) of the time	Frequently	Occasionally	Never
Threatened	4	3	2	1
Self-conscious	4	3	2	1
Insecure	4	3	2	1
Embarassed	4	3	2	1
Vengeful	4	3	2	1

By combining ratings from #1 and #2 on the <u>same</u> chart, you can see where (1) the two of you share common feelings toward each other, and (2) there are discrepancies or imbalances in your mutual feelings.

By combining ratings from #1 and #3, you can identify areas where your feelings might be <u>misunderstood</u> by the other person.

"GETTING TO KNOW YOU"

Most of us tend to think that our beliefs about other people and the feelings that we have toward them arise out of our <u>experience</u> with them: the other person acts in certain ways or treats us in certain ways, and we respond accordingly. However, it is highly likely that you and I have <u>already</u> formed certain beliefs about different "types" of people that can substantially affect the way we experience almost any person we come into contact with. These beliefs, in turn, cause us to express certain feelings toward others and to treat them in particular ways, <u>even if they are complete strangers</u>. Part of the challenge in "getting to know" another person is thus to suspend some of these beliefs long enough to experience the person as he or she really is.

When you meet somebody for the first time, how open are you to seeing them as they "really" are? If you consider yourself to be a fair-minded person with a minimum of prejudices, you might answer, "I'm very open! I don't harbor a lot of preconceived notions about people." But the fact of the matter is that it is very difficult for <u>any</u> of us to view a new acquaintance with a completely "clean slate." The problem here, as I have already suggested, is our <u>beliefs</u>: most of us have developed an elaborate set of beliefs having to do with the various conditions under which we might first encounter someone we have never met before:

- groups to which the person belongs
- appearance/demeanor

- status/occupation
- history/past behavior
- interests/personal habits
- role/relationship to you
- meeting place/context

All of us harbor beliefs (and associated feelings) about each of these things, and there are few of us, if any, who would be able to prevent these beliefs from having at least some effect on how we perceive a new acquaintance and how we behave toward them. And it goes without saying that the same argument would apply to how the other person perceives and behaves toward <u>us</u>: their beliefs would condition the way that they experience us. In other words, **how two complete strangers experience their initial encounter will be substantially affected by the respective beliefs that they bring to that encounter.**

Let us now look a little more closely at the particular circumstances that can affect the way you experience a person whom you are encountering for the first time:

Group Membership

Some of our most powerful beliefs have to do with stereotypic traits that we associate with groupings such as a person's race, gender, age, nationality, or political orientation:

- "Many Asians…"
- "Women are more inclined than men to…"
- "Most old people…"
- "The Irish…"
- "Liberals can be counted on to…"

Other groupings about which you might also hold strong beliefs would include the person's <u>family</u>, <u>religious affiliation</u>, <u>organizational memberships</u> (American Civil Liberties Union, National Rifle Association, etc.), and <u>sexual orientation</u>. There are not many of us who can honestly say that we do not harbor at least some beliefs about such groupings, and many of us hold very strong beliefs that condition the way we experience someone who appears to belong to a particular group. Such preconceptions can be especially powerful when your beliefs are associated with strong feelings. Here are some typical examples:

- If you encounter someone from your <u>own</u> group—whether he or she be of the same race, sex, age, family, religion, nationality, or political or sexual orientation—you may be more likely to feel *connected, trusting,* and *empathic.* Such feelings are especially likely to arise if you are a member of a "minority" group. However, if you happen to harbor negative beliefs about your own group, you may instead feel *suspicious* or *intolerant.*

- If you encounter someone from a group that is <u>different</u> from the one you belong to, and if you hold strong negative beliefs about that group, a wide range of feelings can emerge: *distant, disdainful, superior,* or even *inferior.* If you believe that members of the other group harbor negative beliefs about <u>your</u> group, you might also feel *resentful, suspicious, hateful,* or *insecure.* Finally, if you believe that your group has been persecuted or victimized by the other group, you might also feel *guarded, threatened, fearful, hostile,* or *vengeful.*

- If you believe that the group to which the other person belongs is inferior to your own group, you might feel *intolerant, disdainful,* or *superior.*

- If your encounter is with <u>several</u> people from a particular group that is different from your own group—for example, you happen to be the only man in a group of women, the only white person in a group of African Americans, the only American in a group of Japanese, the only Democrat in a group of Republicans, or the only elderly person in a group of teenagers—you will also be likely to feel *self-conscious* and possibly even *afraid.*

Clearly, if you bring any of these feelings into your initial encounter with another person or group, it will <u>change the way you experience them,</u> regardless of the "true" nature of that person or group.

EXERCISE

(a) **Complete the following sentences:**
   "Fat people…"
   "Sexual attractiveness…"
   "People who dress well…"
(2) **Identify some of the beliefs that are implied in each of the completed sentences. What interpersonal feelings do you associate with these beliefs?**

Appearance/Demeanor

The fact that many of us believe that physical appearance is of great importance is demonstrated in a variety of ways: the highly profitable cosmetics and fashion industries, the proliferation of diet books and diet systems, the rapidly expanding use of cosmetic surgery, and the burgeoning business in body building and body sculpting equipment (as I write this there seems to be a particular fixation on "abs"). No wonder, then, that how someone looks when you first meet them can have such a powerful effect on how you perceive them and how you act toward them.

While the <u>particular</u> beliefs that we harbor about physical appearance or demeanor may vary considerably from person to person, the fact that most of us believe that beauty and sexual attractiveness are very important is underscored by our tendency to "notice" people who are physically very attractive or sexual (recall from chapter 2 that our unconscious mind routinely directs our conscious attention toward anything that we believe to be "important"). Such a widespread belief is not lost, of course, on the advertising and entertainment industries, which try to insure that you'll pay attention to their products and productions by using models and actors who appear to be very beautiful and very sexual.

In short, when you encounter another person who looks very attractive or sexy to you, your experience of that person is likely to be colored by any of several feelings that may arise: *sexual, admiring, envious, or inferior.* Which feeling will arise, and how you will actually <u>behave</u>, depends, of course, on your own unique set of beliefs about beauty, sexuality, and so forth.

EXERCISE

When you initially encounter someone who is very wealthy, powerful, or famous, (a) are you likely to "pay more attention" to them than you would if they did not possess any of the qualities? If your answer is "yes" or "probably," why is this so? What beliefs would cause you to treat them differently? (b) Is it likely that any of the following interpersonal feelings might arise in your consciousness: admiring, envious, angry, inferior, or in awe of? Any other feelings? What beliefs might underlie these feelings? (c) If you think somebody has much less wealth, power, or status than you do, would this affect how you relate to them? Would you be likely to feel superior, disdainful, fortunate, or sympathetic? What beliefs might be involved in such feelings?

EXERCISE

(a) Complete the following sentences:
"The best thing about people who work in my field or profession..."
"The worst thing about people who work in my field or profession..."
(b) What beliefs about your field or profession are implied in your answers?

Other aspects of personal appearance about which you might hold beliefs that could influence the way you experience any stranger would include their <u>dress</u> (how formal, how fashionable, how expensive, how tattered, etc.), <u>grooming</u> (hairstyle, makeup, cleanliness, etc.), <u>stature</u>, <u>weight</u>, <u>body type</u>, and <u>disabilities</u>. Many of us have also formed beliefs about people based upon how they <u>speak</u>—how low- or high-pitched their voice is, whether they speak in a monotone or with a lot of inflection, and whether they speak with an accent (southern, New York, Germanic, French, Spanish, etc.). Once again, these beliefs can affect how we experience people when we first meet them.

It is important to realize that your beliefs about certain groups can affect <u>how you think about</u> any group <u>before</u> you initially encounter a member of that group. While the actual encounter may "surprise" you if it does not confirm your beliefs, the fact that you have already formed beliefs about that group increases the likelihood that you will "notice" things about that person that confirm those beliefs, and "overlook" those things that contradict them.

Status/Occupation

In a country like the United States, there are few people who have not developed strong beliefs about issues such as wealth, power, and status. As a consequence, when it comes to initial contacts between people, their relative social status, wealth, and power can have profound effects on how they view each other and on the manner in which they relate to each other. Although there are potentially important differences among these three attributes, they are also mutually reinforcing: just as great wealth can contribute to your status and power, so can power and status enhance your wealth.

A person's job or occupation can also affect how you relate to them, in part because so many of us tend to "define" ourselves—our sense of "self"—in terms of the work that we do. Thus, when two strangers meet at a social gathering, it is almost assumed that one of the first pieces of information that will be exchanged will concern "what do you do for a living?" Learning what the other person's occupation is will almost certainly affect the way you experience them, simply because there are so many occupations about which people tend to hold stereotypic beliefs: used car salesperson, police officer, politician, college professor, lawyer, physician, school teacher, ballet dancer, rock musician, military officer, and so on. A variety of feelings can be associated with these stereotypic beliefs: *admiring, trusting, suspicious, curious, hateful, threatened, disdainful,* and so on.

Since almost all of us have developed a comprehensive set of beliefs about our <u>own</u> occupation, it is almost inevitable that you would relate in a special way to someone who works at your profession. Upon meeting such person, in contrast to someone from a different field, you would probably be more inclined to feel *connected, trusting, and empathic.*

Closely related to occupation is a person's level of <u>education</u>. In the belief systems of many people, education is the equivalent of status. Thus, some people with high levels of educational attainment may tend to feel *superior* or *disdainful* toward people with less education, and some people with less education are inclined to feel either *admiring, inferior,* or *envious* in the presence of highly educated people. Indeed, when people find themselves in a <u>group</u> whose educational level is very different from their own, they might also be inclined to feel *self-conscious.*

History/Past Behavior

When you know some highly significant fact about another person's past, it is very difficult—at least in your initial encounter—to view them or treat them like any other person. Again, this is because most of us have developed strong beliefs about certain kinds of behavior or experience. This is particularly true in the case of emotionally-loaded events that you have personally experienced: a serious illness, loss of a close relative, caring for a parent with Alzheimer's disease, having an abusive parent or spouse, and so on. In such cases there is a good chance that you will manifest one or more of the following feelings: *connected, caring, trusting, loving (nonromantic), empathic, or sympathetic.*

We have already discussed what can happen when you encounter someone who has attained high status of prestige (see the previous section), and you can expect to experience similar feelings when you run into someone who has been very successful or accomplished some remarkable feat: *admiring,* and possibly *envious, in awe,* or *inferior.* But what kinds of feelings might emerge if you know something negative or embarrassing about the person's past? Consider just a few of the possibilities that might affect your feelings, for example, if the person:

- has served time in prison
- recently flunked out of school or college
- has been a drug or alcohol abuser
- has been married four or five times
- is receiving public assistance
- has been hospitalized for mental illness
- has declared bankruptcy
- was recently fired from his job

Few of us could honestly say that, upon encountering a person whom we know to have done one or more of these things, we would not experience at least some of the following feelings: *suspicious, fearful, distant, unsympathetic, disdainful, fortunate, superior,* or *threatened* or—under some conditions—*empathic* or *sympathetic.*

Interests/Personal Habits

Knowledge of a new acquaintance's interests and personal habits can affect the way you initially experience them in much the same way that knowledge of their occupation can. This is particularly true when their interests and habits are the same or similar to yours. Consider just some of the many ways in which you might find a "match" between your and the other person's interests and habits:

- Hobbies (collecting, hunting, rock climbing, computers, body building, etc.)
- Spectator sports (especially if you support the same team!)
- Musical/literary/artistic tastes
- Personal values

One again, knowing that you and the other person share such things makes it likely that you will experience feelings such as the following: *connected, trusting,* and *empathic.*

Role/Relationship to You

How you approach almost any interpersonal encounter, including the feelings that you are likely to experience, will obviously be affected by the respective roles that you and the other person play in relation to each other. Among the more obvious relationships that can affect such encounters are <u>familial</u> (are you a parent, child, sibling, or other relation?), <u>job or work</u> (are you a supervisor, subordinate, or coworker?), and <u>friendship status</u> (are you a close friend, casual friend, acquaintance, or adversary?).

When it comes to encounters with strangers or with people you do not know very well, there is very often some kind of <u>service</u> involved. In such situations, you can be either a service <u>provider</u> or service <u>recipient</u>. Consider how many different service relationships there are that can affect how you are likely to feel toward the other person and the way you approach the encounter (the provider is listed first and the recipient second):

- lawyer/client
- doctor, health care provider/patient
- teacher/student
- salesperson/customer
- postal or other public employee/citizen
- telephone receptionist or operator/customer
- driver/passenger
- tour guide/tourist
- clergy/parishioner
- waiter, bartender, maitre d'/patron
- police officer/citizen
- you/panhandler
- you/stranger seeking help or advice
- stranger/you, in search of help or advice
- housekeeper, gardener, personal servant/homeowner

Most of us harbor beliefs about such relationships—what constitutes "proper" conduct on the part of the two parties, how much respect and consideration each party has a right to expect from the other, how much "service" the provider should be prepared to render—that can substantially affect not only how you feel and act toward the other person, but also how the other person feels about and treats you.

EXERCISE

(a) **Pick one of the relationships listed on the previous page and recall a recent encounter where you experienced one or more of the following: anger, a good deal of frustration, or a feeling of having been taken advantage of. List some of your beliefs about "proper" conduct that you feel were violated.**

(b) **Pick another one of the relationships and recall a recent encounter when you felt one or more of the following: appreciative, charmed, or flattered. List some of the beliefs that might have led you to react in this way.**

Meeting Place/Context

This final category covers a wide variety of situations under which you might encounter a stranger or person you do not know well:

- the street or other public place
- social gathering (informal-formal, large-small, intimate-impersonal)
- professional consultation (private office, telephone, restaurant, etc.)
- bar or club
- sporting event
- office
- theater
- in transport (taxi, bus, train, plane, boat)
- your home
- other private home

Again, the beliefs that you hold about these different venues—including what constitutes "normal" or "proper" conduct in each—can substantially affect your feelings and the manner in which you approach the other person.

Summary

This somewhat detailed examination of the factors that can predispose you to feel and act in certain ways when you initially encounter other people has been presented to underscore a very critical point about your relationships with other people: **Since much of your experience of new people—including the feelings that you direct toward them and the way that they react to you—is dependent on a complex web of beliefs that <u>you</u> bring to the encounter, becoming more aware of these beliefs and their associated feelings can help to make these encounters much more positive and personally satisfying.**

"GETTING ALONG TOGETHER"

Before leaving the subject of "consciousness and community" I would like to acknowledge one other set of interpersonal "feelings" that have enormous significance, not only for each of us personally, but also for our communities, our nation, and the world at large: **the sense that you "get along," or "don't get along," with another person.** I put "feelings" in quotes because "getting along" is not, strictly speaking, a "feeling" in the same sense as love, hate, and caring are feelings. "Getting along" is, of course, usually associated with positive interpersonal feelings such as liking and trust, just as not getting along is usually associated with negative interpersonal feelings such as disliking and suspicion.

The challenge of getting along has to do not only with two individuals, but also with (1) an individual and any larger group to which that individual belongs, and (2) any two groups. Indeed, many of our national and world conflicts arise because various national, racial, cultural, or religious groups or communities are not able to "get along" with each other. However, since in this book we are focusing on the consciousness of the individual, I would like to conclude this chapter with an essay that considers the dilemma of the individual and the community: **since any group or community consists of individuals with different beliefs, feelings, needs, desires, and talents, what has to happen in order for these individuals to "get along" with each other? What has to happen for the group not just to survive, but to prosper?** I offer this essay as possible "food for thought" as you consider the many groups and communities of which you are a member.

RECONCILING INDIVIDUALISM AND COMMUNITY: A MUSICAL METAPHOR

One of the major dilemmas confronting any community is how to reconcile the differing beliefs and needs of the individuals within that community. Another way of posing this question is to ask how a community or group of individuals can <u>collaborate</u> effectively, in order to fulfill group needs and aspirations, while simultaneously honoring and cultivating the individuality and uniqueness of its members. This challenge is probably inherent in any human collectivity, whether it be an individual family or an entire nation. If you happen to be married or living with a partner, your individual needs—for example, for love, sexual fulfillment, self-development and creative expression—have to be reconciled with a variety of "community" needs having to do with maintenance of the home, child care, finances, and your partner's need for love and sexual fulfillment. For larger collectivities of people, individual needs become more diverse and group needs much more complex.

In the traditional marriage ceremony both partners pledge to "honor and cherish" each other. Similarly, the U.S. Constitution guarantees each citizen "liberty and the pursuit of happiness," not to mention a variety of "freedoms." While it is easy for any group to say that it "celebrates" diversity and "honors" the uniqueness and individuality of each member, it is quite another thing to make such claims work in practice. Is it really possible for people to collaborate on behalf of "community goals" without completely sacrificing their individuality? Is it even possible that the collaborative effort can be strengthened and enhanced by the diversity of the individuals who make up the community? What are your beliefs about such matters?

In thinking about these questions I have tried to search for real-life examples of successful community or group efforts that also value and celebrate individuality. The field of human endeavor that immediately came to mind was music. Practically all forms of music, from rock to country to jazz to classical, afford us an opportunity to see not only how collaboration and individualism can coexist, but also how these two values can be mutually enhancing. It goes without saying that good ensemble music requires collaboration. Yet, a successful musical ensemble does not merely "honor" the individuality of its members; it requires it. The very essence of beautiful music is that it simultaneously combines uniquely different sounds. These sounds are diverse not only with respect to rhythm and pitch but also with respect to the quality of sound produced by each different instrument or voice. Imagine how awful an ensemble would sound if everybody always played or sang the same notes or played the same instrument in exactly the same way. And even when we have people playing the same notes with the same instrument, as, for example, when the violin section of a symphony orchestra plays in unison, the richness and beauty of the overall sound depends in part upon the diversity of tones produced by the different violinists. If every player in a violin section produced exactly the same quality of tone, the subjective effect would be boring, if not unpleasant.

Practically every type of ensemble music can also "showcase" individual virtuosity. In classical music the concerto form celebrates the virtuoso pianist or violinist, while grand opera celebrates vocal virtuosity. The individual virtuoso is, of course, supported by the larger ensemble—the full chorus or full orchestra—as part of the "community effort." In this case, the "individualism" of the soloist is actually enhanced and enriched by the addition of the accompanying ensemble. In that uniquely American musical form that we call improvised jazz, we often find a more "democratic" showcasing of virtuosity, where each member of the jazz ensemble in turn is afforded an opportunity to solo while the other members provide accompaniment.

Another way of using this music metaphor is to see any piece of music as consisting of melody (what the individual creates) and harmony (what the group or "community" of individuals creates). The musical effect of an individual melodic line can be enhanced or enriched if it is "accompanied" by one or more other melodic lines that complement ("harmonize with") it. Similarly, we could say that the musical value or effect of the "accompaniment" is enhanced by the presence of the "melody." The key element here is that the two or more melodies that create the unique "harmonic effect" must be in some way <u>different</u> from each other (i.e., pitch, time, voice, instrument, or tone quality). Once again: the unique beauty of ensemble music does not just "tolerate" such differences; it <u>requires</u> them.

If we were to translate what I have just said about melody and harmony into more general terms, we might argue as follows: **the ideal community is one that <u>captializes</u> on the diversity of its individual members, such that the overall functioning of the community and the functioning of the unique individuals within that community are mutually enhancing.**

Does the metaphor of ensemble music provide us with any general clues as to what individual members need to <u>do</u> in order to create such a community? What are the personal beliefs and actions that are needed to create a genuinely collaborative community that also celebrates the uniqueness and individuality of each member? Some insight into this question can be gained by examining just how it is that musical ensembles are able to function effectively.

To begin with, there must be some <u>agreement</u> among the musicians as to just what music is to be played, in what key, and at what tempo. Members of musical ensembles can and do debate and discuss such issues, but in the absence of any agreement, there is little point in trying to create ensemble music, since both the ensemble and the individual musicians who comprise it will be unable to function effectively.

This basic agreement about goals, purposes, and a modus operandi is clearly analogous to the shared values that we seek to discover in forging a common purpose for any community: Why does the community exist? What are its purposes? How should it function? Unless the members can reach some consensus regarding the basic purposes of the community and agree on how it should function, it will be very difficult to develop a viable community. If we were to express this principle in the terms used in this book, we might say that, if a community is to function effectively, its members need to develop a set of *shared beliefs* concerning its goals and purposes.

Not only must there be some shared understanding of what the group's purposes and mode of functioning will be, but each member must also understand what his or her particular part or contribution will be. We can call this the division of labor. These understandings are analogous, of course, to the agreements that musicians must reach about what music is to be played, what the proper tempo should be, and who will play which instrument or sing which part.

Next we have the very important issue of competence. Unless the individual musicians have achieved a certain level of technical competence in singing or playing their instruments, they can become a drag on the other members and detract from the overall performance of the ensemble. Individual competence in the functioning of groups and communities is an issue that has received far too little attention from educators and social scientists. Thus, while our educational system is designed to help you acquire individual skills in reading, writing, computing, and speaking, it provides very little formal training in listening, not to mention empathy, tolerance, teamwork, mediation, leadership, and other "group skills" that almost any community needs to collaborate effectively. Citizens can draw only two conclusions from these skewed educational priorities: group/community skills are either unimportant or unteachable (or both). Once again we see the importance of beliefs: could it be that many citizens avoid getting involved in collaborative efforts to improve their communities because they believe either (a) that they would not really be very good at it, or (b) that positive change is impossible or impractical? Could it be that citizens would value and enjoy becoming social change agents more if they (a) understood more about how to function effectively in groups and (b) believed that they could really make a contribution to strengthening the community? Clearly, most members of most organizations and communities have had little formal opportunity to develop the critical skills and attitudes that are needed to succeed in any collaborative effort. In other words, if individual community members were more skilled at collaboration and believed that such efforts could produce positive change, perhaps they would find it far more appealing to become "leaders" or active participants in community improvement efforts.

A close correlate of individual technical competence in a musical ensemble is <u>self-knowledge</u>. Each musician must have a good understanding of his or her tastes, competencies, <u>and</u> limitations. Such self-knowledge is needed, first of all, to insure that the individual musician will affiliate with an appropriate musical ensemble, one that would be enjoyable to play or sing with and one that can use the particular skills that the musician has to offer. Self-knowledge also helps the musician either to avoid tackling music that is too difficult or, if the ensemble decides to play such music, to drop out or practice sufficiently to acquire the level of skill needed to play the music competently. Again, to generalize the self-knowledge principle: if you are a member of an organization or community, it is important not only to know what knowledge and talents you can contribute to the collective effort, but also to be able to acknowledge areas where you lack the requisite knowledge and skill and, if necessary, to be willing to exert the effort needed to acquire the needed competence in these areas.

An equally important aspect of self-knowledge concerns your relevant <u>beliefs</u>: How important to you personally is the success of the collaborative effort? Do you believe that the effort can succeed? Do you believe that you and others possess the needed competence and dedication?

Knowledge of self, of course, is closely aligned with <u>knowledge of others</u>. Any competent musician knows that good ensemble work depends in part on knowing each other's skills and proclivities. Such knowledge is important not only in deciding what music the ensemble should play but also in enabling each musician to help other musicians play their parts with maximum effectiveness. The parallel with communities in general is obvious: knowing the values, passions, talents, skills, and limitations of other members of the community is of critical importance in attempting to define a common purpose that is achievable and to which all the members can commit themselves. Furthermore, each member can provide critical <u>feedback</u> to other members as a means of enhancing their self-knowledge.

One of the most important ingredients in an effectively functioning musical ensemble is that the individual players or singers must <u>listen</u> to each other. In some ways this is the most fundamental requirement of all. Imagine how absurd a musical ensemble would sound if the players were either unwilling to listen to each other or unable to hear each other. The analogous requirement for communities in general would to be the willingness and ability of each member to understand and empathize with other group members. As long as the members believe that the community is merely a forum for expressing their individual views, there is no need to "listen" to each other. Unless community members are able and willing to understand and listen to each other, it will be very difficult either to forge a common purpose or to create any real sense of collaboration.

Another important characteristic of a good ensemble player is <u>commitment</u>. It takes a good of time and energy simply to put together a good musical ensemble, and even more time and energy for the musicians to get to know each other and to be able to perform their music in ways that are satisfying to each member. The delays, disappointments, and frustrations that even top ensembles inevitably experience mean that the commitment of each member needs to be sufficiently strong to sustain the group over time. The same is true, of course, for organizations and communities in general: Their long-term viability requires that the individual members be sufficiently committed to the group's basic goals and purposes to sustain it, especially during "hard times."

Still another requirement of a good musical ensemble might be called <u>respect</u>. Each ensemble player or singer intuitively realizes that every other member of the ensemble performs a key role in creating the overall community effort. Respect thus comes not only from understanding that each performer contributes importantly to the whole, but also from the realization that other performers have worked hard to acquire the technical competence needed to play their parts at a high level of excellence. The parallels here for communities in general are obvious.

The final criterion for an effective musical ensemble is that each musician must have a <u>sense of the whole</u>. It is not enough just to know your part and to play it well, but one must also have a sense of how the entire ensemble sounds and of how the performance of each musician contributes to the whole. Similarly, in almost any kind of organization or community, it is important for each participant to have a "big picture" of what is happening within that organization or community: How are we doing? Are we clear about our common purpose? Are we making real progress toward realizing that purpose?

It goes without saying that these nine criteria that have been abstracted from the musical metaphor—shared values, division of labor, competence, self-knowledge, knowledge of other group members, the ability to listen, commitment, respect, and a sense of the whole—are closely interdependent. Thus, your level of commitment to the group and your interest in listening to and understanding your group peers will be greater if you have mutual respect for and understand each other and if you believe that you and they share similar values. At the same time, to identify these areas of shared or common values and to effect a meaningful division of labor, you must first take the trouble to listen to and understand each other. Finally, neither self-knowledge, shared values nor a willingness to listen to each other will be sufficient to form an effective collaborative effort unless you and your fellow community members are able and willing to acquire the knowledge and competencies that allows your community to sustain itself and prosper.

Perhaps the simplest way to see how you might apply these nine principles in your own interpersonal relationships is to paraphrase the discussion of each principle by substituting the name of some significant relationship in your own life—marriage, partnership, friendship, and so forth—for the word "community." Let us illustrate how you could do this by paraphrasing the above discussions of just two of the principles, <u>listening</u> and <u>commitment</u>, and for this particular example, let us assume that you are married:

One of the most important ingredients in an effectively functioning marriage is that the individual partners must <u>listen</u> to each other. In some ways this is the most fundamental requirement of all. Imagine how absurd a marriage would be if the partners were either unwilling to listen to each other or unable to hear each other. The analogous requirement for partnerships in general would to be the willingness and ability of both partners to understand and empathize with each other. As long as either partner believes that the relationship exists primarily as a means for fulfilling his or her individual needs, there is no need to "listen" to or "hear" each other. Unless both partners are able and willing to understand and listen to each other and care about what the other thinks and feels, it will be very difficult either to forge a common purpose or to create any real sense of collaboration.

Another important characteristic of a good marriage is <u>commitment</u>. It takes a good deal of time and energy to create a good marriage, and even more time and energy for the partners to get to know each other and to be able to live together in ways that are satisfying to both of them. The delays, disappointments, hurts, and frustrations that even the best marriages inevitably experience mean that the commitment of each partner needs to be sufficiently strong to sustain the marriage over time.

As an exercise, try paraphrasing these and some of the other paragraphs to fit your own real (or possible future) marriage, partnership, or school or work environment. In relating to these different "communities," how well do you exemplify the nine principles?

NOTES

1. The earliest instance of such a connection would be the "symbiosis" that typically exists between an infant and its mother.
2. When two people feel this way about each other, we sometimes call it "codependency."

CHAPTER 10

CHANGING BELIEFS

In chapter 1 it was suggested that your beliefs are like the "software" of your mind, the elaborate set of rules that you have established for interpreting the events of your life and for making meaning out of your daily experience. Your beliefs thus play a major role in shaping the contents of your conscious mind, especially your feelings, intents, and desires. And given that your daily behavior and the choices that you make in your life are an expression of these feelings, intents, and desires, **your beliefs literally create much of your life experience.**

In this chapter we shall consider various approaches to identifying and changing those beliefs that are not serving you well. Since part of the challenge of changing any belief is to understand how you acquired it in the first place, let us begin by taking a look at the process of belief acquisition.

THE ORIGINS OF BELIEFS

While the question of how people acquire their beliefs is a highly complex one, there are two fundamentally different ways in which you can acquire beliefs. For simplicity I like to call these the "passive" and "active" ways of forming beliefs. "Passive" belief acquisition occurs when you embrace someone else's beliefs either because you trust them or want to <u>please</u>

Mindworks: Becoming More Conscious in an Unconscious World, pp. 205–220

them—to gain their love, acceptance, or approval—or because you <u>fear</u> that they might reject you or punish you if you do not. In other words, when you adopt beliefs passively, the <u>content</u> of the beliefs matters less than the fact that "significant others" hold them (and may also want you to embrace them). Indeed, the influence of these other people or groups can be so great that you may sometimes adopt their beliefs even though they might contradict some of your other beliefs. Since the passive approach to acquiring beliefs is most characteristic of children, the "significant others" typically include parents, older siblings, teachers, clergy, or other adults, as well as peers. Peers, however, represent a potentially powerful source of passive belief acquisition at almost any age.

A common psychological mechanism for passive belief acquisition is <u>identification</u>: you embrace the beliefs of significant others (especially parents or other "role models") because you identify with—want to be like, want to emulate—them. This means of belief acquisition, which usually occurs unconsciously (i.e., without mindful awareness), is most common among children and adolescents, but it can occur at any age.

When you acquire beliefs "actively," your personal assessment of the <u>content</u> of the belief is of paramount importance: does it make sense to you, is it consistent with your experience, does it seem "right?" In other words, the active approach to acquiring beliefs derives from your need to <u>know</u>, to <u>comprehend</u>, and to <u>understand</u>: you embrace a particular belief because your experience, knowledge, reason, and intuition tells you that the idea expressed in the belief is either true, good, or important. (In this view, beliefs about "possibility" would fall under beliefs about "truth").

Some of your beliefs, of course, are acquired both actively and passively, in the sense that you might be influenced simultaneously by your identification with others (or need to please them) <u>and</u> by your desire to know, comprehend, and understand. The tricky part of this, of course, is that, **even if you initially acquired a belief passively—say, because you identified with a particular parent or peer—that belief will tend to shape your experience so as to generate "evidence" that supports it.** In other words, **just because your experience tells you that a particular belief is "true" does not mean that you acquired that belief actively.**

Beliefs About What is True

We tend to take most of our beliefs about "truth" for granted, by which I mean that we usually do not subject them to critical scrutiny or otherwise question them. For certain types of beliefs about the physical world, of course, there are indeed ways that you can "test" them. For example, you can believe that the earth is flat, if you like, and some people apparently still do. However, the physical sciences have provided us with rules and procedures for <u>testing</u> beliefs about the nature of physical reality, and in the case of this particular belief it can be shown to be false.

When in comes to beliefs about human nature and social organizations, however, the physical scientists' tools are of little use. This is not to say that many social and behavioral scientists have not tried to formulate theories and deduce the "laws" of human nature and organizations, but simply that their formulations have not served to settle any of the controversy about what we are "really" like as human beings. Some of these theories have enjoyed considerable popularity at various times, but the popularity of a theory probably says more about our shared belief systems than it does about the "validity" of the theory itself.

When it comes to beliefs that you have acquired passively, beliefs about what is true or what is possible can sometimes be challenged by your everyday experience: a physical event that suggests that the belief may be false. However, passively acquired beliefs about what is good—"never take the Lord's name in vain"—or what is important—"I should brush my teeth after every meal"—are usually not subject to confirmation or refutation by means of "objective" information that you get through your five senses. As a result, you may well find it difficult to question some of your beliefs about goodness and importance, especially if they have been acquired passively.

One reason why adolescence can often be a trying time for both children and their parents is that the adolescent child is being exposed to beliefs that may contradict certain parental beliefs that the child has acquired passively. The adolescent can be exposed to such conflicting beliefs in a variety of ways—in school, by reading, from the media, and so forth—but the most common source is the adolescent peer group. Because the child also identifies with and wants the acceptance and approval of peers, she passively embraces beliefs that are at variance with parental beliefs.[1] These belief conflicts, which can become especially severe if the child <u>acts</u> on the contrary beliefs, are at the heart of what we call "adolescent rebellion."

The Chicken or the Egg?

A dilemma which has intrigued psychologists and philosophers alike is the causal connection between belief and social "reality." Are our beliefs about human nature and society shaped by the society, or is the society a <u>manifestation</u> of those beliefs? At first glance it might appear that we are all like amateur scientists, observing objectively what the society is like and formulating our beliefs accordingly. In other words, it might seem like our beliefs about the world around us are simply shaped by our encounter with that world, that is, by our experience:

Experience → Belief

Upon closer examination, however, such an analysis turns out to be greatly oversimplified. To begin with, our perceptions and understanding of each encounter with a life event will be greatly affected by the concepts, beliefs, and expectations that we <u>bring</u> to that encounter. Consider for a moment the various opinions and other reactions that different people are likely to have to a given movie, book, speech, painting, television show, political candidate, parent, child, teacher, or new acquaintance. Why would you and someone else react differently to the same person or event? Because your mental "software"—your <u>beliefs</u>—is different. Further, the fact that your reactions to a person are shaped by your particular beliefs means that that person's subsequent reactions to <u>you</u> are also likely to be affected by these same beliefs. But there is more. Not only are your reactions to a given person or event likely to differ from someone else's as a function of your beliefs, but your beliefs will also ultimately influence <u>which</u> person or event you are likely to come into contact with. A person who believes that competitive sports are a waste of time is not likely to attend sporting events or to attract or hang out with sports-minded people, a person who harbors strongly conservative beliefs is not likely to attract or hang out with leftists, and so on. In short, **much of your experience is shaped by your beliefs:**

Belief → Experience

How, then, can you go about the process of understanding how you acquired particular beliefs? How can you determine whether you believe something simply because your experience has led you "objectively" to that conclusion, rather than because you wanted to please others or to gain their approval? Following are some questions you might want to ask yourself in order resolve such questions:

- **Who else in my life holds the same belief?** If "significant others" in your life—parents, spouse, peers, close friends, or other people or groups with which you identify—share the same belief, then what is the possibility that you have embraced this belief in part because you identify with them or want their approval and acceptance?
- **Do I agree with these same people on most other things?** One way to assess the degree to which you may have acquired certain

beliefs passively—to secure the love, approval, acceptance, and so forth, of significant others and/or because you identify with them—is to assess your own willingness to *disagree* with these same people or groups. The more you tend to embrace a similar package of beliefs, and the greater your reluctance to take positions that might be contrary to the beliefs of these significant others, the greater the likelihood that you have acquired at some of these beliefs passively.

- **What *evidence* do I have from my experience that supports the belief?** Can you cite any contrary evidence?
- **Can I remember *when* I first acquired the belief?** Can you remember a time when you did <u>not</u> hold the belief? How aware were you of the "evidence" (cited in the previous question) *before* you acquired the belief? (If you have held the belief for as long as you can remember, then there is a very good chance you acquired it passively.)

GETTING STARTED

One way to begin the process of belief change is first to take an inventory of some of your core beliefs. I have found it convenient to categorize beliefs in terms of the "concept" (see chapter 2) that the belief focuses on:

- Beliefs about <u>yourself</u>: "I'm a hard worker."
- Beliefs about <u>others</u>: "My boss has a bad temper."
- Beliefs about <u>groups</u>: "Employees should always respect their boss."
- Beliefs about <u>things</u>: "My company is a terrible place to work."
- Beliefs about <u>activities</u>: "The work I do is not really very important."
- Beliefs about <u>past events</u>: "My boss really treated me badly."
- Beliefs about <u>future events</u>: "I'm not going to last long in this job."
- Beliefs about <u>abstract concepts</u>: "Loyalty is the most important virtue."

By using these eight general categories, you can take any subject—your work, your school, yourself, or some other important person in your life—and write down some of your core beliefs in each category. In conducting this exercise, keep in mind the following two principles:

- **Any belief or set of beliefs that consistently causes you to experience negative feelings, or to behave in ways that you later regret, are <u>dysfunctional</u> beliefs;**
- **Any core belief that is highly critical or derogatory, that focuses on what you or others should *not* do, or that *limits* your sense of what is possible, is a <u>potentially</u> dysfunctional belief.**

Some of the exercises presented in the previous five chapters (5-9) were designed to help you identify such beliefs. The challenge posed by dysfunctional beliefs is, of course, threefold: (1) to identify beliefs that are potentially dysfunctional, (3) to assess critically the effect that they are having on your feelings, behavior, and life experience; and (3), for beliefs that are found to be dysfunctional, to find ways either to minimize their negative effect on your life, to abandon (or suspend) them, or to replace them with beliefs that are less dysfunctional. These can all be formidable challenges.

IDENTIFYING DYSFUNCTIONAL BELIEFS

There are many different strategies available for getting in touch with your dysfunctional beliefs. In this section we will discuss how you can employ some of these strategies as a first step toward suspending or replacing some of the beliefs that are presently not serving you well.

Beliefs About What is True and What is Possible

At first glance, the idea of changing or suspending any of your beliefs about "truth" presents an insurmountable dilemma: if something is "true," how can you bring yourself <u>not</u> to believe it? With a little reflection, however, it becomes clear that there are very few dysfunctional beliefs about "what's true" that cannot be successfully challenged.

Your beliefs about truth or "reality" are of three major kinds: <u>Memories</u> of "what happened" in your past, assertions about what is <u>currently</u> true in the present moment, and beliefs about <u>future</u> "truths." This latter group includes (a) your expectations about what is going to happen and (b) your beliefs about <u>what is possible</u>. When it comes to memories, most of us are aware that they are subject to a considerable amount of error. Take, for example, the common case where you cannot be sure that an early childhood memory is something you actually experienced or something you have merely been told about by your parents. Indeed, since your memories are necessarily present <u>constructions</u> or <u>representations</u>

(re-present!) of "past" events, **there is no way to be sure that any memory is accurate or completely "true."**

But what about the present? The fact that your "current" reality is in a continuous state of flux means that **any belief about what is "true" in the present moment is also subject to error or distortion.** Many beliefs about the present, of course, can be safely assumed to be virtually error free, especially those that have to do with the physical world: "It's cold in Antarctica," "the earth is round," and so on. Many other beliefs about the present—while theoretically subject to error—must necessarily be assumed to be true simply to allow you to get through an ordinary day: "The bus or train I take to work today will not crash," "the building I work in will not collapse," and so on. And the "truth" of such beliefs can readily be demonstrated in your daily experience.[2] There is, however, a very large group of dysfunctional beliefs that you might embrace about current "truths" that could be much more open to dispute, but which nevertheless have very important effects on your conscious experience and behavior. Take the following five examples:

1. Bad luck seems to follow me wherever I go.
2. People are always taking advantage of me.
3. I am not an attractive person.
4. He is completely insensitive to other people's feelings.
5. People are basically selfish.

The reason why such beliefs tend to be dysfunctional is that they limit and therefore <u>distort</u> your experience in ways that are likely to "confirm" the beliefs. Let us see how this might work with the same five negative beliefs:

1. You will tend to disempower yourself by (a) attributing most of your problems and difficulties to "bad luck" rather than to the choices you make; and (b) avoiding situations and choices that might bring you "good luck."
2. Your interpersonal relationships will suffer because you will find it difficult to trust other people.
3. The social/sexual/romantic aspects of your life will suffer because you will tend to (a) put little effort into grooming and personal appearance ("What's the use?"); and (b) misinterpret—and there-fore not be open or responsive to—the positive overtures of others who may be attracted to you.
4. Your relationships with that person will suffer because you will tend to (a) focus on anything he does that suggests "insensitivity" and

misinterpret (or ignore) the things he does that are not consistent with this belief; and (c) elicit negative feelings from him because of the negative belief that you bring to your contacts with him.

5. Your experience of others <u>and</u> of yourself will become distorted because will tend to (a) focus your attention on the "selfish" things you and they you do and misinterpret (or ignore) acts of generosity or selflessness; and (b) <u>resist</u> impulses to be giving and generous with others.

Still another way of getting in touch with your dysfunctional beliefs about "truth" and "possibility" is to work <u>backwards</u> from your strongest negative emotions. Feelings of *fear* or *anxiety*, for example, can often be traced to beliefs about things that <u>might</u> happen.[3] Similarly, feelings of *depression* can often be traced to beliefs either about things that happened in the past or about future (negative) possibilities. And when it comes to strongly negative feelings about other people such and *hate* and *suspicion*, you can usually trace such feelings to negative beliefs either about things others have <u>done</u> or about their <u>intentions</u>.

Dysfunctional Beliefs About Goodness and Importance

Some of our most dysfunctional beliefs have to do with our ethics and morality, our sense of right and wrong. Feelings of *anger* or *outrage*, for example, can often emerge in your consciousness if you believe that someone has committed a serious violation of your beliefs about "what's right" or "what's good." If you believe that <u>you</u> have violated some of these same beliefs, you may well experience strong feelings of *guilt, shame, remorse,* or *depression.* One could argue, of course, that it is "natural" or "normal" to experience such powerful feelings when your beliefs about right and wrong have been violated in some significant way, and there can indeed be times when such feelings lead to constructive change. On the other hand, such beliefs become dysfunctional when the feelings they give rise to persist to the point where they dominate your consciousness and interfere with your daily life.

Using the Exercises From Earlier Chapters

A major purpose of chapters 5 through 9 was to encourage you to undertake an exhaustive analysis of your intents, desires, and virtually all of your feeling states and to reflect on some of the beliefs that might give rise to these feelings. If you have read these chapters and done some of the suggested exercises, you have probably already identified some of your dysfunctional beliefs. If you have not done these exercises and are still not sure that you have identified some of your most dysfunctional beliefs, some good ways to start would be:

- To complete the chart on **General Feeling States** (chapter 5, p. 118) and do the exercises that follow;
- To complete the chart on **"Bodily" Feelings** (chapter 7, p. 155) and answer the questions that follow;
- To (a) think of <u>someone important in your life with whom you are currently having</u> difficulties, and (b) perform the exercise described in chapter 9 under the section, "Taking Stock of Your 'Feeling Relationships' With Others" (p. 187);
- To complete the chart on **Topics You Might Think About** (chapter 8, p. 166) and carry out the exercise, "Taking Stock of Your Thinking Tendencies" (pp. 169-171).

When it comes to this last strategy, if you believe that you spend "too much time" thinking about a topic like sex, money, food, your personal appearance, or success, you may be harboring incompatible or contradictory motives or beliefs about that topic. For example:

- You may believe that the topic is important, but that it is "not good."
- You may believe that the topic is important, but "not attainable."
- You may believe that the topic "not important," in which case there would almost certainly be other, <u>unrecognized</u> motives, desires, or beliefs involved.

One way to begin identifying such hidden motives or desires is to complete sentences like the following: "When it comes to [*topic*], what I really want is…," or "As far as [*topic*] is concerned, my greatest desire would be…" In the case of hidden beliefs, you can similarly begin to identify them by completing sentences like the following: "What [*topic*] really means to me is…," or "In my opinion, [*topic*]…"

Still another approach to identifying dysfunctional beliefs is through an analysis of your <u>desires</u> and <u>intents</u> (chapter 6). One way to start is to take a thorough inventory of your intents and desires with respect to one of more of the following: your relationships with others, money/possessions, work/career, leisure activities/avocations, and personal development (see p. 140 in chapter 6). Even if you initially limit such a survey to just one of these areas, the results can tell you a lot about your beliefs, given that you usually desire something because you believe it is either good or important (or both). However, your beliefs about what is <u>possible</u> highlight an important difference between merely desiring, on the one hand, and actually intending, on the other. Thus, when you desire something because you believe that it is important, whether or not you will actually form an intention to attain it will reveal a lot concerning your beliefs about its attainability <u>and</u> goodness. In other words, **desiring something without forming an intention to make it happen implies a conflict in beliefs.** Exploring such "motivational inconsistencies"(see p. 138 in chapter 6) can be of great help in identifying dysfunctional or conflicting beliefs.

CHANGING (OR SUSPENDING) DYSFUNCTIONAL BELIEFS

One of the fascinating things about trying to change your beliefs is that you will often have to contend first with your *beliefs about your beliefs*! For example, if you have been able to identify a particular dysfunctional belief, you might hesitate to take any action to change or suspend it because you <u>also</u> hold one or more of the following kinds of beliefs:

1. "I'll never be able to change or suspend that belief."
2. "Since the belief's 'true,' how can I <u>not</u> believe it?"
3. "Change is going to be a long, agonizing process."
4. "I'm going to have to "give up" something that's very important to me."

Such "beliefs about beliefs" tend to be "self-fulfilling prophesies," primarily because they <u>prevent you from taking appropriate action</u>. It is also important to realize that, since embracing any of these four "beliefs about beliefs" will tend to prevent you from making any serious attempt at belief change, you may cling to them because you realize that they protect you from experiencing any of the fear or anxiety that is typically associated with belief change by giving your life a certain degree of <u>predictability</u>. You thus achieve a kind of emotional "safety" by maintaining the same beliefs, no matter how dysfunctional they might be.

There are, however many ways in which you can counter or at least suspend such limiting beliefs by considering other, competing beliefs. A few examples:

1. "I'll never know if I don't try."
2. "If I take the trouble to examine it critically, maybe I can find some evidence that it's not really true."

3. "Only if I choose to make it that way."

4. "Maybe I need to understand better why something dysfunctional can be so 'important.' Also, I might find that it's not so important after all."

Possible Strategies

Once you have decided that it is time to try changing or suspending a dysfunctional belief, it is important to realize that what you really need to do is to find ways to <u>disempower</u> that belief. Here are several strategies for doing this:

<u>Objectification</u>. The point of "objectifying" any belief is to "distance" yourself from it psychologically. Writing down your belief on a sheet of paper is a good first step. Not only write it down, but also write down any associated beliefs and any other related thoughts about it in as much detail as you can. Discussing your belief with someone else can also help to objectify it.

<u>Find out: What positive function(s) is it serving?</u> You can always count of the fact that, while a belief may be dysfunctional, it is <u>always</u> performing some kind of positive function for you. For example, if you believe that certain major problems in your life have been caused by others (the "blame game") or by "bad luck," this protects you in two ways: (1) you can avoid the psychic pain involved in admitting to yourself that your problems have arisen because of choices that <u>you</u> have made; and (2) you can put off the hard work that would be involved in taking charge of your own life (interestingly, the belief that you are "helpless" or "inadequate" can serve this same "positive" function!). Similarly, if you believe that you are unattractive because you are overweight, but also believe that "there's no way I'll ever be able to lose weight and keep it off," the latter belief may be protecting you from the anxiety or fear that you might experience if other people were to make sexual advances to you.

<u>Involve others</u>. Tell someone that you are planning to change. It is particularly useful to discuss your plans with people who <u>do not </u>share your dysfunctional belief or who hold opposing beliefs.

<u>Visualize and imagine</u>. The idea behind this strategy is to disempower your belief by imagining how your life would be different without it. Conjure up visual images of a "future you" who no longer holds that belief. For example, if you want something new or different in your life but do not make any effort to attain it because you believe you are lacking something—ability, money, time, and so forth,—imagine how your life would be different if this limitation <u>did not</u> exist. If you carry out this imaginative exercise at least once a day, it can be an especially powerful tool in

belief change. In other words, rather than merely reminding you about everything that is <u>wrong</u> with the belief that you want to change or suspend, visualization begins to show you all of the positive new life <u>possibilities</u> that lay ahead. At the same time, this creative use of your imaginative skills helps to free up your conscious and unconscious minds to begin charting a "path" of choices that will lead in the direction of those new possibilities.

<u>Take action; do something "physical."</u> The idea behind this strategy is to go beyond a purely "cerebral" approach to belief change by getting your <u>body</u> involved in the process. For instance, if you want to suspend or change some dysfunctional negative belief that you have about yourself (such beliefs usually have to do with your motives, your limitations, or "mistakes" that you have made in the past), carry out some physical action that <u>contradicts</u> that belief. For example, if you believe you are too selfish or greedy, perform some act of generosity. Or, if you want to give up smoking but believe you are incapable of it, decide not to smoke for some very limited period—an hour, 2 hours—or for just one time give up your "favorite" cigarette (e.g., after a meal). This particular strategy is a good one to use in conjunction with the imagination/visualization strategy (above).

Confronting Your Fear of Change

There are many reasons why most of us will have some apprehension about letting go of any of our core beliefs. Changing your beliefs—especially those core beliefs about yourself, others, and the world around you that define your worldview—inevitably means changing your life in some way, and life change always carries with it a degree of uncertainty: Just <u>how</u> will my life be different? How will my relationships with other people change? Will I be prepared for these changes? The idea of changing our beliefs, in other words, tends to make us uneasy because it threatens the sense of safety, predictability, and comfort that we tend to associate with our familiar routines and habits.

While the prospect of changing almost any kind of core belief can make you uneasy, your greatest fears are likely to be associated with changing beliefs about <u>yourself</u>. Virtually all of us have developed a sense of self that comprises a complex web of beliefs about our personality, our past successes and failures, our talents and limitations, and so forth. And here is where the fear arises: "If I change my concept of who I am in any substantial way, then *will I still be me?*" The real paradox here is that, **the stronger your sense of self, the greater your fear of self-change is likely to be.**" If you are extremely dissatisfied with your current life or if you have a low opinion of yourself—as reflected in many critical and negative beliefs about who you are and what you have done—you may be quite open to the possibility of significant life change. But if you believe in general that you are basically a good person and that you have been successful in your work and in your personal life, you may be highly resistant to revising your concept of who you are in any significant way. You may be strongly attached, in other words, to your current notion of who you are.

WHO *ARE* YOU?

During my doctoral training in psychology and for many years thereafter I was very involved in "personality assessment," a subfield of psychology that specializes in "measuring" people's personalities, usually by means of tests or inventories such as the Rorschach (the so-called "inkblot" test) or the Minnesota Multiphasic Personality Inventory (MMPI). The underlying assumption that drives the use of such instruments is that each of us has an unique "personality" consisting of such things as attitudes, self concept, beliefs, values, fears, interests, desires, and behavioral inclinations. Since our personality is supposed to predispose us to respond to others and the world around us in certain distinctive ways, making an accurate assessment of someone's personality presumably enables us to (a) understand or "diagnose" why that person feels or behaves in a certain way (especially if the person is anxious or depressed or if the behavior is considered bizarre or antisocial) and (b) "predict" how the person will behave in some future situation.

Another, perhaps more critical assumption in the field of personality assessment is that each individual's personality is relatively fixed and unchanging, or at least very resistant to change. The belief that our personalities are permanent features of ourselves—much like our facial features or eye color—is widespread in our society and reflected in almost all aspects of our lives.

Take yourself as an example. If someone were to ask you to "describe yourself" or to "tell me what kind of person you are," you would probably have little trouble answering with words like "intelligent," "hard-working," "outgoing," "optimistic," "considerate," "serious," or whatever. Many personality "tests," in fact, rely heavily on the belief that our personalities are more or less "set" and that we are able and willing to describe them to others. In fact, the very phrase, "describe yourself," implies that "you"—your personality—is fixed and unchanging, much like a painting or a sculpture. These beliefs about personality, which are deeply ingrained in our culture, are continually reinforced, not only by psychologists, but also by most institutions of our society. For example, if you were to apply for a job or for admission to a selective college or university, you would ordinarily have to go through some kind of screening process requiring you to provide information about your "past performance," take "tests," and get letters of recommendation. When employers rely on such information, they are implicitly assuming that your personal qualities are relatively fixed: the use of tests and letters of recommendation is thus based on the belief that your job performance will depend on your "abilities" (as revealed in the tests) and "what kind of person your are" (as revealed by the letters), and the use of job histories is based on the belief that your "future performance" will be like your "past performance." In modern society the most extreme proponents of this belief that you have a relatively "fixed" personality are probably either the astrologers, who contend that certain basic aspects of your personality are determined at birth, or the geneticists, who believe that many personality features are determined at the moment of conception!

CAN YOU *REALLY* CHANGE?

Let me now suggest an alternative view which may at first seem radical, if not preposterous:

> **your "personality" is fixed or unchanging only to the extent that you are unwilling to change your beliefs.**

In other words, if you were to describe yourself to me as "optimistic" or "lazy" or as anything else, what you would really be doing is telling me about your current beliefs. Keep in mind that your beliefs are just that: beliefs. Nothing more and nothing less. As we have already seen, beliefs are not the same as objective facts (although we sometimes "believe" that they are); rather, they are assertions about the nature of reality—how things are, were, will be, could be, or ought to be.

Now you might want to argue with me about all of this, defending your beliefs about yourself by citing "evidence" from your past behavior: "See how much time I have wasted in the past. See how much I have procrastinated in the face of difficult tasks. Obviously, I'm a 'lazy' person." I could, of course, argue with your interpretation of your past behavior, pointing out that it probably relies on a set of other beliefs (about work, play, "responsibility," etc.) that need to be examined as well. But for purposes of argument let us assume that you are objectively "right": that a neutral, independent panel of behavior experts would examine your past behavior closely and agree that you did indeed exhibit a good deal of "laziness."

Now what does this have to do with who you <u>are</u>? Does the fact that you and others who know you believe that you have acted in a lazy fashion in the past mean that you—the you that is reading this sentence—are <u>currently</u> lazy, or that you <u>must</u> act in a lazy fashion the next time you are presented with an opportunity to do so? Is someone pointing a gun at your head, ordering you to "act lazy or else!?" Do not you reserve the right to choose <u>not</u> to act this way? Do you not have the option to act differently?

It is important to realize that the argument presented in the last two paragraphs could be applied to almost <u>any</u> aspect of your "personality." In other words, in theory it would be possible to refute almost any claim that you might care to make about your personality. If this is true, then is there anything we could say about you that is "true?"

Now let me suggest for your consideration a simple but even more radical proposition: The next time someone asks you to describe yourself, or the next time you ask yourself, "who am I?, there are only two responses you can give that are literally "true":

"I am nothing."
or
"I am everything."

"I am nothing" is really a shorthand way of saying, "nothing in my past life *forces* me to be a certain way in my present life; I always have the freedom to choose to be different."

"I am everything" is really a shorthand way of saying, "all options remain open to me. I can be lazy or be a workaholic, I can be optimistic or pessimistic, I can be honest or I can be a liar. I have the potential to be whatever I want. I am free to choose." (About the only limitations on your ability to make such choices would be physical ones: if you are a man you would not be able to get pregnant, if you are blind you would not be able to become an airline pilot, and so on.)

Note that the only obstacle that can stand in the way of your embracing these two responses is, once again, your beliefs: your belief that you "have" a personality that is relatively fixed and unchanging, your belief that your past determines your present, and your belief about whether you are really free in the present moment to choose among alternative patterns of behavior.

One way to approach this problem is to see your beliefs about who you are simply for what they are: a set of beliefs, a "story," if you will, that you tell yourself about who you are. It would be one thing if you were to tell this story in strictly factual and historical terms—"I have done these things and had these experiences so far in my life"—but it is quite another to draw conclusions and generalizations from this history: "therefore this is the kind of person I am; this is <u>me</u>." The fact is that **you are in truth only who and what you choose to be in this moment, and nothing else.**" In short: you <u>have</u> a past—a set of memories or current beliefs about "what happened" and "what I have done"—but **you are <u>not</u> your past.**

The key to freeing yourself up from the limiting conceptions that you may have about yourself is to create a little "psychological distance" between yourself—the consciousness that reads these words, on the one hand—and the "story' that you tell yourself about who you are—your "personality," your strengths and limitations, and so forth—, on the other. Learn to look at this story as you would your clothes, your car, or any other object or personal possession: <u>as something that you "have," but not as something that *defines* (and therefore limits) you.</u> Just as you can change your clothes or your car (or get rid of them altogether!), so can you either (a) change the story that you have been telling yourself about who you are, or (b) simply realize that this story "defines" you only to the extent that you *allow* it to through your beliefs. In other words, it is only your limiting beliefs that prevent you from acknowledging the real truth about who you are: **a conscious being who is always free in the present moment to choose your course of action.**

NOTES

1. What developmental psychologists call "individuation"—the lengthy process whereby the child gradually develops a sense of self that is distinctive and not just a reflection of parental values and beliefs—typically gives rise to this kind of conflict, where parental beliefs are questioned and challenged in part because the parents hold them.

2. It should be mentioned here that there are a few people—those who suffer from a psychological condition known as agoraphobia—who are unable to embrace such "obvious" truths about everyday realities and who are consequently afraid to venture out of doors.

3. You can also experience fear or anxiety in relation to past events, but such feelings are often associated with the possibility that the events might recur.

CHAPTER 11

THE EXPERIENCE OF TIME

"Hold every moment sacred. Give each clarity and meaning, give each the weight of thine awareness, each its true and due fulfillment."

—Thomas Mann (1940)

There are two main reasons why I have chosen to devote this final chapter to the subject of time. First, when it comes to the totality of your conscious experience—your waking life, if you will—**time is all you have!** That we all recognize the "value" of time is reflected not only in our language—we speak of "spending," time, "saving" time, and "wasting" time—but also in our reverence for youth (they "have" a lot of time) and in our shared desire to live a "long time." The second reason is that, since time has important implications for almost all of the subjects covered in the earlier chapters, the way we perceive and experience time provides a good vehicle for reviewing and summarizing many of the basic ideas presented in the book. Another reason for leaving the subject of time until the end of the book is to encourage to you take a critical look at some of your **beliefs** about time!

What is time? Physicists tell us that time is not really something that can be defined in any absolute sense, but rather is a human invention. And, since Albert Einstein formulated his theories of relativity, physicists now believe that what we think of as time is intimately connected with

Mindworks: Becoming More Conscious in an Unconscious World, pp. 221–237

space and that space can actually be "bent" and time "slowed down" by the gravitational pull of large heavenly bodies. But what about "time" as you personally <u>experience</u> it? And how do you conceive of time, that is, what do you <u>believe</u> about it? In this chapter we will address both of these questions, with the ultimate aim of enhancing your understanding of how your conscious experience and your actions are affected by your sense of time and your beliefs about it.

YOUR BELIEFS ABOUT TIME

Most of us believe that time is something that can be divided into three parts: past, present, and future. If you think of your awareness or consciousness as being composed of an ever-changing stream of <u>events</u>—ideas, perceptions, sensations, feelings—events that are happening now constitute "the present," events that have already happened make up "the past," and events that have not yet happened represent "the future." If you were to use the analogy of a video tape, the "past" would be represented by that part of the tape you have already viewed, the "present" by whatever part you are currently viewing, and the future by the remaining part that you have not yet viewed. So far, so good.

But upon closer inspection, this particular way of looking at time turns out to present certain difficulties. The main problem concerns the meaning of "the present": Just *where* is the dividing line between the present and the past? And *where* is the dividing line between the present and the future? Another way of putting this question is to ask: How "wide" is the present? In the videotape analogy, the part of the tape you are viewing—the "present"—is pretty narrow, perhaps no more than one "frame."

When you try to answer this question by reflecting on your own consciousness, it becomes difficult to figure out just what "the present" is, because, unlike a video tape, you cannot "freeze frame" your conscious experience. As soon as a "future" event become "present," it seems to become "past" almost instantaneously as it is replaced by another "future" event. Thus, the more you reflect on your experience of the "passage of time," the more the past and the future seem to come closer and closer together, squeezing the present into a narrower and narrower space.

What, then, *is* "the present?" For me, the best resolution of this dilemma is contained in poem I composed several years ago:

Time and the Now

The Now is everything.
And it is nothing.
It is the knife edge between past and future—

dimensionless, timeless—
nudging everything ahead or behind,
leaving nothing for itself.
Yet behind is only present memory,
And ahead is only present fantasy,
Leaving All That Is
In the spacious Now.

Another way of looking at "time" and "the Now" is to realize that **everything happens in the now.** What we call "the past" was once "now," but it is not happening anymore. And what we call "the future" will someday be "now," but it has not happened yet. You can, of course, say that your present life situation—your thoughts, your emotional state, your work, your personal relationships with others—is a reflection of your past choices and actions. And in exactly the same way you can say that where you end up in the future will reflect the choices you make right now. In other words, your future will be shaped by what you choose to do in the present moment, in the next moment, and in each moment after that.

Note that I am <u>not</u> saying that your past determines your future. I said, rather, that **it is your <u>present</u> that determines your future**, and that just as your present reflects the choices you made in your previous "presents," so will the course of your future be determined by the choices you make right now and in each moment to come.

It is possible, of course, to "let" your future reflect past patterns of behavior, which is to say that you can choose to continue doing things in the present the same way you have done them in previous moments. When you consistently choose to think or act in the same way without much awareness—without being "mindful" that you are in fact making a choice to think or act as you have in the past— we would say that you have "developed the habit" of thinking or acting in that way. The fact that we all exhibit such habitual patterns of behavior helps to create the <u>impression</u> that "your past determines your future." If some of these past patterns have served you well, then there may be every reason to continue them in the present. But if you feel that your life has become "routine" or "boring" or that you are "in a rut," then there may be good reason for you to take a closer look at these patterns. **If you fail to realize that you are always <u>choosing</u> in the present moment to maintain past patterns of behaving and reacting to the events of your life, then you are basically <u>disempowering</u> yourself.**

While it might seem a bit odd to say that your present determines your future, it is no less odd to realize that **your present also determines your past.** In other words, just as your present life experiences define what you

---

EXERCISE

(1) Write down at least two "bad habits" or repetitive patterns of behavior that you would like to change. (2) For each pattern, think of the most recent time when you exhibited that behavior and ask yourself, "What was my attention focused on at the time? What was I thinking and feeling? Was I thinking about something in the past? In the future? How mindful was I of the fact that I was practicing the same behavior? (3) Promise yourself that the next time a situation arises when you might practice the same pattern, you will try to become fully mindful of your inclination and, if you once again engage in that behavior, to be fully mindful of the fact that you are making a conscious choice to do it.

---

used to refer to as the "future," so do they define the events that you will subsequently refer to as the "past."

Consider what you are doing right now in *this* present moment: reading this book, maybe pausing every now and then to think about what you are reading. Do you *have* to read this page in this moment? Is someone putting a gun to your head telling you to read this sentence at this moment or else? Of course not. The fact is that you are freely making a <u>choice</u> to read, and that you are also completely free, in this present moment, to choose to do something else! You can choose to read another part of the book, to make notations on the book or in a notebook, to read something else, to take a break, to meditate on your breathing or on some other part of your body, or—depending on the physical environment in which you find yourself right now—to get up and stretch, take a walk, get something to eat, call someone on the phone, and so on. On the other hand, you can also choose to refocus your attention away from the present moment by thinking about some past or future event.

FOCUSING ON THE MOMENT

Imagine the present conscious moment as your own private drama taking place on a brightly lit stage. Like any good drama, each moment in the show is alive and full of interesting possibilities. Now imagine your consciousness as the audience that is viewing this drama in your own private theater. Since this is your theater, you can not only <u>participate</u> actively in the play (the present moment) but you can also <u>control the curtain.</u> With this particular curtain, the left side represents your "past" and the right side represents your "future." The left side of the curtain is painted with all kinds of scenes from your past, and the right side contains all kinds of fantasies about your future. The more you choose to close the curtain—that is, the more you focus your consciousness on the past or the future—the less of the stage (the present moment) you are able to see and the fewer possibilities there are for you to participate in the play. And if you choose to prevent yourself from viewing any of the play by closing the curtain completely—that is, if you choose to focus your full attention on the past or the future—you take yourself completely out of the present moment and are no longer able to be a conscious participant in it.

TIME AND EMOTIONS

Why do so many of us deprive ourselves of the opportunity to experience and explore the richness of the present moment by "closing the curtains of our consciousness?" What is it about the past and the future that so easily draws us away from what is happening in the now? What gives our thoughts about the past and future—our memories and fantasies—so much power? The answer, of course, is that **thoughts about the past and the future get their "drawing power" from the <u>feelings</u> that are associated with them**. And while past or future events can certainly be associated with positive feelings, the feelings that have the greatest power to distract your attention away from the present moment are often negative ones.

Feelings That Draw You Into the Past

Some of your most powerful negative feelings are associated with "past" events. For example, if you believe that someone has harmed you

---

EXERCISE

(1) Think of a recent time when you felt guilty, sorry, or remorseful about something. What are some of your beliefs about "right and wrong" that were involved? Can you remember what you were doing during those times when you experienced these feelings? How did your feeling affect what you were doing? (2) Repeat the exercise using a recent time when you felt nostalgic or were reminiscing.

or done you wrong, there are several such feelings that can arise: **anger, outrage, hate, hurt,** and **resentment.** On the other hand, if you believe that you have done something wrong, a different but equally powerful type of negative feeling can arise: **guilt, remorse,** or **sorrow.** Finally, if you believe that you have suffered a tremendous loss or simply that something has gone terribly wrong, you can experience a feeling of **despondence.** Note that each of these feelings is associated with memories or thoughts about "past" events.

Attachment to the past, it should be stressed, does not always have to involve negative feelings; you can also occupy your conscious attention with thoughts of prior events that are associated with positive feelings. While all of us engage in such "reminiscing" or "nostalgia" from time to time as a means of generating positive feeling states, being excessively preoccupied with "the good old days" not only limits your ability to live fully in the moment, but may also signify that your present (and possibly future) life circumstances are not fulfilling.

Feelings That Draw you Into the Future

There are two very different kinds of "future oriented" feelings that can distract your attention away from the present moment: **fear** and **desire.** In the case of fear, your attention is focused on negative events that might occur; in the case of desire, it is focused on future events that you regard as positive. There are several variations on the theme of fear—**worry, anxiety, insecurity, uncertainty**—but each shares a common concern with negative events that might occur in the future. In some cases, anxiety or insecurity can arise even though there are no particular events that you have in mind; rather, you experience a kind of generalized foreboding about the future.

When in comes to **desire,** there are also several variations: **craving, yearning, wishing,** and **hoping** (see chapter 6). In each instance the feeling is connected to thoughts about some future situation or outcome that you believe to be either important or good (or both). However, as mentioned in Chapter 6, such feelings can usually be traced to a belief that in the present moment you are personally lacking something or that your current existence is somehow either unfulfilling or incomplete.

Feelings That can Draw you Both ways

There are a few powerful feelings that can distract your attention away from the present moment in both directions at once, that is, toward the

EXERCISE

(1) Think of a recent time when you felt worried, fearful, or apprehensive about something. See if you can identify any relevant beliefs (e.g., about possible future events). Can you remember what you were doing at the time? How did the feeling affect what you were doing? (2) Repeat the exercise using a recent time when you desired, wished for, or craved something.

past <u>and</u> the future. Perhaps the most powerful of these are **vengeful** feelings, which can arise when you want to retaliate against someone who has done you wrong. When you experience such a feeling, you might preoccupy yourself with thoughts about both the past—the wrong things the person has done—<u>and</u> the future—possible actions you might take to exact retribution.

Another powerful feeling can draw you in either direction is **depression**. Such feelings are frequently associated with memories of things that have not gone well in the past, but they can also be associated with negative thoughts about the future: impending doom or a sense of hopelessness. While it is true that depressed people might say that they are depressed about their "present situation," what they are really saying is that they "see no way out" of that situation as they think about the <u>future</u>. In other words, while you might feel "displeased" or "dissatisfied" with your present situation—your current health, finances, work, or personal relationships—you are most likely to experience feelings of depression if you also see no way to improve that situation in the <u>future</u>.

In short, feelings that draw you away from the present moment into either the past or the future share one common element: they focus your attention on thoughts—memories and fantasies—of past and possible future events. The more you focus your conscious attention on such thoughts, the less able you become to live in, and be fully mindful of, the present moment.

Being distracted by feelings that draw your conscious attention toward the past or the future comes very close to what the eastern religious and spiritual traditions—Buddhism and Hinduism, in particular—would call *attachment*. According to these traditions, since most human suffering is caused by such attachments, the key to achieving happiness and "enlightenment" is to free yourself from these attachments. While we typically tend to think of attachment in terms of the future—cravings and desires—you can also be "attached" to your possessions or to certain people in your life, as well as to feelings of anger, guilt, and disappointment that are associated with past events. Your <u>degree</u> of attachment depends

---

EXERCISE

(1) Write down a past event or experience that you tend to think a lot about; (2) list any of the feelings or emotions that you can associate with that event; (3) try to identify any relevant beliefs (about the event, yourself, or others who might have been involved); (4) repeat the exercise using some future event or outcome that you tend to think about a lot.

---

on the extent to which your waking consciousness is preoccupied with such feelings and thoughts.

What are you Missing?

This discussion raises a very practical and important question: when you are being distracted from "the present moment" by thoughts and feelings that have to do with the past or future, just what is it that you are missing in the present? Why, in other words, is it generally preferable to be mindful, to "live fully in the moment," to "be here now"? Since this is a very important but complex question, let us consider the answer in some detail.

One of the most obvious things that differentiates "the now" from the past and the future is sensory experience. The sights, sounds, smells, tastes, tactile feelings, and other bodily sensations that are transmitted through your sense organs are all experienced in the now. Whether you happen to be looking at a flower, listening to beautiful music, tasting a wonderful meal, or caressing a loved one, all sensory experiences happen "in the now." In certain respects these sensory experiences are the most "real" thing about being alive and being conscious. While it is true that you can "remember" sensory experiences that you have had in the past and "imagine" sensory experiences that you might have in the future, such thoughts are seldom as intense or as real as the sensations that you experience in the present moment. In fact, your capacity to fully experience and appreciate your momentary sensory contact with the flower, the music, the food, and the lover—to be fully "mindful" of how the flower looks, how the music sounds, how the food tastes, and how the lover's body feels—can be severely compromised by "distracting" thoughts and feelings, *even if these thoughts and feelings have to do with the experience itself:* "This reminds me of flowers my mother used to grow," "I wonder who composed this music," "This meal is probably very fattening," "I hope my lover is enjoying this." All such thoughts tend to dilute or water down the sensations that you are experiencing in the moment.

While it is true that sensory experiences can also be unpleasant, especially those that cause physical discomfort or pain, one of the powerful attractions of being alive and conscious is your capacity to have positive sensory experiences in the moment. While it can be helpful to find ways to "distract" your attention when sensory experiences are unpleasant, in modern technological society many of us find ourselves so continuously distracted by our gadgets that we cannot fully appreciate many of our most positive sensory experiences. Perhaps the prototypic example of this would be the many ways in which we have learned to "splinter" our consciousness while eating: reading, watching television, talking on the telephone, and so on.

Another important aspect of "the present moment" is the kind of <u>feeling</u> states that can emerge. While some of your most powerful negative feelings tend to be associated with past memories or future fantasies, many of your most positive feeling states are connected directly to the present moment. Among general feeling states (chapter 5), for example, we could include joy, transcendence, inspiration, playfulness, serenity, and peacefulness. The same goes for many positive interpersonal feelings (chapter 9)—love, caring, empathy, trust, and connectedness—all of which are best experienced in the present moment rather than in connection with past memories or future fantasies. Finally, positive "bodily" feelings (chapter 7) are, almost by definition, connected directly to the present moment: terrific, energetic, exhilarated, clear-headed, sexual, relaxed, and comfortable.

In short, being able to focus your full attention on the present moment enables you to experience fully not only the rich variety of sensory stimulation produced by your physical environment, but also the many positive feeling states that can emerge in the "spacious now."

Another, more subtle benefit of being fully aware of what is happening in the present moment is that it puts you in closer touch with what we might call "truth" or "reality." What most of the great spiritual traditions have called "ignorance," or "delusion," is a condition where your present experience is either:

1. being distorted by your beliefs, or
2. being ignored because your conscious attention is constantly being driven by the nonstop flow of your thoughts about the past or future.

Given that all things are in a constant state of change and flux, the present moment is necessarily different from all past moments and from all possible future moments. By freeing yourself, even for a few moments, from preoccupations about the past and the future and from the need to constantly interpret and analyze your present experience—by allowing your "pure observer" to replace your "judge" and your "analyst"—you allow yourself to witness the "truth" of the present moment by seeing it exactly as it is. **The more you are able to *be* fully in the moment in this way, the more wisdom you acquire.**

"TIME AWARENESS": TOO FAST OR TOO SLOW?

Whenever you become consciously aware of the passage of time, it is usually because you believe that it passing either too slowly ("time on my hands") or too rapidly ("there's not enough time..."). Let us first consider those times when you feel it is passing too slowly.

"Waiting"

Perhaps the most familiar situation when time seems to pass too slowly occurs when you have to "wait." (Waiting also presents one of the most challenging situations for "living in the moment.") To say that you are "waiting" implies that you are waiting <u>for</u> something, that is, that your consciousness in "attached" to some future event or outcome. Common "waiting" situations that we all experience from time to time include standing in line, being stuck in traffic, being put on hold, waiting in a doctor's office, receiving slow service in a store or restaurant, or waiting for an event to begin or for a person to show up for an engagement or appointment. In each of these situations there is some goal or outcome that you have to "wait for." The more "attached" you are to that outcome, the more likely you will be to find it difficult to wait, "difficulty" here meaning that you will be inclined to experience negative feeling states such as impatience, boredom, frustration, irritation, and anger. And if you are on a "schedule"—by which I mean that the waiting might interfere with your ability either to attain the outcome that you are waiting for or to fulfill other obligations or commitments—then having to wait could also give rise to feelings of uncertainty, anxiety, or worry. The more focused ("attached") you are on these outcomes, the more likely you will be to spend your waiting time in some kind of negative emotional state. And when you express these negative feelings by saying "I'm wasting my time," this is indeed what you are doing. But keep in mind: **it is *you* who has <u>chosen</u> to "waste" that time.**

Since it is pretty much impossible for any of us <u>not</u> to have goals and timetables, and since the realities of modern living mean that delays are inevitable, **all of us will be required to wait, and many of us have to do a lot of waiting**. The question, then, is whether there are ways to avoid or at least minimize the negative feeling states that often arise when you have to wait. One way to approach this question is first to realize that:

- Since time is all you ever have, why waste *any* of it?

The next thing to realize is that:

- The main reason why you believe that you are "wasting" your time waiting and why you experience negative feeling states is that you are not being mindful and you are not living in the moment.

Clearly, when you find yourself "waiting" for something, the first step in coping effectively is to become <u>mindful,</u> both of that fact that you are waiting and especially of any related feelings that you might be experiencing (impatience, worry, irritation, etc.). The next step is to choose <u>how</u> you are going to "live fully in the moment." In most waiting situations you have a variety of options. If you are waiting with other people, it can be interesting simply to observe the others: how they appear, what they are doing, how they might be feeling, and so on. You could even engage others in a conversation about current events, whatever it is that you are waiting for, or even how it feels to wait! Depending on the physical environment in which you find yourself, you might even find it interesting to focus your attention fully on the sounds, sights, or smells of your surroundings. Alternatively, you can choose to focus your attention "inward" in a variety of different ways, for example, by meditating, saying a prayer, being mindful about how different parts of your body feel, or quietly reciting affirmations to yourself. While "mindfulness" strategies such as these tend to be highly effective because they involve "living in the moment," you can also spend your waiting time reading or doing "work." This latter

EXERCISE

Think of a recent time when you had to wait for something. (1) What feelings did you experience? (2) What did you "do" during the time you were waiting? Did you feel like you were "wasting" your time? (3) How else might you have handled the situation?

strategy requires, of course, that you anticipate ahead of time that you might have to wait so that you can bring appropriate reading or work materials with you. (In recent years I have noticed that increasing numbers of people make calls on their cell phones while they are waiting, a coping strategy which I personally avoid in group situations because it can be extremely annoying to the people around you.)

Hurrying

The prototypic situation when time seems to pass too rapidly occurs when you believe that there is "not enough" time available to accomplish some task. In chapter 7 we considered at length the possible beliefs and lifestyle patterns that might cause you frequently to feel hurried or rushed; now let us examine such feelings in relationship to your perceptions of time. Like waiting, hurrying occurs because your attention is focused on—you are strongly "attached" to—some <u>future</u> goal or event: completing a project by a particular deadline or getting to some destination by a certain time. You hurry because you believe that you may not have "enough" time to realize that goal. The more importance you place on the goal, and the greater the perceived gap between the time needed to achieve that outcome and the time available to achieve it, the more rushed you will feel. Acting on such feelings—working or driving at a more rapid pace, "cutting corners," and so forth,—might conceivably help to close this gap, but it also runs at least three risks:

- You increase your chances of experiencing other negative feelings: worry, anxiety, panic, frustration, irritation, and possibly even regret (see the next two). These feelings, in turn, can interfere with effective performance;
- You increase the odds of making mistakes or causing injury or accident (as, for example, when you speed or take chances while driving); and
- The quality of the eventual outcome might be degraded (as, for example, when you get sloppy or careless when you are hurrying to finish a project).

One of the most difficult challenges arises when you have to wait <u>while</u> you feel hurried. Waiting, of course, tends to make you feel all the more hurried! A common example of this dilemma is when you are hurrying to drive to a destination by a certain time and you encounter delays—red lights, construction, traffic jams—that slow your progress. As long as you remain strongly "attached" to your goal—the belief that you <u>must</u> get to

EXERCISE

Think of a recent time when you were hurrying to get somewhere. (1) What feelings did you experience? How did these feelings affect: (a) your ability to enjoy the trip? And (b) the manner in which you traveled? (2) In retrospect, was all the hurrying "worth it? How might you handle a similar situation the next time?

your destination by a certain time or "as soon as possible"—such delays will almost certainly give rise to feelings of frustration, impatience, irritability, anxiety, or anger.

WAITING, HURRYING, AND "CONTROL"

The negative feelings that arise when you are waiting or hurrying are often exacerbated by beliefs about whether or not you are (or should be) "in control" of the situation. "Time binds"—believing that there is too much or too little available time—can be especially anxiety-producing for those of us who believe that we always need to "be in control" of our lives. Most of us accept the fact that we really have no control over the passage of time: we may <u>feel</u> that it is passing "too fast" or "too slowly," but we know that it will "march on" at its usual pace regardless of what we do. The issue of control, then, really has to do with our beliefs about the extent to which we can (or should) control <u>what happens</u> while time passes. For example, if you get impatient while you are waiting for some event to happen or begin, you may try to <u>make</u> it happen sooner by taking some kind of action: complaining, breaking into line, and so forth. When you do this, it is usually because you believe that you <u>can</u> or <u>should</u> exert some degree of personal control over the situation. A similar process operates when you are rushing or hurrying: if you believe that you can (or should be able to) exert some control over the situation, you may take action in response to this belief. Thus, in the above example when you are hurrying to get to some destination, you may drive faster or more aggressively, take shortcuts, and so forth.

The key to coping most effectively with any of these "time bind" problems is to **be clear about your beliefs and how they are affecting your response**:

- <u>Beliefs about personal control.</u> **Do you *really* need to control the situation? How much control do you *really* have? Are the risks *really* worth it?**

- **<u>Beliefs about importance.</u>** If you are waiting: **How important is it,** *really,* **that the delay end as soon as possible?** If you are hurrying: **How important is it,** *really,* **that you make that deadline, or get to that destination as soon as possible? How important,** *really,* **is the time that you might be able to save by rushing? How does that "saved time" compare in importance to the risks that you may be taking?**

It is useful to keep in mind that the most important "control issue" could well be <u>controlling the quality of your experience in the moment</u>. Being too strongly "attached" to ending the delay or reaching your goal as soon as possible, and persisting in the belief that you should exert some kind of control over the situation, can help to degrade the quality of your experience by filling the present moment with all kinds of negative emotions. On the other hand, **you can greatly improve the quality of your experience in the moment by "letting go" of both your attachment to the goal or outcome <u>and</u> your belief that you must exert some control over the situation.**

One way to accomplish this is to embrace an alternative belief: "I really cannot exert much control over the situation." Or, "even if I can somehow manage to end the delay or get to my goal a bit sooner, what little time I might gain isn't worth all of the downside risks (including sacrificing the present moment to a lot of negative emotional states)." "Instead, if I choose to 'surrender' to my 'time bind,' I can make better use of the present moment by relaxing, meditating, enjoying the scenery, watching the people, listening to music, having a good conversation, or doing high quality work." In other words, by simply <u>accepting</u> the fact that you are being delayed or that you are going to be late, you "regain control" by freeing yourself up to live in the present moment in a much more positive and fulfilling way. Again, **the choice is yours.**

THE "LIFE INSURANCE" MENTALITY

In our fast-paced, achievement-oriented society, our conscious attention is often drawn away from what we are experiencing or doing in the present moment because it is focused more on "future" events that we believe are "better" than whatever is happening in moment. As small children we "can't wait" to grow up to be "big kids." As adolescents we "can't wait" for the greater personal freedom that comes with being an adult. Later we go to college and work hard at our studies "so that" we can get a good job. When we get married we "can't wait" to have children. Then we "can't wait" for our children to grow up so we can experience more independence. We become workaholics "so that" we can live a more affluent life "later on" and eventually enjoy a comfortable retirement. What is ironic about this way of living is that often when we reach those "future goals," we continue to find it difficult to live in the moment, so we "look back" nostalgically: "Now that I'm a workaholic with a family and a mortgage I yearn for the days when I was young and footloose with few responsibilities." Or, "Now that I'm retired I long for the days when I was young and energetic with my whole life ahead of me."

I like to call this way of dealing with the present as living according to the "life insurance mentality" because, like buying life insurance, what we are doing in the present (spending money on premiums) has no intrinsic value, but is instead seen as a means to achieving some more desirable end in "the future" (leaving money to others when we die). The life insurance metaphor also reminds us that this manner of looking at the present—that we are always "getting ready" for some future time—implies that the ultimate purpose and meaning of life is to get ready for death!

THE PARADOX OF LIVING IN THE NOW

To some readers the emphasis on mindfulness and "living fully in the present moment" that permeates this chapter and, indeed, the entire book, would appear to contradict some of the advice that one frequently finds in popular psychology and self-help books. Some treatises on psychopathology, in fact, would seem to be arguing that many of us need to be more focused on the past and future. "Psychopaths," "sociopaths," and other types of antisocial personalities, for example, are said to exhibit negative personal traits such as irresponsibility, selfishness, and excessive hedonism because they "live only for the moment," "can't learn from the past," and have "little concern for the future consequences of their actions." In other words, criminals and substance abusers—not to mention those who smoke or overeat—are seen as focusing only on present pleasure or personal gain, as failing to learn from past mistakes, and as ignoring the longer-term (future) consequences of their behavior. Socially and personally responsible people, by contrast, are viewed as being able to "control their impulses," to "learn from past experience," and to "think about the future consequences of their actions."

A similar "time orientation" is characteristic of many of the self-help books that emphasize the importance of focusing our attention on the future: to be successful in work and in life each of us must formulate clearly defined future goals for ourselves and develop specific plans for realizing these goals. Failing to develop and implement such goals ("living only in the present?") is seen as a sign of "immaturity."

At face value this advice would seem to be at variance not only with what is being advocated in this book, but also with the philosophical perspectives of many of the great religious traditions, which, as we have already pointed out, maintain that human suffering is a consequence of our being too "attached" either to memories of past events or to fantasies about future events (i.e., "cravings"). Is there any way to reconcile these apparently contradictory viewpoints?

To begin with, **to advocate "mindfulness" or "living in the moment" is *not* to reject planning or thinking about the future**. As we saw in chapter 6, future-oriented motives and intentions are a fundamental component of consciousness. In fact, intentions and plans have a critical and essential relationship to the present moment, in the sense that they help to give <u>meaning</u> to your actions: you get in your car in the morning (action) <u>in order to</u> get to work (intention). The question of being "mindful in the moment," then, is not one of being without motives and intentions; it is, rather, a question of <u>paying close attention to what is happening in the present moment</u>. Since you—your consciousness, your actions, your very life—are in a process of continuous unfolding from moment to moment, the challenge of being mindful is to be <u>fully aware of where you are and what is happening from moment to moment</u>.

Since there will always be times when you need to be thinking about the future, becoming more "mindful" is really a matter of degree. If you are constantly fantasizing about the future, it will be very difficult to remain mindful in the present moment. In other words, it is one thing to <u>have</u> motives and intents—we all have them because they are an essential part of living—but it is quite another to focus your attention on them to the extent that you are seldom mindful of what is happening in the moment. Since "what is happening," in this case, <u>includes</u> the fact that you may be preoccupied with your goals, cravings, or ambitions, simply becoming <u>aware</u> of the fact that this is what you are focused on represents an important first step toward becoming more mindful: "Here I am, fantasizing about something in the future!" The same goes, incidentally, for memories of past events: while being able to remember is necessary to effective functioning in the world, it is very difficult to be mindful in the present if you are constantly thinking about the past. And if your awareness tends to be preoccupied with past events, the first step toward achieving greater mindfulness is to recognize it: Here I am, focusing my attention on the past!"

The interesting thing about mindfulness is that it actually <u>enhances</u> effective functioning in the future. Look at it this way: **if your are not fully aware of "where you are"—how you are feeling, what you are** thinking, and what is happening around you in the present moment—how can you expect to make intelligent choices about what to do in the next moment and in each moment after that? In short, when you are not being mindful and your attention is "somewhere else," you run a significant risk of taking actions that are not in your best interests. Paradoxically, a lack of mindfulness also impedes your ability to "learn from the past," in the following way: if you are not fully aware of where you are and what is happening in the present moment, then your <u>memory</u> of that moment will be similarly distorted.

A FINAL EXERCISE

Getting into the Moment

Once a day, give yourself a gift: Tell yourself that for 20 seconds, a minute, or 5 minutes, you are not going to <u>do</u> anything. For that time, you have no projects, no commitments, no deadlines, no responsibilities, nothing that you have to do. Instead, take the time just to <u>be</u> with whatever there is in the moment: your breathing, how each part of your body feels, whatever thoughts or feelings come into your mind, whatever is happening around you. Do not bother to analyze or judge any of it; just allow everything—yourself, your surroundings—to <u>be</u> exactly as they are in that moment. And whenever you feel that the "gift" time is up, *let your next actions flow naturally from that open, mindful space that you have created for yourself.*

POSTSCRIPT

The Outer Reaches of Consciousness

"The most beautiful thing we can experience is the mysterious.
It is the source of all true art and science."

—Albert Einstein (1949)

I have added this postscript to remind the reader about some of the very important and fascinating aspects of consciousness that have not been covered in this book. Up to this point we have looked at aspects of your conscious experience that can be described reasonably well with words: feelings, beliefs, concepts, sensations, and so on. There is, however, a whole class of conscious experiences that are extremely difficult to describe in words, not only because of the inherent limitations of language—the experiences are difficult to put into words because they are extremely subtle or complex—but also because many of them are relatively rare—only a few of us have had the experience. Among the more familiar of these experiences would be intuition, inspiration, dreaming, drug-induced states, and what are called "peak" experiences. The less common states would include various kinds of "spiritual," "mystical" or "higher" states as well as phenomena such as clairvoyance, telepathy, hyp-

Mindworks: Becoming More Conscious in an Unconscious World, pp. 239–249

nosis, lucid dreaming, trance states, precognition, "channeling," remote viewing, near death experiences (NDEs), out-of-body experiences (OBEs), visions, hallucinations, and other "altered" or "nonordinary" states of consciousness.

Rather than attempting to provide a comprehensive look at each of these states—a task which would necessarily consume many volumes (hundreds, if not thousands, of books have already been written about these topics), the overview presented in this postscript will focus on just two issues: (1) what some of these states can teach us about the way the mind works, and (2) the <u>phenomenology</u> of some of these states, that is, how people describe the actual experience. Given that many readers will not have had an opportunity to experience many of these nonordinary states, I will also rely heavily on the firsthand accounts of others in discussing such states.

In many respects this postscript brings us full circle back to the central topic of chapter 1: the relationship between the conscious and nonconscious parts of the mind. We have already seen the great power of the nonconscious mind: to serve as a "storehouse" for all of your memories, intentions, concepts, and beliefs; to "screen" the mass of information that continuously comes in through your senses; and to "decide" much of what your conscious mind pays attention to from moment to moment. Now, in looking at phenomena such as intuition, creativity, and the various "nonordinary" states of consciousness, we are once again forced to conclude that the nonconscious mind is a major player in bringing about these various states.

"SPIRITUAL" EXPERIENCES

Have you ever had a "spiritual" experience? This can be a difficult question for some people to answer, in part because the word "spiritual" is subject to a variety of meanings. (My unabridged dictionary gives 12 different definitions of "spiritual" and 31 different definitions of "spirit!") Some people are reluctant to consider themselves as "spiritual" because they equate the word with "religious" or with something supernatural. Conversely, some people consider themselves to be spiritual <u>because</u> they are religious.

Following is a list of typical situations when people are likely to feel spiritual. As you read each item in the list, ask yourself, "Have I ever had a spiritual experience in such a situation?"

- When you are in a house of worship.
- When you look up at the sky on a clear night.

EXERCISE

(a) Think of the last time when you felt "spiritual" (or the closest thing to it). What happened to make you feel that way? (b) When was the earliest time that you can remember having such an experience? Do you see any parallels between the two events? (c) Complete the following sentence: "To me spirituality..." (d) What beliefs are implied in your answer?

- When you hear beautiful music.
- When you view a great work of art.
- When you witness a stunning athletic or artistic performance (gymnastics, dance, figure skating, poetry, theatre).
- When you <u>participate</u> in a remarkable musical, athletic or artistic event.
- When you contemplate the beauty and harmony of the universe.
- When you see a newborn baby.
- When you make love.
- When you are "communing with nature" (walking in a dense forest, watching the clouds in the sky, viewing a beautiful garden, near a great desert or body of water, high up in the mountains, viewing wildlife in their natural habitat, looking at a beautiful flower).
- When you are praying or meditating.
- When you witness a "miraculous" event (someone recovering from an "incurable" disease, a "lost soul" who turns his life around, etc.).
- When you feel that you have *really* discovered or understood something for the first time.

While spiritual experiences are in many ways beyond description, some of the feeling terms that were discussed in earlier chapters might capture at least some of what you might experience in such situations: *transcendent, blissful, joyous, awed, inspired, exhilarated, enthralled, transported, uplifted, enraptured,* and so on.

DREAMING

Where do dreams come from? The fact that most of us dream while we sleep leaves us almost no alternative except to conclude that dreams are generated by the nonconscious part of our minds.[1] Although some dreams can seem very "realistic" while we are having them, the fact that the dream state usually "feels" very different from normal waking consciousness helps us, once we awaken, to distinguish dreams from waking "reality." There is, however, one situation where the dream state and the waking state intersect, and it is generally known as "lucid" dreaming. In this state you are indeed dreaming, but you are also <u>aware</u> of the fact that you are experiencing a dream. Moreover, in many cases the person who is having a lucid dream is often able to <u>control</u> some of the events of the dream. By "knowing" that "this is just a dream," the lucid dreamer also realizes that the action is not subject to the same physical constraints that operate in the waking state. Thus, the lucid dreamer is able to "will" certain things to happen—flying, traveling great distances in an instant, etc.—that would be physically impossible in the normal waking world. It is thus not surprising that most people find lucid dreaming to be interesting and enjoyable, if not exciting. Although lucid dreams tend to be relatively uncommon, some investigators (LeBerge, 1985; Morris, 1985) claim that almost anyone can <u>learn</u> how to have such dreams on a regular basis.

INTUITION, INSPIRATION, AND CREATIVITY

The by-play between the conscious and nonconscious parts of the mind is also clearly illustrated in the case of intuition, inspiration, and creativity. The intuitive idea, the inspiration, and the creative product or idea all have to originate ("come from") somewhere, and that "somewhere" is the nonconscious part of your mind.

Intuition

Although dictionary definitions of "intuition" vary somewhat, they generally agree on two points:

- Intuition involves a direct perception, apprehension, or "knowing" of some fact, truth, insight, or understanding.
- Intuition generally occurs <u>without</u> conscious reasoning.

This second quality is especially important, since we typically think of knowledge as something we either get directly through the senses—"I saw it happen"—or arrive at through logic or reason—"All the facts point to it." Intuitive knowing, on the other hand, occurs in the <u>absence</u> of relevant sensory information or logical reasoning. Thus, **when you have a** strong "hunch" or when you feel that you "just know" something without being able to prove or justify it logically, you are experiencing your intuition at work.

The importance of intuition in your daily life becomes especially obvious when you realize that **you form many of your values and morals— your beliefs about goodness—intuitively**. Thus, while you can no doubt give logical <u>reasons</u> for many of your beliefs about right and wrong, the decision to <u>embrace</u> particular beliefs and values is typically arrived at intuitively: "I just *know* that it's the right thing to do." "It just *feels* right."

There are wide differences among us in the extent to which we are willing to <u>trust</u> our intuition. Some of us want physical "proof" or "evidence" before we can accept certain ideas that come to us, while others of us are willing to accept what our intuition tells us as long it "feels" right. Whatever your own views about the "accuracy" of your intuition might be, the fact is that **<u>much</u> of your daily living is in fact intuitive**. If you have any doubts about this, consider for a moment all of the different choices that you make in a typical day: what to wear, what to eat, what to say to people you meet, and so on. Normally when you make such "mundane" decisions you do not first ask for "evidence" or go through a logical reasoning process before you decide how to act. Intuition is also involved in many of the more important life choices that you make: selecting a career, choosing a romantic partner, deciding where to live, and so on. Many of us, of course, make such decisions <u>primarily</u> on an intuitive basis. And while it is true that some people may invoke a good deal of logic and reasoning in making such choices—"I want a romantic partner who is young, tall, slim, beautiful, intelligent, honest, confident, humorous, trustworthy, kind, etc."—the fact is that even in such "objective" decision making there is inevitably a substantial intuitive element—"I'm in love," "We have good chemistry," "It just feels good being together." And if a hard-core "objective" person were to argue that his or her choice of a life partner was based solely on the "objective facts," then we need to ask, "Given that you might well have found someone with even <u>more</u> of the qualities you desire, why <u>this</u> particular person?"

Inspiration and Creativity

Intuition is intimately connected to inspiration and creativity. While doing something creative can sometimes involve a good deal of logical thought or reasoning—a scientist, for example, who is attempting to devise a theory to explain certain observations—many people, especially those in the fine and performing arts, believe that thinking can actually <u>interfere</u> with creativity. Indeed, when you read personal accounts of what people experience in their waking consciousness during the creative process (see below), it becomes clear that intuition is almost always a part of that process.

But what, exactly, is creativity? While different dictionaries once again present somewhat different definitions, in this discussion we shall refer to creativity as the process whereby we bring into existence something new or original. That "something" can be a creative product such as a painting, poem, sculpture, musical composition, dance routine, or theatrical production, but it can also be something less tangible such as a scientific theory, an idea for urban renewal, or a new way of relating to others (parenting, leading, collaborating, mediating, serving those in need, etc.). Viewed in this way, **creativity is a fundamental part of human existence.** Or, as several people have observed, "your life is your own greatest work of art."

What role, then, does the creative process play in your conscious experience? Following are some verbatim accounts of what people in various fields experience during the process of creating:

- [an artist/writer] "I love looking at something from as many sides as possible, lifting up an observation and shaking it until a revelation falls out. It's a form of play I've always relished ... a mental state where all the elements of play are present but raised to richly fulfilling heights" (Ackerman, 2000, p. 45).

- [a painter/sculptor] "there's something flowing through you that's not you. To me, the feeling is tangible proof of the existence of spirit: something we can tap into that's beyond ourselves and our senses. The highest goal we can aspire to is to be transmitter of that" (Miller, 1997, p. 7).

- [composer Aaron Copland] "Well, I work at the piano...But something directs your fingers...Some musical idea in your head which does not take reality until you actually hear it." (John-Steiner, 1985, p. 155).

- [an experimental psychologist] "Most of the things that I think of that are any good happen when I talk ... I may get a new idea when I am lecturing. It might be triggered off by the overall topic or task which produces within me a wealth of associations" (John-Steiner, 1985, p. 190).

- [a choreographer] "This happens spontaneously. Movements are not intellectually contrived but are evoked by emotional images" (John-Steiner, 1985 p. 164).

- [a poet] "when I had barely learned to read, I felt an intense emotion and set down a few words.... Overcome by a deep anxiety, I wrote them neatly on a piece of paper" (John-Steiner, 1985 p. 154).

- [another writer] I think creativity is spiritual ... a synonym for inspiration ... suddenly it comes clear to me what I need to say and how to say it. I feel awe when this happens, it's an inspiring experience.... I'm tempted to say it comes from God. For me this is an experience of divine self-disclosure" (Wakefield, 1996, p. 212).

- [composer Johannes Brahms] "I ... feel that a higher power is working through me.... It cannot be done merely by will power working through the conscious mind.... I immediately feel vibrations that thrill my whole being.... Those vibrations assume the forms of distinct mental images ... the ideas flow in upon me, directly from God ... measure by measure the finished product is revealed to me.... I have to be in a semi-trance condition to get such results ... the conscious mind is in temporary abeyance and the subconscious is in control, for it is through the subconscious mind ... that the inspiration comes. I have to be careful, however, not to lose consciousness, otherwise the ideas fade away" (Abell, 1987, pp. 4-6).

- [composer Richard Struass] "When in my most inspired moods, I have definite compelling visions, involving a higher selfhood. I feel at such moments that I am tapping the source of Infinite and Eternal energy from which you and I and all things proceed. Religion calls it God" (Abell, 1987, p. 86).

Despite the considerable variation in these accounts, at least four themes are apparent:

- No informants speak of conscious, logical thought or analysis as a precursor to creativity.
- Most informants say that creation is accompanied by strong <u>feelings</u>: "awe," "thrill," "anxiety," "play," "emotional images."

EXERCISE

(a) **Think of something creative that you have done in the recent past. How did you feel at the time?**

(b) **Complete the following sentences:**
 • **"When it comes to creativity, I..."**
 • **"My most creative..."**
 • **"I would like to create..."**

(c) **What beliefs about yourself are implied in your answers?**

- Most informants report (or imply) that the creative material comes from "somewhere else"—which, in the context of this book, we can assume to be the nonconscious part of the mind.
- Some informants see the source of their creative inspiration in spiritual or religious terms.

MYSTICISM AND THE "HIGHER" STATES OF CONSCIOUSNESS

I shall conclude this brief excursion into the "outer reaches" of consciousness by considering some of the "higher" states of consciousness that have been described over the centuries by mystics of almost all religious persuasions. In most of the great spiritual and religious traditions—Christianity, Buddhism, Hinduism, Judaism, Islam, Taoism, and others—there have been practitioners who have sought a closer connection with, or a more direct realization of, God, Spirit, Truth, "ultimate Reality," or "the Infinite." Mystical states can occur spontaneously or with the aid of various kinds of rituals or drugs, but most religious mystics typically achieve such states by means of lengthy and highly disciplined contemplation or meditation. There are a great many different terms that have been used to label these mystical or "higher" states of consciousness: for example: enlightenment, self-realization, *samhadi, nirvikalpa, satori,* "pure emptiness," "no mind," nondual and so on. Whatever one chooses to call such mystical states, my interest here is to give you some notion of what these mystics actually <u>experience</u> when they reach such states. Ken Wilber (1995), who is arguably the foremost contemporary student of these higher states of consciousness, concludes that, regardless of the particular meditative techniques or theology of the spiritual practitioner, mystics are remarkably consistent in their experiential accounts of these higher (or what he also refers to as "transpersonal") states. Wilber has identified four successively higher "levels" of consciousness in the transpersonal realm, which he labels, respectively, as the psychic, the subtle, the causal, and the nondual. Each successively higher realm incorporates the ones below it. Perhaps the best way to get some sense of what is experienced in these higher realms is to quote below some excerpts from Wilber's writing. **As you read these accounts, ask yourself, "Have I ever felt anything like this?"**

The Psychic Realm

in some deep, awesome, mysterious way, everything that happens is all of a piece ... "good"...and ... "bad"... are necessary pieces of this great work of

Art called manifestation.... In the deepest part of my own awareness, I am one with the Whole. I do not see the world. I am the world.... I am unmoved in my Confidence and Equanimity of the basic All Rightness of the universe.... The quiet bliss of the simple feeling of Being is [my] constant companion; [I am] one with the sun and the moon and the radiant stars ... one with all the wonders of manifestation ... a Joy that is so overpowering.... [I] find it hard to breathe" (Wilber, 2001, para. 4-14).

Wilber also quotes Jesus from the *Gospel of St. Thomas*:

"Jesus said to them:
When you make the two one, and
when you make the inner as the outer
and the outer as the inner and the above
as the below, and when
you make the male and the female into a single one
then you shall enter the Kingdom. (para. 8)

The Subtle Realm

It is not just that everything is All Right. Everything is All Right because everything issues from the same divine Ground and Source ... the God of this world is found within, and you *know* it is found within: in those hushed silent times when the mind becomes still, the body relaxes into infinity, the senses expand to become one with the world—in those glistening times, a subtle luminosity, a serene radiance, a brilliant transparent clarity shimmers as the true nature of all manifestation, erupting every now and then in a compassionate Radiance before whom all idols retreat, a love so fierce it adoringly embraces both light and dark, both good and evil, both pleasure and pain equally.... The real secret of the subtle Divine: the light and the sun and the stars and all of nature comes directly from your very own Heart. (Wilber, 2001, para. 129).

The Causal Realm

Language becomes increasingly problematic as a means of conveying how people experience these last two realms. Perhaps the best way to get a sense of the causal realm is to realize that it is intimately connected to something that was discussed in chapter 3: The pure observer or "witness." As Wilber (1999) describes it:

as you rest in the Witness—realizing, I am not objects, I am not feelings, I am not thoughts—all you will notice is a sense of Freedom, a sense of Liberation, a sense of Release—release from the terrible constriction of identifying with these puny little finite objects, your little body and little mind and little ego, all of which are objects that can be seen, and thus are not the true seer, the real self, the pure Witness, which is what you really are ... that witnessing awareness is not itself anything specific you can see. It is just a vast background sense of freedom—or <u>pure Emptiness</u>—and in that pure Emptiness, which you are, the entire manifest world arises. You <u>are</u> that Freedom. Openness, Emptiness—and not any ... thing that arises in it. (p. 87)

The Nondual Realm

In describing this "highest" state of consciousness, which he also refers to as "One Taste," Wilber (1999) states that "the Witness itself disappears into everything that is witnessed, subject and object become One Taste, or simple Suchness, and this is the nondual estate" (p. 96.) He then goes on to describe a nondual state he experienced while swimming in the warm waters off the south coast of Florida:

There is no time in this estate, though time passes through it. Clouds float by in the sky, thoughts float by in the mind, waves float by in the ocean, and I am all of that. I am looking at none of it, for there is no center around which perception is organized. It is simply that everything is arising, and I am all of that.... There is nothing outside of me, there is nothing inside of me, because there is no me—there is simply all of this, and it has always been so."

My ankle hurts from dancing last might, so there is pain, but the pain doesn't hurt me, for there is no me. There is simply pain, and it is arising just like everything else—birds, waves, clouds, thoughts. I am none of them, I am all of them, for it's all the same One Taste. This is not a trance, or a lessening of consciousness, but rather an intensification of it—not subconscious but superconscious...There is a crystal-clear awareness of everything that is arising, moment to moment, it's just not happening to anybody. This is not an out-of body experience; I am not above looking down; I am not looking at all; and I am not above or below anything—I am everything. There is simply all of this, and I am that.... There is always this sense, with One Taste, that you have never left it, no matter how confused you get, and therefore there is never really the sense that you are entering it or leaving it. It is just so, always and forever, even now, and unto the ends of the world. (pp. 96-97)

NOTE

1. Given that dreaming is so common, one might expect a book on human consciousness to devote a good deal of attention to this fascinating and important topic. However, I have—somewhat reluctantly—chosen not to

devote much attention to dreaming for two principal reasons: (1) neither the meaning of dreams, nor the relationship between dreaming and normal waking consciousness, is well understood; and (2) I do not consider myself to be either an expert dreamer or an expert on dreams.

REFERENCES

Abell. A. M. (1987). *Talks with great composers*. New York: Philosophical Library.

Ackerman, D. (2000, March-April). Flights of fancy: Confessions of a creativity junkie. *Modern Maturity*, 44-46.

Boorstein, S. (1995). *It's easier than you think: The Buddhist way of life*. San Francisco: Harper.

The Dalai Lama, H. H. (1999). *Ethics for the new milliennium*. New York: Riverhead Books.

Einstein, A. (1949). *The world as I see it*. New York: Philosophical Library.

Gunaratana, V. H. (1992). *Mindfulness in plain english*. Boston: Wisdom.

Hanh, T. N. (1987). *The miracle of mindfulness: A manual on meditation*. Boston: Beacon Press.

John-Steiner, V. (1985). *Notebooks of the mind: Explorations of thinking*. New York: Harper & Row.

Kabat-Zinn, J. (1994). *Wherever you go, there you are: Mindfulness meditation in everyday life*: New York: Hyperion.

Leavitt, R. K. (2007). Retrieved February 10, 2005, from http://www
.quoteworld.org/
category/evil/author/robert_keith_leavitt

Leberge, S. (1985). *Lucid dreaming: The power of being awake and aware in your dreams*. New York: New Ballentine Books.

Mann, T. (1940). *The beloved returns*. New York: Albert A. Knopf.

McDonald, K. (1990). *How to meditate: A practical guide*. Boston: Wisdom.

Miller, D. P. (1997, April, 7). The clear path to creativity: An interview with Dan Wakefield. *The Sun*, 256, 4-8.

Morris, J. (1985). *The dream workbook: Discover the knowledge and power hidden in your dreams*. New York: Fawcett Crest.

Surya Dass, L. (1997). *Awakening the Buddha within: Eight steps to enlightenment*. New York: Broadway Books.

Tariqavi. (1970). When a man meets himself. In I. Shah (Ed.), *Wisdom of the idiots* (pp. 122-123). London: Octagon Press.

Taylor, E. (1997). *A psychology of spiritual healing*. West Chester, PA: Chrysalis Books.

Wakefield, D. (1996). *Creating from the spirit: A path to creative power in art and life*. New York: Ballantine Books.

Webster's New World Dictionary. (1998). College edition. New York: World.

Wilber, K. (1995) *Sex, ecology, and spirituality: The spirit of evolution*. Boston: Shambhala.

Wilber, K. (1999). *One taste: The journals of Ken Wilber*. Boston: Shambhala.

Wilber, K. (2001). *The deconstruction of the World Trade Center* (Part III). Boston: Shambhala. Retrieved December 14, 2002, from http://wilber.shambhala.com/html/books/boomeritis/wtc/part3.cfm/

ABOUT THE AUTHOR

Psychologist Alexander Astin is the Allan M. Cartter professor of higher education, emeritus at the University of California at Los Angeles. He is also the founding director of the Higher Education Research Institute at UCLA and is the author of 20 books and more than 300 other articles. His articles have been published in leading psychological and educational journals as well as in *The Saturday Review, Psychology Today,* and the *Los Angeles Times.* Readers of *Change* magazine voted Dr. Astin as the person "most admired for creative, insightful thinking" in the field of higher education and a recent study in the *Journal of Higher Education* identified him as the most-frequently-cited author in his field. Dr. Astin has lectured at more than 250 colleges and universities here and abroad, and his writing has earned him awards from 10 different national associations. A fellow of the American Psychological Association, Dr. Astin has also been a fellow at the Center for Advanced Study in the behavioral sciences at Stanford University and is the recipient of 11 honorary degrees.

Printed in the United States
85861LV00002B/70-87/A